BEING SINGULAR PLURAL

MERIDIAN

Crossing Aesthetics

Werner Hamacher

& David E. Wellbery

Editors

Translated by
Robert D. Richardson
and Anne E. O'Byrne

Stanford
University
Press

———

Stanford
California
2000

BEING SINGULAR PLURAL

Jean-Luc Nancy

Stanford University Press
Stanford, California

© 2000 by the Board of Trustees
of the Leland Stanford Junior University

Being Singular Plural was originally published as *Être singulier pluriel*
© 1996, Éditions Galilée.

Assistance for the translation was provided by the French Ministry of Culture.

Printed in the United States of America on acid-free, archival-quality paper.

Library of Congress Cataloging-in-Publication Data

Nancy, Jean-Luc.
   [Être singular pluriel. English]
   Being singular plural / Jean-Luc Nancy ; translated by Robert D. Richardson
and Anne E. O'Byrne
      p.   cm. — (Meridian, crossing aesthetics)
   Includes bibliographical references and index.
      ISBN 0-8047-3974-9 (alk. paper) — ISBN 0-8047-3975-7 (pbk. : alk. paper)
   1. Ontology.   2. Philosophical anthropology.   I. Title.   II. Meridan
(Stanford, Calif.)
B2430.N363 E8713   2000
194—dc21   00-057326

Original printing 2000

Last figure below indicates year of this printing:
09

Typeset by James P. Brommer
in 10.9/13 Garamond and Lithos display

Contents

Lead, as I do, the flown-away virtue back to earth—
yes, back to body and life; that it may give the earth its
meaning, a human meaning! May your spirit and your
virtue serve the meaning of the earth. . . . Man and
man's earth are still unexhausted and undiscovered.

—Nietzsche

This epigraph is chosen quite deliberately. I run the risk of its seeming to lend itself to a certain Christian, idealist, and humanist tone, a tone in which it is easy to recognize those well-meaning virtues and values that have loosed upon the world all the things that have driven the humanity of our century to despair over itself, where these values are both blind to and complicit in this letting loose. In his own way, Nietzsche himself would have undoubtedly participated in this dubious, moralizing piety. At any rate, the word "meaning" rarely appears in his work, and still more rarely in any positive sense. One would do well, therefore, not to give any hasty interpretations of it here. The above excerpt appeals to a "human meaning," but it does so by affirming that the human [*l'homme*] remains to be discovered.[1] In order for the human to be discovered, and in order for the phrase "human meaning" to acquire some meaning, everything that has ever laid claim to the truth about the nature, essence, or end of "man" must be undone. In other words, nothing must remain of what, under the title of meaning, related the earth [*la terre*] and the human to a specifiable horizon. Again, it is Nietzsche who said that we are now "on the horizon of the infinite"; that is, we are at that point where "there is no more 'land,'" and where "there is nothing more terrible than the infinite."[2]

Are we finally going to learn this lesson? Are we perhaps finally able to hear it, or is it now impossible for us to learn anything else? Can we think an earth and a human such that they would be only what they are—*nothing but* earth and human—and such that they would be none of the various horizons often harbored under these names, none of the "perspectives" or "views" *in view* of which we have disfigured humans [*les hommes*] and driven them to despair?

"The horizon of the infinite" is no longer the horizon *of the whole*, but the "whole" (all that is) as put on hold everywhere, pushed to the outside *just as much as* it is pushed back inside the "self." It is no longer a line that is drawn, or a line that will be drawn, which orients or gathers the meaning of a course of progress or navigation. It is the opening [*la brèche*] or distancing [*l'écartement*] of horizon itself, and in the opening: *us*. We happen as the opening itself, the dangerous fault line of a rupture.

∽

I want to emphasize the date on which I am writing this. It is the summer of 1995, and as far as specifying the situation of the earth and humans is concerned, nothing is more pressing (how could it really be avoided?) than a list of proper names such as these, presented here in no particular order: Bosnia-Herzogovina, Chechnya, Rwanda, Bosnian Serbs, Tutsis, Hutus, Tamil Tigers, Krajina Serbs, Casamance, Chiapas, Islamic Jihad, Bangladesh, the Secret Army for the Liberation of Armenia, Hamas, Kazakhstan, Khmers Rouges, ETA militia, Kurds (UPK/PDK), Montataire, the Movement for Self-determination, Somalia, Chicanos, Shiites, FNLC-Canal Historique, Liberia, Givat Hagadan, Nigeria, the League of the North, Afghanistan, Indonesia, Sikhs, Haiti, Roma gypsies of Slovenia, Taiwan, Burma, PLO, Iraq, Islamic Front Salvation, Shining Path, Vaulx-en-Velins, Neuhof. . . . Of course, it would be difficult to bring this list to an end if the aim was to include all the places, groups, or authorities that constitute the theater of bloody conflicts among identities, as well as what is at stake in these conflicts. These days it is not always possible to say with any assurance whether these identities are intranational, infranational, or transnational; whether they are "cultural," "religious," "ethnic," or "historical"; whether they are legitimate or not—not to mention the question about which law would provide such legitimation; whether they are real, mythical, or imaginary; whether they are independent or "instrumentalized" by other groups who wield political, economic, and ideological power. . . .

This is the "earth" we are supposed to "inhabit" today, the earth for which the name Sarajevo will become the martyr-name, the testimonial-name: this is us, we who are supposed to say *we* as if we know what we are saying and *who* we are talking about. This earth is anything but a sharing of humanity. It is a world that does not even manage to constitute a world; it is a world lacking in world, and lacking in the meaning of world. It is an enumeration that brings to light the sheer number and proliferation of these various poles of attraction and repulsion. It is an endless list, and everything happens in such a way that one is reduced to keeping accounts but never taking the final toll. It is a litany, a prayer of pure sorrow and pure loss, the plea that falls from the lips of millions of refugees every day: whether they be deportees, people besieged, those who are mutilated, people who starve, who are raped, ostracized, excluded, exiled, expelled.

What I am talking about here is compassion, but not compassion as a pity that feels sorry for itself and feeds on itself. Com-passion is the contagion, the contact of being with one another in this turmoil. Compassion is not altruism, nor is it identification; it is the disturbance of violent relatedness.

~

What does the above-named proliferation require of us, this proliferation that seems to have no other meaning than the indeterminate multiplication of centripetal meanings, meanings closed in on themselves and supersaturated with significance—that is, meanings that are no longer meaningful because they have come to refer only to their own closure, to their horizon of appropriation, and have begun to spread nothing but destruction, hatred, and the denial of existence?

What if this autistic multiplicity, which tears open and is torn open, lets us know that we have not even begun to discover what it is to be many, even though "la terre des hommes"[3] is exactly this? What if it lets us know that it is itself the first laying bare [*mise à nu*] of a world that is only the world, but which is the world absolutely and unreservedly, with no meaning beyond this very Being of the world: singularly plural and plurally singular?

Preface

The first and principal essay of this book, which gives it its title, was not composed in an altogether sequential manner, but rather in a discontinuous way, repeatedly taking up several themes. To a certain extent, then, the sections can be read in any order, since there are repetitions here and there. But this is the result of a fundamental difficulty. This text does not disguise its ambition of redoing the whole of "first philosophy" by giving the "singular plural" of Being[1] as its foundation. This, however, is not *my* ambition, but rather the necessity of the thing itself and of our history. At the very least, I hope to make this necessity felt. At the same time, apart from the fact that I do not have the strength to deliver the treatise "of the singular plural essence of Being," the form of the ontological treatise ceases to be appropriate as soon as the singular of Being itself, and therefore also of ontology, is in question. This is nothing new. At least since Nietzsche, and for all sorts of reasons that no doubt come together in the reason I invoke, philosophy is at odds with its "form," that is, with its "style," which is to say, finally, with its address. How does thinking address itself to itself, to thinking (which also means: how does thinking address itself to everyone, without its being a matter of a "comprehension" or "understanding" that might be called "common")? How is thinking addressed? (The philosophical treatise, and "philosophy" as such, is the neutralization of address, the subjectless discourse of

Being-Subject [*l'Etre-Sujet*] itself.) Put another way, what is the "dialogue of the soul with itself" that Plato talks about, which demonstrates that this question, or this worry, has always been part of our history? If thinking is addressed, then it is because there is meaning in this address, and not in discourse (but it is in the address of discourse). This obeys the primordial, ontological condition of being-with or being-together, which is what I would like to talk about. A treatise, therefore, is not sufficiently discursive. Nor is it enough to dress discourse in the form of an address (for me to address you with the familiar "you" [*tu*] the whole way through). The address means that thinking itself addresses itself to "me" and to "us" at the same time; that is, thinking addresses itself to the world, to history, to people, to things: to "us." Another ambition springs from this or, better yet, another, more restricted, attempt: to allow thinking's address to be perceived, an address that comes to us from everywhere simultaneously, multiplied, repeated, insistent, and variable, gesturing only toward "us" and toward our curious "being-with-one-another," [*être-les-uns-avec-les-autres*], toward our addressing-one-another.[2]

(By the way, the logic of "with" often requires heavy-handed syntax in order to say "being-with-one-another." You may suffer from it as you read these pages. But perhaps it is not an accident that language does not easily lend itself to showing the "with" as such, for it is itself the address and not what must be addressed.)

In this, there is an illusion that lies in wait, the illusion of willing the adequation of "form" and "content," of willing truth itself into presence: as if I could write to every addressee a seismographical account of our upsets, our agitations, our troubles, and our addresses without addressees. My only response is no: no will, "on my life I did not know what it was to will" (Nietzsche). Or I might say the following: willing (or desire) is not a thinking; it is a disturbance, an echo, a reverberating shock.

The latter essays were chosen because their subjects converge with that of the primary essay. As you will see, the first two are connected to the exact circumstances of the most violent events of these last years.

BEING SINGULAR PLURAL

§ Of Being Singular Plural

It is good to rely upon others. For no one can bear this life alone.

—Hölderlin

Since human nature is the true community of men, those who produce thereby affirm their nature, human community, and social being which, rather than an abstract, general power in opposition to the isolated individual, is the being of each individual, his own activity, his own life, his own joy, his own richness. To say that a man is alienated from himself is to say that the society of this alienated man is the caricature of his real community.

—Marx

We Are Meaning

It is often said today that we have lost meaning, that we lack it and, as a result, are in need of and waiting for it. The "one" who speaks in this way forgets that the very propagation of this discourse is itself meaningful. Regretting the absence of meaning itself has meaning. But such regret does not have meaning only in this negative mode; denying the presence of meaning affirms that one knows what meaning would be, were it there, and keeps the mastery and truth of meaning in place (which is the pretension of the humanist discourses that propose to "rediscover" meaning.) Whether it is aware of it or not, the contemporary discourse on meaning goes much further and in a completely different direction: it brings to light the fact that "meaning," used in this absolute way, has become the bared [dénudé] name of our being-with-one-another. We do not "have" meaning anymore, because we ourselves are meaning—entirely, without reserve, infinitely, with no meaning other than "us."

This does not mean that we are the content of meaning, nor are we its fulfillment or its result, as if to say that humans were the meaning (end, substance, or value) of Being, nature, or history. The meaning of this meaning—that is, the signification to which a state of affairs corresponds and compares—is precisely what we say we

I

have lost. But we are meaning in the sense that we are the element in which significations can be produced and circulate. The least signification just as much as the most elevated (the meaning of "nail" as well as the meaning of "God") has no meaning in itself and, as a result, is what it is and does what it does only insofar as it is communicated, even where this communication takes place only between "me" and "myself." Meaning is its own communication or its own circulation. The "meaning of Being" is not some property that will come to qualify, fill in, or finalize the brute givenness of "Being" pure and simple.[1] Instead, it is the fact that there is no "brute givenness" of Being, that there is no desperately poor *there is* presented when one says that "there is a nail catching. . . . " But the givenness of Being, the givenness inherent to the very fact that we understand something when we say "to be" (whatever it may be and however confused it might be), along with the (same) givenness that is given with this fact—cosubstantial with the givenness of Being and the understanding of Being, that we understand one another (however confusedly) when we say it, is a gift that can be summarized as follows: *Being itself is given to us as meaning*. Being does not *have* meaning. Being itself, the phenomenon of Being, is meaning that is, in turn, its own circulation—and *we* are this circulation.

There is no meaning if meaning is not shared,[2] and not because there would be an ultimate or first signification that all beings have in common, but because *meaning is itself the sharing of Being*. Meaning begins where presence is not pure presence but where presence comes apart [*se disjoint*] in order to be itself *as* such. This "as" presupposes the distancing, spacing, and division of presence. Only the concept of "presence" contains the necessity of this division. Pure unshared presence—presence to nothing, of nothing, for nothing— is neither present nor absent. It is the simple implosion of a being that could never have *been*—an implosion without any trace.

This is why what is called "the creation of the world" is not the production of a pure something from nothing—which would not, at the same time, implode into the nothing out of which it could never have come—but is the explosion of presence in the original multiplicity of its division. It is the explosion of *nothing*, in fact, it is the spacing of meaning, spacing *as* meaning and circulation. The *nihil* of creation is the *truth* of meaning, but meaning is the originary sharing of this truth. It could be expressed in the following way: Being cannot *be* anything but being-with-one-another, circulating in the *with* and as the *with* of this singularly plural coexistence.

If one can put it like this, there is no other meaning than the meaning of circulation. But this circulation goes in all directions at once, in all the directions of all the space-times [*les espace-temps*] opened by presence to presence: all things, all beings, all entities, everything past and future, alive, dead, inanimate, stones, plants, nails, gods—and "humans," that is, those who expose sharing and circulation as such by saying "we," by *saying we to themselves* in all possible senses of that expression, and by saying we for the totality of all being.

∼

(*Let us say we for all being, that is, for every being, for all beings one by one, each time in the singular of their essential plural. Language speaks for all and of all: for all, in their place, in their name, including those who may not have a name. Language says what there is of the world, nature, history and humanity, and it also speaks for them as well as* in view of *them, in order to lead the one who speaks, the one through whom language comes to be and happens ("man"), to all of being, which does not speak but which is nevertheless—*stone, fish, fiber, dough, crack, block, and breath. *The speaker speaks for the world, which means the speaker speaks to it, on behalf of it, in order to make it a "world." As such, the speaker is "in its place" and "according to its measure"; the speaker occurs as its representative but also, at the same time (and this has all the values of* pro in Latin), *in anticipation of it, before it, exposed to it as to its own most intimate consideration. Language says the world; that is, it loses itself in it and exposes how "in itself" it is a question of losing oneself in order to be of it, with it, to be its meaning—which is all meaning.*)

∼

Circulation goes in all directions: this is the Nietzschean thought of the "eternal return," the affirmation of meaning as the repetition of the instant, nothing but this repetition, and as a result, nothing (since it is a matter of the repetition of what essentially does not return). But it is a repetition already comprised in the affirmation of the instant, in this affirmation/request (*re-petitio*) seized in the letting go of the instant, affirming the passing of presence and itself passing with it, affirmation abandoned in its very movement. It is an impossible thought, a thinking that does not hold itself back from the circulation it thinks, a thinking of meaning right at [*à même*][3] meaning, where its eternity occurs as the truth of its passing. (For instance, at the moment at which I am writing, a brown-and-white cat is crossing the garden, slipping mockingly away, taking my thoughts with it.)

It is in this way that the thinking of the eternal return is the inaugural thought of our contemporary history, a thinking we must repeat (even if it means calling it something else). We must reappropriate what already made us who "we" are today, here and now, the "we" of a world who no longer struggle to have meaning but to be meaning itself. This is *we* as the beginning and end of the world, inexhaustible in the circumscription that nothing circumscribes, that "the" nothing circumscribes. *We make sense* [nous faisons sens], not by setting a price or value, but by exposing the absolute value that the world *is* by itself. "World" does not mean anything other than this "nothing" that no one can "mean" [*vouloir dire*], but that is said in every saying: in other words, Being itself as the absolute value in itself of all that is, *but this absolute value as the being-with of all that is* itself bare and impossible to evaluate. It is neither meaning [*vouloir-dire*] nor the giving of value [*dire-valoir*], but value *as such*, that is, "meaning" which is the meaning of Being only because it is Being itself, its existence, its truth. Existence *is with*: otherwise nothing exists.

Circulation—or eternity—goes in all directions, but it moves only insofar as it goes from one point to another; spacing is its absolute condition. From place to place, and from moment to moment, without any progression or linear path, bit by bit and case by case, essentially accidental, it is singular and plural in its very principle. It does not have a final fulfillment any more than it has a point of origin. It is the originary plurality of origins and the creation of the world in each singularity, creation continued in the discontinuity of its discrete occurrences. From now on, *we, we others*[4] are charged with this truth—it is more *ours* than ever—the truth of this paradoxical "first-person plural" which makes sense of the world as the spacing and intertwining of so many worlds (earths, skies, histories) that there is a taking place of meaning, or the crossing-through [*passages*] of presence. "We" says (and "we say") the unique event whose uniqueness and unity consist in multiplicity.

People Are Strange

Everything, then, passes *between us.*[5] This "between," as its name implies, has neither a consistency nor continuity of its own. It does not lead from one to the other; it constitutes no connective tissue, no cement, no bridge. Perhaps it is not even fair to speak of a "connection" to its subject; it is neither connected nor unconnected; it falls short of both; even better, it is that which is at the heart of a connection, the *inter*lacing [l'entre*croisment*] of strands whose extremities remain separate even at the very center of the knot. The "between" is the stretching out [*distension*] and distance opened by the singular as such, as its spacing of meaning. That which does not maintain its distance from the "between" is only immanence collapsed in on itself and deprived of meaning.

From one singular to another, there is contiguity but not continuity. There is proximity, but only to the extent that extreme closeness emphasizes the distancing it opens up. All of being is in touch with all of being, but the law of touching is separation; moreover, it is the heterogeneity of surfaces that touch each other. *Contact* is beyond fullness and emptiness, beyond connection and disconnection. If "to come into contact" is to begin to make sense of one another, then this "coming" penetrates nothing; there is no intermediate and mediating "milieu." Meaning is not a milieu in which we are immersed. There is no *mi-lieu* [between place]. It is a matter of one or the other, one and the other, one with the other, but by no means the one in the other, which would be something other than one or the other (another essence, another nature, a diffuse or infuse generality). From one to the other is the syncopated repetition of origins-of-the-world, which are each time one or the other.

The origin is affirmation; repetition is the condition of affirmation. I say "that is, that it is." It is not a "fact" and has nothing to do with any sort of evaluation. It is a singularity taking refuge in its affirmation of Being, a touch of meaning. It is not an other Being; it is the singular of Being by which the being *is*, or it is of Being, which *is being* in a transitive sense of the verb (an unheard of, inaudible sense—the very meaning of Being). The touch of meaning brings into play [*engager*] its own singularity, its distinction, and brings into play the plurality of the "each time" of every touch of meaning, "mine" as well as all the others, each one of which is "mine" *in turn*, according to the singular turn of its affirmation.

Right away, then, there is the repetition of the touches of meaning, which meaning demands. This incommensurable, absolutely heterogeneous repetition opens up an irreducible strangeness of each one of these touches to the other. The other origin is incomparable or inassimilable, not because it is simply "other" but because it is an origin and touch of meaning. Or rather, the alterity of the other is its originary contiguity with the "proper" origin.[6] You are absolutely strange because the world begins *its turn with you*.

We say "people are strange."[7] This phrase is one of our most constant and rudimentary ontological attestations. In fact, it says a great deal. "People" indicates everyone else, designated as the indeterminate ensemble of populations, lineages, or races [*gentes*] from which the speaker removes himself. (Nevertheless, he removes himself in a very particular sort of way, because the designation is so general—and this is exactly the point—that it inevitably turns back around on the speaker. Since I say that "people are strange," I include myself in a certain way in this strangeness.)

The word "people" does not say exactly the same thing as the Heideggerian[8] "one,"[9] even if it is partly a mode of it. With the word "one," it is not always certain whether or not the speaker includes himself in the anonymity of the "one." For example, I can say "someone said to me" ["on m'a dit"] or else "it is said that" ["on dit que"] or else "that is how it is done" ["c'est comme ça qu'on fait"] or else "one is born; one dies" ["on naît, on meurt"]. These uses are not equivalent and, moreover, it is not certain that it is always the case that the "one" speaks of himself (from and about himself). Heidegger understood that "one" would only be said as a response to the question "who?" put to the subject of *Dasein*, but he does not pose the other inevitable question that must be asked in order to discover *who* gives this response and who, in responding like this, removes himself or has a tendency to remove himself. As a result, he risks neglecting the fact that there is no pure and simple "one," no "one" in which "properly existing" existence [*l'existant* "proprement existant"] is, from the start, purely and simply immersed. "People" clearly designates the mode of "one" by which "I" remove myself, to the point of appearing to forget or neglect the fact that I myself am part of "people." In any case, this setting apart [*mise à l'ecart*] does not occur without the recognition of identity. "People" clearly states that we are all precisely *people*, that is, indistinctly persons, humans, all of a common "kind," but of a kind that has its existence only as numerous, dispersed, and indeterminate in its generality. This existence can only be grasped in the paradoxical simultaneity of togetherness (anonymous, confused, and indeed massive) and disseminated singularity (these or those "people(s)," or "a guy," "a girl," "a kid").

"People" are silhouettes that are both imprecise and singularized, faint outlines of voices, patterns of comportment, sketches of affects, not the anonymous chatter of the "public domain." But what is an affect, if not each time a sketch? A comportment, if not each time a pattern? A voice, if not each time a faint outline? What is a singularity, if not each time its "own" clearing, its "own" imminence, the imminence of a "propriety" or propriety itself as imminence, always touched upon, always lightly touched: revealing itself *beside*, always beside. ("Beside himself" ["a côté de ses pompes"[10]], as the saying goes. The comedy of this expression is no accident, and, whether it masks an anxiety or liberates the laughter of the ignorant, it is always a matter of an escape, an evasion, and an emptying out of what is closest, an oddity presented as the rule itself.)

"I" take refuge in an exception or distinction when I say "people," but I also confer this distinction on each and every person, although in just as obscure a way. This is undoubtedly why people so often make the judgment "people are strange" or "people are incredible." It is not only, or even primarily, a question of the tendency (however evident) to set up our own *habitus* as the norm. It is necessary to uncover a more primitive level of this particular judgment, one where what is apprehended is nothing other than singularity as such. From faces to voices, gestures, attitudes, dress, and conduct, whatever the "typical" traits are, everyone distinguishes himself by a sort of sudden and headlong precipitation where the strangeness of a singularity is concentrated. Without this precipitation there would be, quite simply, no "someone." And there would be no more interest or hospitality, desire or disgust, no matter who or what it might be for.

"Someone" here is understood in the way a person might say "it's him all right" about a photo, expressing by this "all right" the covering over of a gap, making adequate what is inadequate, capable of relating only to the "instantaneous" grasping of an instant that is precisely its own gap. The photo—I have in mind an everyday, banal photo—simultaneously reveals singularity, banality, and our curiosity about one another. The principle of indiscernability here becomes decisive. Not only are all people different but they are also all different from one another. They do not differ from an archetype or a generality. The typical traits (ethnic, cultural, social, generational, and so forth), whose particular patterns constitute another level of singularity, do not abolish singular differences; instead, they bring them into relief. As for singular differences, they are not only "individual," but infraindividual. It is never the case that I have met Pierre or Marie per se, but I have met him or her in such and such a "form," in such and such a "state," in such and such a "mood," and so on.

This very humble layer of our everyday experience contains another rudimentary ontological attestation: what we receive (rather than what we perceive) with singularities is the discreet passage of *other origins of the world.* What occurs there, what bends, leans, twists, addresses, denies—from the newborn to the corpse—is neither primarily "someone close," nor an "other," nor a "stranger," nor "someone similar." It is an origin; it is an affirmation of the world, and we know that the world has no other origin than this singular multiplicity of origins. The world always appears [*surgit*][11] each time according to a decidedly local turn [of events]. Its unity, its uniqueness, and its totality consist in a combination of this reticulated multiplicity, which produces no result.

Without this attestation, there would be no first attestation of *existence* as such, that is, of the nonessence and non-subsistence-by-itself that is the basis of being-oneself. This is why the Heideggerian "one" is insufficient as the initial understanding of *existentielle* "everydayness." Heidegger confuses the everyday with the undifferentiated, the anonymous, and the statistical. These are no less important, but they can only constitute themselves in relation to the differentiated singularity that the *everyday* already is by itself: each day, each time, day to day. One cannot affirm that the meaning of Being must express itself starting from everydayness and then begin by neglecting the general differentiation of the everyday, its constantly renewed rupture, its intimate discord, its polymorphy and its polyphony, its relief and its variety. A "day" is not simply a unit for counting; it is the turning of the world—each time singular. And days, indeed every day, could not be similar if they were not first different, difference itself. Likewise "people," or rather "peoples," given the irreducible strangeness that constitutes them as such, are themselves primarily the exposing of the singularity according to which existence exists, irreducibly and primarily—and an exposition of singularity that experience claims to communicate with, in the sense of "to" and "along with," the totality of beings. "Nature" is also "strange," and we exist there; we exist *in* it in the mode of a constantly renewed singularity, whether the singularity of the diversity and disparity of our senses or that of the disconcerting profusion of nature's species or its various

picture = text

metamorphoses into "technology." Then again, we say "strange," "odd," "curious," "disconcerting" *about* all of being.

Themes of "wonder" and the "marvel of Being" are suspect if they refer to an ecstatic mysticism that pretends to escape the world. The theme of scientific curiosity is no less suspect if it boils down to a collector's preoccupation with rarities. In both cases, desire for the exception presupposes disdain for the ordinary. Hegel was undoubtedly the first to have this properly modern consciousness of the violent paradox of a thinking whose own value is as yet unheard of, and whose domain is the grayness of the world. This ordinary grayness, the insignificance of the everyday—which the Heideggerian "one" still bears the mark of—assumes an absent, lost, or far away "grandeur." Yet, truth can be nothing if not the truth of being in totality, that is, the totality of its "ordinariness," just as meaning can only be right at [*à même*] existence and nowhere else. The modern world asks that this truth be thought: that meaning is right at. It is in the indefinite plurality of origins and their coexistence. The "ordinary" is always exceptional, however little we understand its character as origin. What we receive most communally as "strange" is that the ordinary itself is originary. With existence laid open in this way and the meaning of the world being what it is, the exception is the rule. (Is this not the testimony of the arts and literature? Is not the first and only purpose of their strange existence the presentation of this strangeness? After all, in the etymology of the word *bizarre*,[12] whether the word comes from Basque or Arabic, there is a sense of valor, commanding presence, and elegance.)

Gaining Access to the Origin

As a consequence, gaining access to the origin,[13] entering into meaning, comes down to exposing oneself to this truth.

What this means is that we do not gain access to the origin: access is refused by the origin's concealing itself in its multiplicity. We do not gain access; that is, we do not penetrate the origin; we do not identify with it. More precisely, we do not identify ourselves in it or as it, but *with* it, in a sense that must be elucidated here and is nothing other than the meaning of originary coexistence.

The alterity of the other is its being-origin. Conversely, the originarity of the origin is its being-other, but it is a being-other *than* every being *for* and *in crossing through* [à travers] all being. Thus, the originarity of the origin is not a property that would distinguish a being from all others, because this being would then have to be something other than itself in order to have its origin in its own turn. This is the most classic of God's aporias, and the proof of his nonexistence. In fact, this is the most immediate importance of Kant's destruction of the ontological argument, which can be deciphered in a quasi-literal manner; the necessity of existence is given right at the existing of all existences [*l'exister de tout l'existant*], in its very diversity and contingency. In no way does this constitute a supplementary Being. The world has no supplement. It is supplemented in itself and, as such, is indefinitely supplemented by the origin.

This follows as an essential consequence: the being-other of the origin is not the alterity of an "other-than-the-world." It is not a question of an Other (the inevitably "capitalized Other")[14] *than* the world; it is a question of the alterity or alteration *of* the world. In other words, it is not a question of an *aliud* or an *alius*, or an *alienus*, or an other in general as the essential stranger who is opposed to what is proper, but of an *alter*, that is, "one of the two." This "other," this "lowercase other," is "one" among many insofar as they are many; it is *each one*, and it is *each time* one, one *among* them, one among all and one *among* us all. In the same way, and reciprocally, "we" is always inevitably "us all," where no one of us can be "all" and each one of us is, in turn (where all our turns are simultaneous as well as successive, in every sense), the other origin of the same world.

The "outside" of the origin is "inside"—in an inside more interior than the extreme interior, that is, more interior than the *intimacy* of the world and the intimacy that belongs to each "me." If intimacy must be defined as the extremity of coincidence with oneself, then what exceeds intimacy in interiority is the distancing of coincidence itself. It is a coexistence of the origin "in" itself, a co-existence of origins; it is no accident that we use the word "intimacy" to designate a relation between several people more often than a relation to oneself. Our being-with, as a being-many, is not at all accidental, and it is in no way the secondary and random dispersion of a primordial essence. It forms the proper and necessary status and consistency of originary alterity as such. *The plurality of beings is at the foundation* [fondment] *of Being.*

A single being is a contradiction in terms. Such a being, which would be its own foundation, origin, and intimacy, would be incapable of *Being*, in every sense that this expression can have here. "Being" is neither a state nor a quality, but rather the action according to which what Kant calls "the [mere] positing of a thing"[15] takes place ("is"). The very simplicity of "position" implies no more, although no less, than its being discrete, in the mathematical sense, or its distinction *from*, in the sense of *with*, other (at least possible) positions, or its distinction *among*, in the sense of *between*, other positions. In other words, every position is also dis-position, and, considering the appearing that takes the place of and takes place in the position, all appearance is co-appearance [*com-parution*]. This is why the meaning of Being is given as existence, being-in-oneself-outside-oneself, which *we* make explicit, we "humans," but which we make explicit, as I have said, *for* the totality of beings.

If the origin is irreducibly plural, if it is the indefinitely unfolding and variously multiplied intimacy of the world, then not gaining access to the origin takes on another meaning. Its negativity is neither that of the abyss, nor of the forbidden, nor of the veiled or the concealed, nor of the secret, nor that of the unpresentable. It need not operate, then, in the dialectical mode where the subject must retain in itself its own negation (since it is the negation of its own origin). Nor does it have to operate in a mystical mode, which is the reverse of the dialectical mode, where the subject must rejoice in its negation. In both of these, negativity is given as the *aliud*, where alienation is the process that must be reversed in terms of a reappropriation. All forms of the "capitalized Other" presume this alienation from the proper as their own; this is exactly what constitutes the "capitalization" of the "Other," its unified and broken transcendence. But, in this way, all forms of the capitalized "Other" represent precisely the exalted and overexalted mode of the propriety of what is proper, which persists and consists in the "somewhere" of a "nowhere" and in the "sometime" of a "no time," that is, in the *punctum aeternum* outside the world.

The outside is inside; it is the spacing of the dis-position of the world; it is our disposition and our co-appearance. Its "negativity" changes meaning; it is not converted into positivity, but instead corresponds to the mode of Being which is that of disposition/co-appearance and which, strictly speaking, is neither negative nor positive, but instead the mode of being-together or being-*with*. The origin is together with other origins, originally divided. As a matter of fact, we do have access to it. We have access exactly in the mode of having access; we get there; we are on the brink, closest, at the threshold; we *touch* the origin. "(Truly) we have access (to the truth). . . . "[16] ["À la verité, nous accédons . . . "] is Bataille's phrase,[17] the ambiguity of which I repeat even though I use it in another way (in Bataille, it precedes the affirmation of an immediate loss of access). Perhaps everything happens between loss and appropriation: neither one nor the other, nor one and the other, nor one in the other, but much more strangely than that, much more simply.

"To reach[18] [*toucher*] the end" is again to risk missing it, because the origin is not an end. End, like Principle, is a form of the Other. To reach the origin is not to miss it; it is to be properly exposed to it. Since it is not another thing (an *aliud*), the origin is neither "missable" nor appropriable (penetrable, absorbable). It does not obey this logic. It is the plural singularity of the Being of being. We reach it to the extent that we are in touch with *ourselves* and in touch with the rest of beings. We are in touch with ourselves insofar as we exist. Being in touch with ourselves is what makes us "us," and there is no other secret to discover buried behind this very touching, behind the "with" of coexistence.

We have access to the truth of the origin as many times as we are in one another's presence and in the presence of the rest of beings.

Access is "coming to presence," but presence itself is dis-position, the spacing of singularities. Presence is nowhere other than in "coming to presence." We do not have access to a thing or a state, but only to a coming. We have access to an access.

"Strangeness" refers to the fact that each singularity is another access to the world. At the point where we would expect "something," a substance or a procedure, a principle or an end, a signification, there is nothing but the manner, the turn of the other access, which conceals itself in the very gesture wherein it offers itself to us—and whose concealing *is* the turning itself. In the singularity that he exposes, each child that is born has already concealed the access that he is "for himself" and in which he will conceal himself "within himself," just as he will one day hide under the final expression of a dead face. This is why we scrutinize these faces with such curiosity, in search of identification, looking to see whom the child looks like, and to see if death looks like itself. What we are looking for there, like in the photographs, is not an image; it is an access.

Is this not what interests us or touches us in "literature" and in "the arts"? What else interests us about the disjunction of the arts *among* themselves, by which they are what they are as arts: plural singulars? What else are they but the exposition of an access concealed in its own opening, an access that is, then, "inimitable," untransportable, untranslatable *because* it forms, each time, an absolute point of translation, transmission, or transition of the origin *into origin*. What counts in art, what makes art art (and what makes humans the artists of the world, that is, those who expose the world for the world), is neither the "beautiful" nor the "sublime"; it is neither "purposiveness without a purpose" nor the "judgment of taste"; it is neither "sensible manifestation" nor the "putting into work of truth." Undoubtedly, it is all that, but in another way: it is access to the scattered origin in its very scattering; it is the plural touching of the singular origin. This is what "the imitation of nature" has always meant. Art always has to do with cosmogony, but it exposes cosmogony for what it is: necessarily plural, diffracted, discreet, a touch of color or tone, an agile turn of phrase or folded mass, a radiance, a scent, a song, or a suspended movement, exactly because it is the birth of a *world* (and not the construction of a system). A world is always as many worlds as it takes to make a world.

We only have access to ourselves—and to the world. It is only ever a question of the following: full access is there, access to the whole of the origin. This is called "finitude" in Heideggerian terminology. But it has become clear since then that "finitude" signifies the infinite singularity of meaning, the infinite singularity of access to truth. Finitude *is* the origin; that is, it is an infinity of origins. "Origin" does not signify that from which the world comes, but rather the coming of each presence of the world, each time singular.

The Creation of the World and Curiosity

The concept of the "creation of the world"[19] represents the origin as originarily shared, spaced between us and between all beings. This, in turn, contributes to rendering the concept of the "author" of the world untenable. In fact, one could show how the motif of creation is one of those that leads directly to the death of God understood as author, first cause, and supreme being. Furthermore, if one looks at metaphysics carefully, there is not a God who simply and easily conforms to the idea of a producer. Whether in Augustine, Aquinas, Descartes, Malebranche, Spinoza, or Leibniz, one always finds that the theme of creation is burdened with and misrepresented as a problem of production, right up until the decisive moment of the ontological argument's downfall. (Hegel's restoration of the argument, the one to which Schelling assigned significant importance, is nothing but an elaboration of the concept of creation.)

The distinctive characteristic of the concept of creation is not that it posits a creator, but that, on the contrary, it renders the "creator" indistinct from its "creation." (It has to be said, here, in a general way, that the distinctive characteristic of Western monotheism is not the positing of a single god, but rather the effacing of the divine as such in the transcendence of the world. With respect to the question of origin, this is surely the precise point at which the link is forged that makes us unfailingly Jew-Greek in every respect. And, with respect to the question of destination, this is the point from which we are sent into the "global" space as such.[20]) In mythological cosmogonies, a god or demiurge makes a world starting from a situation that is already there, whatever this situation may be.[21] In creation, however, it is the being-already-there of the already-there that is of concern. In fact, if creation is *ex nihilo*, this does not signify that a creator operates "starting from nothing." As a rich and complex tradition demonstrates, this fact instead signifies two things: on the one hand, it signifies that the "creator" itself is the *nihil*; on the other, it signifies that this *nihil* is not, logically speaking, something "from which" ["d'où"] what is created would come [*provenir*], but the very origin [*provenance*], and destination, of some thing in general and of everything. Not only is the *nihil* nothing prior but there is also no longer a "nothing" that preexists creation; it is the act of appearing [*surgissement*], it is the very origin— insofar as this is understood only as what is designated by the verb "to originate." If the nothing is not anything prior, then only the *ex* remains—if one can talk about it like this—to qualify creation-in-action, that is, the appearing or arrival [*venue*] *in nothing* (in the sense that we talk about someone appearing "in person").

The nothing, then, is nothing other than the dis-position of the appearing. The origin is a distancing. It is a distancing that immediately has the magnitude of all space-time and is also nothing other than the interstice of the intimacy of the world: the *among-being* [l'entre-étant] of all beings. This among-being itself is nothing but [a] being, and has no other consistency, movement, or configuration than that of the being-a-being [*l'etre-étant*] of all beings. Being, or the among, shares the singularities of all appearings. Creation takes place everywhere and always—but it is this unique event, or advent, only on the condition of being each time what it is, or being what it is only "at each time," each time appearing singularly.

One can understand how the creation, as it appears in any Jewish-Christian-Islamic theologico-mystic configuration, testifies less (and certainly never exclusively) to a productive power of God than to his goodness and glory. In relation to such power, then, creatures are only effects, while the love and glory of God are deposited right at [*à même*] the level of what is created; that is, creatures are the very brilliance [*éclat*]²² of God's coming to presence. It is necessary, then, to understand the theme of the "image of God" and/or the "trace of God" not according to the logic of a secondary imitation, but according to this other logic where "God" is itself the singular appearance of the image or trace, or the disposition of its exposition: place as divine place, the divine as strictly *local*. As a consequence, this is no longer "divine," but is the dislocation and dis-position of the world (what Spinoza calls "the divine extension") as that opening and possibility [*ressource*] which comes from further away and goes farther, infinitely farther, than any god.

If "creation" is indeed this singular ex-position of being, then its real name is *existence*. Existence is creation, *our* creation; it is the beginning and end that *we* are. This is the thought that is the most necessary for us to think. If we do not succeed in thinking it, then we will never gain access to who we are, we who are no more than us in a world, which is itself no more than the world—but we who have reached this point precisely because we have thought *logos* (the self-presentation of presence) as creation (as singular coming).

This thinking is in no way anthropocentric; it does not put humanity at the center of "creation"; on the contrary, it transgresses [*traverse*] humanity in the excess of the appearing that appears on the scale of the totality of being, but which also appears as that excess [*demesure*] which is impossible to totalize. It is being's infinite original singularity. In humanity, or rather right at [*à même*] humanity, existence is exposed and exposing. The simplest way to put this into language would be to say that humanity speaks existence, but what speaks through its speech says the whole of being. What Heidegger calls "the ontico-ontological privilege" of *Dasein* is neither its prerogative nor its privilege [*apanage*]: it gets Being on its way [*il engage l'être*], but the Being of *Dasein* is nothing other than the Being of being.

If existence is exposed as such by humans, what is exposed there also holds for the rest of beings. There is not, on the one side, an originary singularity and then, on the other, a simple being-there of things, more or less given for our use. On the contrary, in exposing itself as singularity, existence exposes the singularity of Being as such in all being. The difference between humanity and the rest of being (which is not a concern to be denied, but the nature of which is, nevertheless, not a given), while itself being inseparable from other differences within being (since man is "also" animal, "also" living, "also" physio-chemical), does not distinguish true existence from a sort of subexistence. Instead, this difference forms the concrete condition of singularity. We would not be "humans" if there were not "dogs" and "stones." A stone is the exteriority of singularity in what would have to be called its mineral or mechanical actuality [*litter-alité*]. But I would no longer be a "human" if I did not have this exteriority "in me," in the form of the quasi-minerality of bone: I would no longer be a human if I *were* not a body, a spacing of all other bodies and a spacing of "me" in "me." A singularity is always a body, and all bodies are singularities (the bodies, their states, their movements, their transformations).

Existence, therefore, is not a property of *Dasein*; it is the original singularity of Being, which *Dasein* exposes for all being. This is why humanity is not "in the world" as it would be in a milieu (why would the milieu be necessary?); it is *in* the world insofar as the world is its own exteriority, the proper space of its being-out-in-the-world. But it is necessary to go farther than this in order to avoid giving the impression that the world, despite everything, remains essentially "the world of humans." It is not so much the world of humanity as it is the world of the nonhuman to which humanity is exposed and which humanity, in turn, exposes. One could try to formulate it in the following way: *humanity is the exposing of the world; it is neither the end nor the ground of the world; the world is the exposure of humanity; it is neither the environment nor the representation of humanity.*

Therefore, however far humanity is from being the end of nature or nature the end of humanity (we have already tried all the variations of this formula), the end is always being-in-the-world and the being-world of all being.

Even supposing one still wished to take the world as the representation of humanity, this would not necessarily imply a solipsism of humanity: because, if that is the case, then it is the representation itself that instructs me about what it necessarily represents to me, an irrefutable exteriority as my exteriority. The representation of a spacing is itself a spacing. An *intuitus originarius*, which would not be a representation but rather an immersion in the thing-itself, would exist alone and would be for itself the origin and the thing: this was shown above to be contradictory. Descartes himself testifies to the exteriority of the world as the exteriority of his body. Because he hardly doubts his body, he makes a fiction of doubting it, and this pretension as such attests to the truth of *res extensa*. It is also not surprising that for Descartes the reality of this world, about which God could not deceive me, is maintained in Being by the *continuous creation* on the part of this very God. Reality is always in each instant, from place to place, each time in turn, which is exactly how the reality of *res cogitans* attests to itself in each "ego sum," which is each time the "I am" of each one in turn [*chaque fois de chacun à son tour*].

Once again, this is the way in which there is no Other. "Creation" signifies precisely that there is no Other and that the "there is" is not an Other. Being is not the Other, but the origin is the punctual and discrete spacing *between us*, as *between us and the rest of the world*, as *between all beings*.[23]

We find this alterity primarily and essentially intriguing. It intrigues us because it exposes the always-other origin, always inappropriable and always there, each and every time present as inimitable. This is why we are primarily and essentially *curious* about the world and about ourselves (where "the world" is the generic name of the object of this ontological curiosity). The correlate of creation, understood as existence itself, is a curiosity that must be understood in a completely different sense than the one given by Heidegger. For him, curiosity is the frantic activity of passing from being to being in an insatiable sort of way, without ever being able to stop and think. Without a doubt, this does testify to being-with-one-another, but it testifies to it without being able to gain access to the existent opening that characterizes *Dasein* in the "instant."[24] It is necessary, then, to disconnect the most primitive layer of curiosity, the level on which we are primarily *interested* by what is interesting par excellence (the origin), from this inconsistent curiosity and also from the attention that takes care of others (*Fürsorge*). At this level, we are interested in the sense of being intrigued by the ever-renewed alterity of the origin and, if I may say so, in the sense of having an affair with it. (It is no accident that sexual curiosity is an exemplary figure of curiosity and is, in fact, more than just a figure of it.)

As English [and French] allows us to say, other beings are *curious* (or *bizarre*) to me because they give me access to the origin; they allow me to touch it; they leave me before it, leave me before its turning, which is concealed each time. Whether an other is another person, animal, plant, or star, it is above all the glaring presence of a place and moment of absolute origin, irrefutable, offered as such and vanishing in its passing. This occurs in the face of a newborn child, a face encountered by chance on the street, an insect, a shark, a pebble . . . but if one really wants to understand it, it is not a matter of making all these curious presences equal.

If we do not have access to the other in the mode just described, but seek to appropriate the origin—which is something we always do—then this same curiosity transforms itself into appropriative or destructive rage. We no longer look for a singularity of the origin in the other; we look for the unique and exclusive origin, in order to either adopt it or reject it. The other becomes the Other according to the mode of desire or hatred. Making the other divine (together with our voluntary servitude) or making it evil (together with its exclusion or extermination) is that part of curiosity no longer interested in dis-position and co-appearance, but rather has become the desire for the Position itself. This desire is the desire to fix the origin, or *to give the origin to itself*, once and for all, and in one place for all, that is, always outside the world. This is why such desire is a desire for murder, and not only murder but also for an increase of cruelty and horror, which is like the tendency toward the intensification of murder; it is mutilation, carving up, relentlessness, meticulous execution, the joy of agony. Or it is the massacre, the mass grave, massive and technological execution, the bookkeeping of the camps. It is always a matter of expediting the transformation of the other into the Other or making the Other appear in the place of the other, and, therefore, a matter of identifying the Other and the origin itself.

The Other is nothing more than a correlate of this mad desire, but others, in fact, are our *originary interests*. It is true, however, that the possibility of this mad desire is contained in the very disposition of originary interests: the dissemination of the origin upsets [*affole*] the origin in "me" to exactly the same extent that it makes me curious about it, makes "me" a "me" (or a "subject," some*one* in any case). (It follows, then, that no ethics would be independent from an ontology. Only ontology, in fact, may be ethical in a consistent manner. It will be necessary to return to this elsewhere.)

Between Us: First Philosophy

When addressing the fact that philosophy is contemporaneous with the Greek city, one ends up losing sight of what is in question—and rightly so. As is only fitting, however, losing sight of what is in question returns us to the problem in all its acuity after these twenty-eight centuries.

It returns us to the question of the origin of our history. There is no sense of reconstituting a teleology here, and it is not a matter of retracing a process directed toward an end. To the contrary, history clearly appears here as the movement sparked by a singular circumstance, a movement that does not reabsorb this singularity in a universality (or "universal history," as Marx and Nietzsche understood it), but instead reflects the impact of this singularity in renewed singular events. Thus, we have a "future" [*avenir*] and a "to come" [*à venir*]; we have this "future" as a "past," which is not past in the sense of being the starting point of a directed process, but past in the sense of being a "curiosity" ["bizarrerie"] (the "Greek miracle") that is itself intriguing and, as such, remains still "to come." This dis-position of history indeed makes there be *a* history and not a *processus* (here as elsewhere, the Hegelian model reveals itself as uncovering the truth by way of its exact opposite). One can understand, then, Heidegger's "history of Being," and understand that our relation to this history is necessarily that of its *Destruktion*, or deconstruction. In other words, it is a matter of bringing to light this history's singularity as the disassembling law of its unity and understanding that this law itself is the law of meaning.

This clearly supposes that such a task is as demanding and urgent as it is impossible to measure. The task is to understand how history—as a singular, Western accident—"became" what one might call "global" or "planetary" without, at the same time, engendering itself as "universal." Consequently, it is the task of understanding how the West disappeared, not by reciting the formulas of its generalized uniformity, but by understanding the expansion, by and through this "uniformity," of a plural singularity that is and is not, at the same time, "proper" to this "o/accident." And one must understand that this formidable question is none other than the question of "capital" (or of "capitalism"). If one wants to give a full account of "capital"—starting from the very first moments of history that began in the merchant cities—then it is necessary to remove it, far more radically than Marx could have, from its own representation in linear and cumulative history, *as well as* from the representation of a teleological history of its overcoming or rejection. This would appear to be the—problematic—lesson of history. But we cannot understand this task unless we first understand what is most at stake in our history, that is, what is most at stake in philosophy.

According to different versions, but in a predominantly uniform manner, the tradition put forward a representation according to which philosophy and the city would be (would have been, must have been) related to one another as subjects. Accordingly, philosophy, as the articulation of *logos*, is the subject of the city, where the city is the space of this articulation. Likewise, the city, as the gathering of the *logikoi*, is the subject of philosophy, where philosophy is the production of their common *logos*. *Logos* itself, then, contains the essence or meaning of this reciprocity: it is the common foundation of community, where community, in turn, is the foundation of Being.

It is within this uniform horizon, according to different versions (whether strong or weak, happy or unhappy) of this predominant mode of inquiry, that we still understand the famous "political animal" of Aristotle: it is to presume that *logos* is the condition of community, which, in turn, is the condition of humanity; and/or it is to presume that each of these three terms draws its unity and consistency from [its sharing] a communication of essence with the other two (where the world as such remains relatively exterior to the whole affair, presuming that nature or *physis* accomplishes itself in humanity understood as *logos politikos*, whereas *technē* subordinates itself to both).

But this horizon—that of political philosophy in the fullest sense (not as the "philosophy of politics," but philosophy as politics)—might very well be what points to the singular situation where our history gets under way and, at the same time, blocks access to this situation. Or instead, this horizon might be that which, in the course of its history, gives an indication of its own deconstruction and exposes this situation anew in another way.[25] "Philosophy and politics" is the exposition [*énoncé*] of this situation. But it is a disjunctive exposition, because the situation itself is disjunctive. The city is not primarily "community," any more than it is primarily "public space." The city is at least as much the bringing to light of being-in-common *as the dis-position* (dispersal and disparity) of the community represented as founded in interiority or transcendence. It is "community" without common origin. That being the case, and as long as philosophy is an appeal to the origin, the city, far from being philosophy's subject or space, is its problem. Or else, it is its subject or space in the mode of being its problem, its aporia. Philosophy, for its part, can appeal to the origin only on the condition of the dis-position of *logos* (that is, of the origin as justified and set into discourse): *logos* is the spacing at the very place of the origin. Consequently, philosophy is the problem of the city; philosophy covers over the subject that is expected as "community."

This is why philosophical politics and political philosophy regularly run aground on the essence of community or community as origin. Rousseau and Marx are exemplary in their struggle with these obstacles. Rousseau revealed the aporia of a community that would have to precede itself in order to constitute itself: in its very concept, the "social contract" is the denial or foreclosure of the originary division [*déliaison*] between those singularities that would have to agree to the contract and, thereby, "draw it to a close." Although assuredly more radical in his demand for the dissolution of politics in all spheres of existence (which is the "realization of philosophy"), Marx ignores that the separation between singularities overcome and suppressed in this way is not, in fact, an accidental separation imposed by "political" authority, but rather the constitutive separation of dis-position. However powerful it is for thinking the "real relation" and what we call the "individual," "communism" was still not able to think being-in-common as distinct from community.

In this sense, philosophical politics regularly proceeds according to the surreptitious appeal to a metaphysics of the one-origin, where, at the same time, it nevertheless exposes, *volens nolens*, the situation of the dis-position of origins. Often the result is that the dis-position is turned into a matter of exclusion, included as excluded, and that all philosophical politics is a politics of exclusivity and the correlative exclusion—of a class, of an order, of a "community"—the point of which is to end up with a "people," in the "base" sense of the term. The demand for equality, then, is the necessary, ultimate, and absolute gesture; in fact, it is almost indicative of dis-position as such. However, as long as this continues to be a matter of an "egalitarian demand founded upon some generic identity,"[26] equality will never do justice [*ne fait encore pas droit*] to singularity or even recognize the considerable difficulties of wanting to do so. It is here that the critique of abstract rights comes to the fore. However, the "concrete" that must oppose such abstraction is not made up primarily of empirical determinations, which, in the capitalist regime, exhaust even the most egalitarian will: rather, *concrete* here primarily signifies the real object of a thinking of being-in-common, and this real object is, in turn, the singular plural of the origin, the singular plural of the origin of "community" itself (if one still wants to call this "community"). All of this is undoubtedly what is indicated by the word that follows "equality" in the French republican slogan: "fraternity" is supposed to be the solution to equality (or to "equiliberty" ["égaliberté"])[27] by evoking or invoking a "generic identity." What is lacking there is exactly the common origin of the common.[28]

It is "lacking" insofar as one attempts to take account of it within the horizon of philosophical politics. Once this horizon is deconstructed, however, the necessity of the plural singular of the origin comes into play—and this is already under way. But I do not plan to propose an "other politics" under this heading. I am no longer sure that this term (or the term "political philosophy") can continue to have any consistency beyond this opening up of the horizon which comes to us both at the end of the long history of our Western situation *and* as the reopening of this situation. I only want to help to bring out that the combination philosophy-politics, in all the force of its being joined together, *simultaneously exposes and hides the dis-position of the origin* and co-appearance, which is its correlate.

The philosophico-political horizon is what links the dis-position to a continuity and to a community of essence. In order to be effective, such a relation requires an essentializing procedure: sacrifice. If one looks carefully, one can find the place of sacrifice in all political philosophy (or rather, one will find the challenge of the *abstract*, which makes a sacrifice of concrete singularity). But as singular origin, existence is unsacrificable.[29]

In this respect, then, the urgent demand named above is not another political abstraction. Instead, it is a reconsideration of the very meaning of "politics"—and, therefore, of "philosophy"—in light of the originary situation: the bare exposition of singular origins. This is the necessary "first philosophy" (in the canonical sense of the expression). It is an ontology. Philosophy needs to recommence, to restart itself from itself against itself, against political philosophy and philosophical politics. In order to do this, philosophy needs to think in principle about how we are "us" among us, that is, how the consistency of our Being is in being-in-common, and how this consists precisely in the "in" or in the "between" of its spacing.

The last "first philosophy," if one dare say anything about it, is given to us in Heidegger's fundamental ontology. It is that which has put us on the way [*chemin*] to where we are, together, whether we know it or not. But it is also why its author was able to, in a sort of return of *Destruktion* itself, compromise himself, in an unpardonable way, with his involvement in a philosophical politics that became criminal. This very point, then, indicates to us that place from which first philosophy must recommence: it is necessary to refigure fundamental ontology (as well as the existential analytic, the history of Being, and the thinking of *Ereignis* that goes along with it) with a thorough resolve that *starts from the plural singular of origins*, from *being-with*.

I want to return to the issue of "first philosophy" in order to push it even further, but without claiming to be the one who can fully accomplish such an undertaking. By definition and in essence, the above "first philosophy" needs "to be made by all, not by one," like the poetry of Maldoror. For the moment, I only want to indicate the principle of its necessity. Heidegger clearly states that being-with (*Mitsein*, *Miteinandersein*, and *Mitdasein*) is essential to the constitution of *Dasein* itself. Given this, it needs to be made absolutely clear that *Dasein*, far from being either "man" or "subject," is not even an isolated and unique "one," but is instead always the one, each one, with one another [*l'un-avec-l'autre*]. If this determination is essential, then it needs to attain to the co-originary dimension and expose it without reservation. But as it has often been said, despite this affirmative assertion of co-originarity, he gives up on the step to the consideration of *Dasein* itself. It is appropriate, then, to examine the possibility of an explicit and endless exposition of co-originarity and the possibility of taking account of what is at stake in the togetherness of the ontological enterprise (and, in this way, taking account of what is at stake in its political consequences.)[30]

It is necessary to add here that there is a reason for this examination which is far more profound than what first appears to be a simple "readjustment" of the Heideggerian discourse. The reason obviously goes much farther than that, since at its fullest, it is about nothing less than the possibility of speaking "of *Dasein*" in general, or of saying "the existing" or "existence." What would happen to philosophy if speaking about Being in other ways than saying "we," "you," and "I" became excluded? Where is Being spoken, and who speaks Being?

The reason that is foreshadowed has to do precisely with speaking (of) Being. The themes of being-with and co-originarity need to be renewed and need to "reinitialize" the existential analytic, exactly because these are meant to respond to the question of the meaning of Being, or to Being as meaning. But if the meaning of Being indicates itself principally by the putting into play of Being in *Dasein* and as *Dasein*, then, precisely as *meaning*, this putting into play (the "there will be" of Being) can only attest to itself or expose itself in the mode of being-with: because as relates to meaning, it is never for just one, but always for one another, always between one another. The meaning of Being is never in what is said— never said in significations. But it is assuredly in them that "it is spoken," in the absolute sense of the expression. "One speaks," "it speaks," means "Being is spoken"; it is meaning (but does not construct meaning). But "one" or "it" is never other than *we*.

In other words, in revealing itself as what is at stake in the meaning of Being, *Dasein* has already revealed itself as being-with and reveals itself as such before any other explication. The meaning of Being is not in play in *Dasein* in order to be "communicated" to others; its putting into play *is identically being-with*. Or again: *Being is put into play as the "with" that is absolutely indisputable.* From now on, this is the minimal ontological premise. Being is put into play among us; it does not have any other meaning except the dis-position of this "between."

Heidegger writes, *"Dasein's* . . . understanding of Being already implies the understanding of others."[31] But this surely does not say enough. The understanding of Being is nothing other than an understanding of others, which means, in every sense, understanding others through "me" and understanding "me" through others, the understanding of one another [*des uns des autres*]. One could say even more simply that Being is communication. But it remains to be known what "communication" *is*.

For the moment, it is less important to respond to the question of the meaning of Being (if it is a question, and if we do not already basically respond every day and each time . . .) than it is to pay attention to the fact of its exhibition. If "communication" is for us, today, such an affair—in every sense of the word . . . —if its theories are flourishing, if its technologies are being proliferated, if the "mediatization" of the "media" brings along with it an auto-communicational vertigo, if one plays around with the theme of the indistinctness between the "message" and the "medium" out of either a disenchanted or jubilant fascination, then it is because something is exposed or laid bare. In fact, [what is exposed] is the bare and "content"-less web of "communication." One could say it is the bare web of the *com-* (of the *telecom-*, said with an acknowledgment of its independence); that is, it is *our* web or "us" as web or network, an *us* that is reticulated and spread out, with its extension for an essence and its spacing for a structure. We are "ourselves" too inclined to see in this the overwhelming destiny of modernity. Contrary to such meager evidence, it might be that we have understood nothing about the situation, and rightly so, and that we have to start again to understand ourselves—our existence and that of the world, our being disposed in this way.

Being Singular Plural

Being singular plural: these three apposite words, which do not have any determined syntax ("being" is a verb or noun; "singular" and "plural" are nouns or adjectives; all can be rearranged in different combinations), mark an absolute equivalence, both in an indistinct *and* distinct way. Being is singularly plural and plurally singular. Yet, this in itself does not constitute a particular predication of Being, as if Being is or has a certain number of attributes, one of which is that of being singular-plural—however double, contradictory, or chiasmatic this may be. On the contrary, the singular-plural constitutes the essence of Being, a constitution that undoes or dislocates every single, substantial essence of Being itself. This is not just a way of speaking, because there is no prior substance that would be dissolved. Being does not preexist its singular plural. To be more precise, Being absolutely does not *preexist*; nothing preexists; only what exists exists. Ever since Parmenides, one of philosophy's peculiarities has been that it has been unfolding this unique proposition, in all of its senses. This proposition proposes nothing but the placement [*la position*] and dis-position of existence. It is its plural singularity. Unfolding this proposition, then, is the only thing philosophy has to do.[32]

That which exists, whatever this might be, coexists because it exists. The co-implication of existing [*l'exister*] is the sharing of the world. A world is not something external to existence; it is not an extrinsic addition to other existences; the world is the coexistence that puts these existences together. But one could object that there exists something [which does not first coexist]. Kant established that there exists something, exactly because I can think of a possible existence: but the possible comes second in relation to the real, because there already exists something real.[33]

It would also be worth adding that the above inference actually leads to a conclusion about an element of existence's plurality [*un pluriel d'existence*]: there exists something ("me") *and* another thing (this other "me" that represents the possible) to which I relate myself in order for me to ask myself if there exists something of the sort that I think of as possible. This something coexists at least as much as "me." But this needs to be drawn out in the following way: there does not exist just these "me's," understood as subjects-of-representation, because along with the real difference between two "me's" is given the difference between things in general, the difference between my body and many bodies. This variation on an older style of philosophizing is only meant to point out that there has never been, nor will there ever be, any [real] philosophical solipsism. In a certain way, there never has been, and never will be, a philosophy "of the subject" in the sense of the final [*infinie*] closure in itself of a for-itself.

However, there is for the whole of philosophy what is exemplified in Hegel's statement "the I is in essence and act the universal: and such partnership (*Gemeinschaftlichkeit*) is a form, though an external form, of universality."[34] It is well known that dialectical logic requires the passage through exteriority as essential to interiority itself. Nevertheless, within this logic, it is the "interior" and subjective form of the "Me" that is needed in order to finish the project of finding itself and posing itself as the *truth* of the universal and its community. As a consequence, what is left for us to hold onto is the moment of "exteriority" as being of almost essential value, so essential that it would no longer be a matter of relating this exteriority to any individual or collective "me" without also unfailingly attaining [*maintenir*] to *exteriority itself and as such.*

Being singular plural means the essence of Being is only as coessence. In turn, coessence, or *being-with* (being-with-many), designates the essence of the *co-*, or even more so, the *co-* (the *cum*) itself in the position or guise of an essence. In fact, coessentiality cannot consist in an assemblage of essences, where the essence of this assemblage as such remains to be determined. In relation to such an assemblage, the assembled essences would become [mere] accidents. Coessentiality signifies the essential sharing of essentiality, sharing in the guise of assembling, as it were. This could also be put in the following way: if Being is being-with, then it is, in its being-with, the "with" that constitutes Being; the with is not simply an addition. This operates in the same way as a collective [*collégial*] power: power is neither exterior to the members of the collective [*collège*] nor interior to each one of them, but rather consists in the collectivity [*collégialité*] as such.

Therefore, it is not the case that the "with" is an addition to some prior Being; instead, the "with" is at the heart of Being. In this respect, it is absolutely necessary to reverse the order of philosophical exposition, for which it has been a matter of course that the "with"—and the other that goes along with it—always comes second, even though this succession is contradicted by the underlying [*profonde*] logic in question here. Even Heidegger preserves this order of succession in a remarkable way, in that he does not introduce

the co-originarity of *Mitsein* until after having established the originary character of *Dasein.* The same remark could be made about
the Husserlian constitution of the *alter ego,* even though this too is
in its own way contemporaneous (once again, the *cum*) with the
ego in the "single universal community."[35]

To the contrary, it can also be shown that when Hegel begins the
Phenomenology of Spirit with the moment of "sense certainty," where
it appears that consciousness has not yet entered into relation with
another consciousness, this moment is nonetheless characterized by
the language with which consciousness appropriates for itself the
truth of what is immediately sensible (the famous "now it is night").
In doing so, the relation to another consciousness remains surreptitiously presupposed. It would be easy to produce many observations
of this kind. For example, the evidence for the *ego sum* comes down
to, constitutively and co-originarily, its possibility in each one of
Descartes's readers. The evidence as evidence owes its force, and its
claim to truth, precisely to this possibility in each one of us—one
could say, the copossibility. *Ego sum = ego cum.*[36]

In this way, it can be shown that, for the whole of philosophy,
the necessary successivity [*la successivité*] of any exposition does not
prevent the deeply set [*profond*] order of reasons from being regulated by a co-originarity [*soit réglé sur une co-originarité*]. In fact,
in proposing to reverse the order of ontological exposition, I am
only proposing to bring to light a resource that is more or less obscurely presented throughout the entire history of philosophy—
and presented as an answer to the situation described above: philosophy begins with and in "civil" ["concitoyenne"] coexistence as
such (which, in its very difference from the "imperial" form, forces
power to emerge as a problem). Or rather, the "city" is not primarily a form of political institution; it is primarily being-with *as such.*
Philosophy is, in sum, the thinking of being-with; because of this,
it is also thinking-with as such.

This is not simply a matter of clarifying a still faulty exposition. . . . It is just as much a question of doing justice to the essential reasons for why, across the whole history of philosophy, being-
with is subordinated to Being *and,* at the same time and according

to this very subordination, is always asserting [*de faire valoir*] its problem as the very problem of Being. In sum, *being-with is Being's own most problem*. The task is to know why and how this is so.[37]

Let us take up the matter again, then, not beginning from the Being of being and proceeding to being itself being with-one-another [*étant l'un-avec-l'autre*], but starting from being—and all of being—determined in its Being as being with-one-another. [This is the] singular plural in such a way that the singularity of each is indissociable from its being-with-many and *because*, in general, a singularity is indissociable from a plurality. Here again, it is not a question of any supplementary property of Being. The concept of the singular implies its singularization and, therefore, its distinction from other singularities (which is different from any concept of the individual, since an immanent totality, without an other, would be a perfect individual, and is also different from any concept of the particular, since this assumes the togetherness of which the particular is a part, so that such a particular can only present its difference from other particulars as numerical difference). In Latin, the term *singuli* already says the plural, because it designates the "one" as belonging to "one by one." The singular is primarily *each* one and, therefore, also *with* and *among* all the others. The singular is a plural. It also undoubtedly offers the property of indivisibility, but it is not indivisible the way substance is indivisible. It is, instead, indivisible in each instant [*au coup par coup*], within the event of its singularization. It is indivisible like any instant is indivisible, which is to say that it is infinitely divisible, or *punctually* indivisible. Moreover, it is not indivisible like any particular is indivisible, but on the condition of *pars pro toto*: the singular is each time *for* the whole, in its place and in light of it. (If humanity is *for* being in totality in the way I have tried to present it, then it is the exposing of the singular as such and in general.) A singularity does not stand out against the background of Being; it is, when it is, Being itself or its origin.

Once again, it is fairly easy to see to what extent these features answer to those of the Cartesian *ego sum*. The singular is an *ego* that is not a "subject" in the sense of the relation of a self to itself. It is

an "ipseity" that is not the relation of a "me" to "itself."[38] It is neither "me" nor "you"; it is what is distinguished in the distinction,
what is discreet in the discretion. It is being-a-part of Being itself
and in Being itself, Being in each instant [*au coup par coup*], which
attests to the fact that Being only takes place in each instant.

The essence of Being is the shock of the instant [*le coup*]. Each
time, "Being" is always an instance [*un coup*] of Being (a lash, blow,
beating, shock, knock, an encounter, an access). As a result, it is
also always an instance of "with": singulars singularly together,
where the togetherness is neither the sum, nor the incorporation
[*englobant*], nor the "society," nor the "community" (where these
words only give rise to problems). The togetherness of singulars is
singularity "itself." It "assembles" them insofar as it spaces them;
they are "linked" insofar as they are not unified.

According to these conditions, Being as being-with might no
longer be able to say itself in the third person, as in "it is" or "there
is." Because there would no longer be a point of view that is exterior to being-together from which it could be announced that
"there is" being and a being-with of beings, one with the other.
There would be no "it is" and, therefore, no longer the "I am" that
is subjacent to the announcement of the "it is." Rather, it would
be necessary to think the third-person singular in the first person.
As such, then, it becomes the first-person plural. Being could not
speak of itself except in this unique manner: "we are." The truth
of the *ego sum* is the *nos sumus*; this "we" announces itself through
humanity for all the beings "we" are with, for existence in the sense
of being-essentially-with, as a Being whose essence is the with.

("One will speak . . . ": Which one? We will speak: Who is this
"we"? How can I say "us" for those of you who are reading this?
How can I say "us" for me? Although this is what we are in the
process of doing, how do we think together, whether we are "in
accord" or not? How are we with one another? All of this is to ask:
What is at play in our communication, in this book, in its sen-
tences, and in the whole situation that more or less gives them
some meaning? [This is the] question of philosophy as "literature," which is about asking how far it is possible to take the third-

person discourse of philosophy. At what point must ontology become . . . what? Become conversation? Become lyricism? . . . The strict conceptual rigor of being-with exasperates the discourse of its concept. . . .)

~

What is known as "society," therefore, in the broadest and most diffuse sense of the word, is the figure [*chiffre*] of an ontology yet to be put into play. Rousseau presented [a glimpse of] it by making the poorly named "contract" the very event that "made a creature of intelligence and a man . . . from a stupid, limited animal,"[39] and not simply an arrangement between individuals. (Nietzsche confirms this presentation in a paradoxical way when Zarathustra says, "human society: that is an experiment . . . a long search . . . and *not* a 'contract'".[40]) Marx saw it when he qualified humanity as social in its very origin, production, and destination, and when the entire movement and posture of his thinking assigned Being itself to this social being. Heidegger designated it in positing being-with as constitutive of being-there. No one, however, has radically thematized the "with" as the essential trait of Being and as its proper plural singular coessence. But they have brought us, together and individually, to the point where we can no longer avoid thinking about this in favor of that to which all of contemporary experience testifies. In other words, what is at stake is no longer thinking:

   —beginning from the one, or from the other,
   —beginning from their togetherness, understood now as the One, now as the Other,
   —but thinking, absolutely and without reserve, beginning from the "with," *as the proper essence of one whose Being is nothing other than with-one-another* [l'un-avec-l'autre].

The one/the other is neither "by," nor "for," nor "in," nor "despite," but rather "with." This "with" is at once both more and less than "relation" or "bond," especially if such relation or bond presupposes the preexistence of the terms upon which it relies; the "with" is the exact contemporary of its terms; it is, in fact, their contemporaneity. "With" is the sharing of time-space; it is the at-the-same-time-in-the-same-place as itself, in itself, shattered. It is the instant scaling back of the principle of identity: Being is at the same time in the same place only on the condition of the spacing of an indefinite plurality of singularities. Being is with Being; it does not ever recover itself, but it is near to itself, beside itself, in touch with itself, its very self, in the paradox of that proximity where distancing [*éloignement*] and strangeness are revealed. We are each time an other, each time with others. "With" does not indicate the sharing of a common situation any more than the juxtaposition of pure exteriorities does (for example, a bench with a tree with a dog with a passer-by).

The question of Being and the meaning of Being has become the question of being-with and of being-together (in the sense of the world). This is what is signified by [our] modern sense of anxiety, which does not so much reveal a "crisis of society" but, instead, reveals that the "sociality" or "association" of humans is an injunction that humanity places on itself, or that it receives from the world: to have to be only what it is and to have to, itself, be Being as such. This sort of formula is primarily a desperate tautological abstraction—and this is why we are all worried. Our task is to break the hard shell of this tautology. What is the being-with of Being?

In one sense, this is the original situation of the West that is always repeating itself; it is always the problem of the city, the repetition of which, for better or worse, has already punctuated our history. Today, this repetition produces itself as a situation in which the two major elements [*données*] compose a sort of antinomy: on the one hand, there is the exposure of the world and, on the other, the end of representations of the world. This means nothing short of a transformation in the relation [that we name] "politico-philosophy": it can no longer be a matter of a single community, of its essence, closure, and sovereignty; by contrast, it can no longer be a matter of organizing community according to the decrees of a sovereign Other, or according to the *telos* [fins] of a history. It can no longer be a matter of treating sociability as a regrettable and inevitable accident, as a constraint that has to be managed in some way or another. Community is bare, but it is imperative.

On the one side, the concept of community or the city is, in every sense, diffracted. It is that which signifies the chaotic and multiform appearance of the infranational, supranational, para-national and, moreover, the dis-location of the "national" in general. On the other side, the concept of community appears to have its own prefix as its only content: the *cum*, the *with* deprived of substance and connection, stripped of interiority, subjectivity, and personality. Either way, sovereignty is nothing.[41] Sovereignty is nothing but the *com-*; as such, it is always and indefinitely "to be completed," as in com-munism or com-passion.

This is not a matter of thinking the annihilation of sovereignty. It is a matter of thinking through the following question: If sovereignty is the grand, political term for defining community (its leader or its essence) that has nothing beyond itself, with no foundation or end but itself, what becomes of sovereignty when it is revealed that it is nothing but a singularly plural spacing? How is one to think sovereignty as the "nothing" of the "with" that is laid bare? At the same time, if political sovereignty has always signified the refusal of domination (of a state by another or by a church, of a people by something other than itself), how is one to think the bare sovereignty of the "with" and against domination, whether this is the domination of being-together by some other means or the domination of togetherness by itself (by the regulation of its "automatic" control)? In fact, one could begin to describe the present transformation of "political space"[42] as a transition toward "empire," where empire signifies two things: (1) domination without sovereignty (without the elaboration of such a concept); and (2) the distancing, spacing, and plurality opposed to the concentration of interiority required by political sovereignty. The question then becomes: How is one to think the spacing of empire against its domination?

In one way or another, bare sovereignty (which is, in a way, to transcribe Bataille's notion of sovereignty) presupposes that one take a certain distance from the politico-philosophical order and from the realm of "political philosophy." This distance is not taken in order to engage in a depoliticized thinking, but in order to engage in a thinking, the site of which is the very constitution, imagination, and signification of the political, which allows this thinking to retrace its path in its retreat and beginning from this retreat. The retreat of the political does not signify the disappearance of the political. It only signifies the disappearance of the philosophical presupposition of the whole politico-philosophical order, which is always an ontological presupposition. This presupposition has various forms; it can consist in thinking Being as community and community as destination, or, on the contrary, thinking Being as anterior and outside the order of society and, as such, thinking Being as the accidental exteriority of commerce and power. But, in this way, being-together is never properly [brought to the fore as an explicit] theme and as the ontological problem. The retreat of the political[43] is the uncovering, the ontological laying bare of being-with.

~

Being singular plural: in a single stroke, without punctuation, without a mark of equivalence, implication, or sequence. A single, continuous-discontinuous mark tracing out the entirety of the ontological domain, being-with-itself designated as the "with" of Being, of the singular and plural, and dealing a blow to ontology—not only another signification but also another syntax. The "meaning of Being": not only as the "meaning of with," but also, and above all, as the "with" of meaning. Because none of these three terms precedes or grounds the other, each designates the coessence of the others. This coessence puts essence itself in the hyphenation—"being-singular-plural"—which is a mark of union and also a mark of division, a mark of sharing that effaces itself, leaving each term to its isolation *and* its being-with-the-others.

From this point forward, then, the unity of an ontology must be sought in this traction, in this drawing out, in this distancing and spacing which is that of Being and, at the same time, that of the singular and the plural, both in the sense that they are distinct from one another and indistinct. In such an ontology, which is not an "ontology of society" in the sense of a "regional ontology," but ontology itself as a "sociality" or an "association" more originary than all "society," more originary than "individuality" and every "essence of Being." Being is *with*; it is *as the with* of Being itself (the cobeing of Being), so that Being does not identify itself *as such*[44] (*as Being of the being*), but *shows itself* [se pose], *gives itself, occurs, dis-poses itself* (made event, history, and world) as its own singular plural *with*. In other words, *Being is not without Being*, which is not another miserable tautology as long as one understands it in the co-originary mode of being-with-being-itself.

According to this mode, Being is simultaneous. Just as, in order to say Being, one must repeat it and say that "Being is," so Being is only simultaneous with itself. The time of Being (the time that it is) is this simultaneity, this coincidence that presupposes "incidence" in general. It assumes movement, displacement, and deployment; it assumes the originary temporal derivative of Being, its spacing.

In one sense, this is all a matter of repeating the Aristotelian axiom *pollakôs legomenon*; Being is said in many ways. But to say it once more, according to the "with," the "also," the "again" of a history that repeats this excavation and drawing out [*traction*] of Being, the singularity of Being is its plural. But this plurality is no longer said in multiple ways that all begin from a presumed, single core of meaning. The multiplicity of the said (that is, of the sayings) belongs to Being as its constitution. This occurs with each said, which is always singular; it occurs in each said, beyond each said, and as the multiplicity of the totality of being [*l'étant en totalité*].

Being, then, does not coincide *with* itself unless this coincidence immediately and essentially marks itself out [*se remarque*] according to the *co*structure of its occurrence [*l'événement*] (its incidence, encounter, angle of declination, shock, or discordant accord). Being coincides with Being: it *is* the spacing and the unexpected arrival [*survenue*], the unexpected spacing, of the singular plural *co-*.

It might be asked why it is still necessary to call this "Being," since the essence of it is reduced to a prefix of Being, reduced to a *co-* outside of which there would be nothing, nothing but beings or existences [*les existants*], and where this *co-* has none of the substance or consistency proper to "Being" as such. This is, in fact, the matter in question. Being consists in nothing other than the existence of all existences [*tous les existants*]. However, this consistency itself does not vanish in a cloud of juxtaposed beings. What I am trying to indicate by speaking of "dis-position" is neither a simple position nor a juxtaposition. Instead, the *co-* defines the unity and uniqueness of what is, in general. What is to be understood is precisely the constitution of this unique unity as *co-*: the *singular plural.*

(Incidentally, one could show without much trouble that this is a question that has been taken up and repeated throughout a long tradition: in Leibniz's monadology, in all the various considerations of the "originary division," and, most of all, in all the various forms of the difference between the in-itself and the for-itself. But exactly what is important is this repetition, the concentration on and repeated excavation of the question—which does not necessarily signify some sort of progress or degeneration, but rather a displacement, a fit of, or drift toward something else, toward another philosophical posture.)

At the very least, and provisionally, one could try to say it in the following way: it is no more a matter of an originary multiplicity and its correlation (in the sense of the One dividing itself in an arch-dialectical manner, or in the sense of the atoms' relationship to the clinamen) than it is a matter of an originary unity and its division. In either case, one must think an anteriority of the origin according to some event that happens to it unexpectedly (even if that event originates within it). It is necessary, then, to think plural unity originarily. This is indeed the place to think the plural as such.

In Latin, *plus* is comparable to *multus.* It is not "numerous"; it is "more." It is an increase or excess of origin in the origin. To put it in terms of the models just alluded to above: the One is more than one; it is not that "it divides itself," rather it is that one equals more than one, because "one" cannot be counted without counting more than one. Or, in the atomist model, there are atoms *plus* the clinamen. But the clinamen is not something else, another element outside of the atoms; it is not in addition to them; it is the "more" of their exposition. Being many, they cannot but incline or decline; they are ones in relation to others. Immobility or the parallel fall [*la chute parallèl*] would do away with this exposition, would return to the pure position and not distinguish itself from the One-purely-one (or, in other words, from the Other). The One as purely one is less than one; it cannot be, be put in place, or counted. One as properly one is always more than one. It is an excess of unity; it is one-with-one, where its Being in itself is copresent.

The *co-* itself and as such, the copresence of Being, is not presentable as that Being which "is," since it is only in the distancing. It is unpresentable, not because it occupies the most withdrawn and mysterious region of Being, the region of nothingness, but quite simply because it is not subject to a logic of presentation. Neither present nor to be presented (nor, as a result, "unpresentable" in the strict sense), the "with" is the (singular plural) condition of presence in general [understood] as copresence. This copresence is neither a presence withdrawn into absence nor a presence *in* itself or *for* itself.

It is also not pure *presence to*, to *itself*, to *others*, or to the *world*. In fact, none of these modes of presence can take place, insofar as presence takes place, unless copresence first takes place. As such, no single subject could even designate *itself* and *relate itself* to itself as subject. In the most classical sense of the term, a subject not only assumes its own distinction from the object of its representation or mastery, it also assumes its own distinction from other subjects. It is possible, then, to distinguish the ipseity of these other subjects (which is to say, the aesity) *from* [d'avec] its own source of representation or mastery. Therefore, the with is the supposition of the "self" in general. But this supposition is no longer subjacent to the self, in the sense of an infinite self-presupposition of sub-jective substance. As its syntactic function indicates, "with" is the pre-position of the position in general; thus, it constitutes its dis-position.

The "self," of the "self" in general, takes place with before taking place as itself and/or as the other. This "aesity" of the self is anterior to the same and to the other and, therefore, anterior to the distinction between a consciousness and its world. Before phenomenological intentionality and the constitution of the ego, but also before thinglike consistency as such, there is co-originarity according to the with. Properly speaking, then, there is no anteriority: co-originarity is the most general structure of all con-sistency, all constitution, and all con-sciousness.

[This is] presence-with: *with* as the exclusive mode of being-present, such that being present and the present of Being does not coincide in itself, or with itself, inasmuch as it coincides or "falls with" ["tombe avec"] the other presence, which itself obeys the same law. Being-many-together is the originary situation; it is even what defines a "situation" in general. Therefore, an originary or transcendental "with" demands, with a palpable urgency, to be disentangled and articulated for itself. But one of the greatest difficulties of the concept of the with is that there is no "getting back to" or "up to" [*remonter*] this "originary" or "transcendental" position; the with is strictly contemporaneous with all existence, as it is with all thinking.

Coexistence

It is no accident that communism and socialism of all sorts are responsible for an essential part of the set of expectations that belong to the modern world. They are responsible for the hope of a rupture and innovation from which there is no turning back; it is the hope for a revolution, a re-creation of the world. It becomes clearer to us every day that it is not enough to stigmatize the errors, lies, and crimes of "existing versions of socialism" as "national socialisms." Represented primarily in the assured and demanding consciousness of "human rights," moral and political condemnation always runs the risk of using its incontestable legitimacy to mask another legitimacy, which was and still is that of an irreducible demand that we be capable of saying "we," that we be capable of saying we to ourselves (saying it about ourselves to one another), beginning from the point where no leader or God can say it for us. This demand is in no way secondary, and this is what gives it its terrible power to unleash, subvert, resist, or sweep away.

Because not being able to say "we" is what plunges every "I,"
whether individual or collective, into the insanity where he cannot
say "I" either. To want to say "we" is not at all sentimental, not at
all familial or "communitarian." It is existence reclaiming its due
or its condition: coexistence.[45]

If the "socialist" hope as such had to be understood as an illusion
or a trick, then the meaning that carried it along, the meaning which
violently manifested itself through it, was all the better illuminated.
It was not a question of substituting the rule of these people for the
rule of those people, substituting the domination of the "masses" for
that of their masters. It was a question of substituting a shared sovereignty for domination in general, a sovereignty of everyone and of
each one, but a sovereignty understood not as the exercise of power
and domination but as a *praxis* of meaning. The traditional sovereignties (the theologico-political order) did not lose power (which
only ever shifts from place to place), but lost the possibility of making sense. As a result, meaning itself—that is, the "we"—demanded
its due, if one can talk in these ways. What we must remember is
that what Marx understood by alienation was both the alienation of
the proletariat *and* the alienation of the bourgeoisie (indeed, an
alienation of the "we," but one that was asymmetrical, unequal), and
that this is primarily an alienation of meaning. But Marx still left the
question of the appropriation or reappropriation of meaning in suspense—for example, by leaving open the question of what must be
understood by "free labor." In time, this suspense opened onto the
demand for another ontology of the "generic being" of humanity as
"essentially social": a co-ontology.

Thus, the disenchantment or disarray of our fin de siècle cannot
content itself with mourning the passing of socialist visions, any
more than it can comfort itself by replacing them with a naive collection of new "communitarian" themes. This disenchantment
does something else; it designates our major anxiety, the one that
makes "us" what "we" are today; we exist as the anxiety of "social
Being" as such, where "sociality" and "society" are concepts plainly
inadequate to its essence. This is why "social Being" becomes, in a
way that is at first infinitely poor and problematic, "being-in-

common," "being-many," "being-with-one-another," exposing the "with" as the category that still has no status or use, but from which we receive everything that makes us think and everything that gives "us" to thinking.

At the very moment when there is no longer a "command post" from which a "socialist vision" could put forward a subject of history or politics, or, in an even broader sense, when there is no longer a "city" or "society" out of which a regulative figure could be modeled, at this moment being-many, shielded from all intuition, from all representation or imagination, presents itself with all the acuity of its question, with all the sovereignty of its demand.

This question and demand belong to the constitution of being-many as such and, therefore, belong to the constitution of plurality *in* Being. It is here that the concept of coexistence is sharpened and made more complex. It is remarkable that this term still serves to designate a regime or state more or less imposed by extrinsic circumstances. It is a notion whose tone often oscillates between indifference and resignation, or even between cohabitation and contamination. Always subject to weak and unpleasant connotations, coexistence designates a constraint, or at best an acceptable concomitance, but not what is at stake in being or essence, unless in the form of an insurmountable aporia with which one can only negotiate. It is an "unsociable sociability" that probably would not even satisfy Kant himself, now that its paradox no longer serves as a guide to any thinking through of the perfectability of peoples, but rather serves as a *pudendum* to the cynicism known as "liberalism." But liberalism is showing all the signs of exhaustion—at the very least, exhaustion in terms of meaning—since, at the collapse of "socialism," it can only respond by designating the "social" and the "sociological" as relatively autonomous spheres of action and knowledge. Repairing fractures or describing structures will never be able to take the place of a thinking of Being itself as being-together. The liberal response to the collapse of communism, then, involves nothing more than an eager repression of the very question of being-in-common (which so-called real communism repressed under a common Being). Now that this particular question is the only one to have come to light, it will not leave us alone; it will not stop cropping up again, since "we" are in question in it.

What comes to light, then, is not a "social" or "communitarian dimension" added onto a primitive individual given, even if it were to occur as an essential and determining addition. (Just think of the numerous circumstances of ordinary discourse in which this order is imposed on us: first the individual, then the group; first the one, then the others; first the rights-bearing subject; then real relationships; first "individual psychology," then "collective psychology"; and above all, first a "subject," then "intersubjectivity"—as they astonishingly persist in saying.) It is not even a question of a sociality or alterity that would come to cut across, complicate, put into play, or *alter* the principle of the subject understood as *solus ipse*. It is something else and still more. It does not so much determine the principle of the *ipse*, whatever this may be ("individual" or "collective," insofar as one can speak in these ways), as it codetermines it *with* the plurality of *ipses*, each one of which is cooriginary and coessential to the world, to a world which from this point on defines a coexistence that must be understood in a still-unheard-of sense, exactly because it does not take place "in" the world, but instead forms the essence and the structure of the world. It is not a nearness [*voisinage*] or community of *ipses*, but a co-ipseity: this is what comes to light, but as an enigma with which our thinking is confronted.

In twentieth-century philosophy, the Heideggerian ontology of *Mitsein* is still no more than a sketch (I will come back to this). Husserlian coexistence or community retains its status as correlative to *ego*, where "solipsistic" egology remains first philosophy. Outside philosophy, it is remarkable that it is not social and political theory which has most closely approached the enigma of a co-ipseity (and as a result, the enigma of a hetero-ipseity). Rather what has come closest to co-ipseity is, on the one hand, an ethnology that ends up being more engaged with the phenomena of comembership[46] and, on the other, the Freud of the second model, the triple determination of which is constituted according to a mechanical coexistence (what are the "id" and "superego" if not being-with, if not the coconstitution of the "ego"?). The same could be said for the Lacanian theory of "significance," insofar as it does not bring about a return to signification, but a mutually instituting correlation of "subjects" (to the extent that the Lacanian "Other" is anything but an "Other": such a name is a theologizing residue that serves to designate "sociation").

However, it is just as remarkable that psychoanalysis still represents the most individual practice there is, and, moreover, represents a sort of paradoxical privatization of something the very law of which is "relation" in every sense of the word. Curiously, what happens here may be the same as what happens in the economy: "subjects" of exchange are the most rigorously co-originary; *and* this mutual originarity vanishes in the unequal appropriation of exchange, such that this coexistence vanishes in a strong sense. It is no accident, then, if Marx and Freud represent two different, yet symmetrical, projects; each puts forth an indissociably theoretical and practical attempt to get at "being-in-common" as a critical point (of disorder in one, of sickness in the other) of history or civilization. If a brief summary is allowed here, I would say that, because there has been no "socialist economy" (but only state capitalism), just as there has been no "collective psychoanalysis" (unless by means of a projection of an individual model), there lies between economics and psychoanalysis the bare space of a "being-together" whose theologico-political presupposition has been exhausted, and which reappears only in reactive spurts. This space has become global, which does not simply mean it has spread out over the entire surface of the planet and beyond, but that it has emerged as the surface of what is at play in the depths: the essence of being-with.

This process of globalization results in a coalescence, a concentration that seems to be both uniform and anonymous and, at the same time, an atomization, a codispersion that seems to be given over to idiocy. This is idiocy in the sense of the Greek *idiotes*, meaning private or ignorant person, as well as idiocy in the modern sense of stupid impenetrability ("private property" as deprived of meaning). It seems, then, that the dialectic Marx thought he foresaw unfolding appears to be definitively blocked, the dialectic of an "individual" appropriation that would mediate within itself the moments of private property and collective property. At the same time, this seems to confirm definitively the Freudian contrast between a possible cure of the nervous individual and the incurable malaise of civilization. This dialectic, this contrast, and their uncommunicative and paralyzing confrontation indicate the knot of questions, expectations, and anxieties of an epoch. How can being-together appropriate itself as such, when it is left up to itself to be what it is, when it is presented in a formulation that is stripped down and has no substantial presupposition or, in other terms, lacks symbolic identification? What becomes of being-with when the *with* no longer appears as a com-position, but only as a dis-position?

How are we to understand the co- as *dis-*? Which one of these is the "as such" of Being that exposes it as its own sharing and which expresses that, as Being, it is between Being and Being itself? And moreover, what is it that brings together in Being that "as" = "as such" and "as" = "similarly"? Each time, Being as such is Being as the Being of *a* being, and it is this each time, similarly. What is it that makes Being as such a being-similar which circulates from being to being and which, thereby, implies the disparity, discontinuity, and simultaneity required for gauging a "resemblance"? What is this com-plication (co-implication and complexity) by which humans exhibit—within the discourse of the similar and the dissimilar, a discourse which is very difficult and puts "humanity" as such into play—a certain (dis)similarity of Being that crosses through all being? How can Being as such be anything other than the (dis)similarity of being in its simultaneity?

To say that this question is an ontological question—or even that it is *the* ontological question, absolutely—does not mean we have to leave the realm of economics and sickness, any more than we have to abandon the order of *praxis*. On the contrary, as I have already said, this question is simply that of what is called "capital," and even the question of "history" and "politics." "Ontology" does not occur at a level reserved for principles, a level that is withdrawn, speculative, and altogether abstract. Its name means the thinking of existence. And today, the situation of ontology signifies the following: to think existence at the height of this challenge to thinking that is globalness [*mondialité*] as such (which is designated as "capital," "(de-)Westernization," "technology," "rupture of history," and so forth).

Conditions of Critique

The retreat of the political and the religious, or of the theologico-political, means the retreat of every space, form, or screen into which or onto which a figure of community could be projected. At the right time, then, the question has to be posed as to whether being-together can do without a figure and, as a result, without an identification, if the whole of its "substance" consists only in its spacing. But this question cannot be articulated in a completely appropriate way until the full extent of the withdrawal of its figure and identity has been grasped. Today, when thinking moves too quickly, when it is fearful and reactionary, it declares that the most commonly recognized forms of identification are indispensable and claim that the destinies proper to them are used up or perverted, whether it be: "people," "nation," "church," or "culture," not to mention the confused "ethnicity" or the tortuous "roots." There is a whole panorama of membership and property, here, whose political and philosophical history has yet to be written[47]: it is the history of the representation-of-self as the determining element of an originary concept of society.

The retreat presents itself in two ways at once: on the one hand, the theologico-political withdraws into the realm of law[48]; on the other, it withdraws into a self-representation that no longer refers to an origin, but only to the void of its own specularity.

Passing into the realm of law effectively divides the "political" in two: there is the formal abstraction of the law, which undoubtedly "does right" by every particularity and every relation, but without giving this right any meaning other than itself; and then the reality of the relation of forces—whether economic, technical, or the forces of passion—stands out in a pronounced and autonomous fashion, that is, unless law itself undertakes to set itself up as an origin or foundation, in the form of an absolute Law [*la Loi*]. (It is here that psychoanalysis seeks, in a remarkable way, to facilitate a substantial and authoritarian vision of society.) Law as such is necessarily the Law of an Other, or the Law as Other. The Other implies its nonrepresentability. In a theological realm, this can give rise to an "interdiction of representation" that supposes the sacred nature of the Other and, along with it, an entire economy of the sacred, sacrificial, hierarchical, and heirophantic, even where the theophany and theology are negative. Access to Presence, and even to a "super-presence," is always preserved. But within an atheological realm, this interdiction becomes a denial of representation; the alterity of the law either retrieves, represses, or denies its origin, and ends in the singular presence of each one to the others. In this sense, something "unrepresentable" or "unfigurable" runs the risk of revealing itself as completely oppressive and terrifying, if not terrorist, open to the anguish of an originary Lack. In contrast, the "figure" proves itself to be capable of opening onto the "with" as its border, the very limit of its outline.

(Of course, these two "realms" do not just follow one another in a history. They are each and both implicated in the interdiction against representation and/or the anxiety about it, that is, in the question about gaining access to the origin(s), a question about its possibility/impossibility.)

So it is not so much a question of denying law itself, it is more a question of "doing right" by the singular plural of the origin. As a result, it is a matter of questioning law about what we might call its "originary anarchy" or the very origin of the law in what is "by all rights without any right": existence unjustifiable as such. To be sure, the derivation or deduction of law from the unjustifiability of existence is not immediate or obvious. In essence, it may even escape the process of a "deduction" altogether. But this remains to be thought; in the meantime, law without ontology reabsorbs Being and its meaning into the empty truth of Law. To assume that politics is entirely a question of "human rights" is also to assume surreptitiously that "man" is entirely a question of the Other. This is what is most often at work in any call to "ethics": a transcendental unpresentability of that most concrete presence.

On the other side of this retreat, however, it is representation that triumphs, absorbing entirely both the transcendental and the concrete. What does the impoverished word "society" now say when it is emptied of all "sociation" or "association," not to mention emptied of the "communities" and "fraternities" that constitute our images of primitive life (the construction of which has, in general, shown itself to be fantastical)? What is left seems to be nothing more than this "society" face to face with itself, being-social itself defined by this game of mirrors, and losing itself in the scintillating play of light and images. It is not a matter of the Other or others, but of a singular plural that is subsumed by means of its own curiosity about itself, subsumed within a generalized equivalence of all the representations of itself that it gives itself to consume.

This is called "the spectacular-market society" or "the society of the spectacle." This is the post-Marxist or meta-Marxist intuition of Situationism. It thinks of "commodity fetishism," or the domination of capital, as being accomplished by the general commodification of fetishes, in the production and consumption of material and symbolic "goods" that all have the character of being an image, illusion, or appearance (and where, in fact, democratic rights tops the list of such "goods"). The "good," of which the "spectacle" is the general illusion, is only the real self-appropriation of social Being. An order structured according to a visible division of society, the justification for which is found only in an invisible beyond (religion, ideal), is succeeded by an immanent order that, like visibility itself, imitates its self-appropriation at every point. The society of the spectacle is that society which achieves alienation by an imaginary appropriation of real appropriation. The secret of the illusion consists in the fact that real appropriation must consist only in a free, self-creating imagination that is indissociably individual and collective: the spectacular commodity in all its forms consists essentially in the imagery [*imaginaire*] that it sells as a replacement for authentic imagination. As such, then, universal commerce is constituted by a representation wherein existence is both an invention and a self-appropriating event. A subject of representation, that is, a subject reduced to the sum or flux of representations which it purchases, is the placeholder that functions as a subject of Being and history. (This is why the reply to the spectacle is formulated as the free creation of the "situation": the appropriating event abruptly removed from the logic of the spectacle. This is also why Situationism, the offspring of several artistic movements, refers to a paradigm of artistic creation that is nonaesthetic or maybe even antiaesthetic.)

In this way, Situationism (which I do not really want to go into here, but want to treat as a symptom[49]), and some of its offshoots into various sorts of analyses concerning the self-simulation and self-control of our society, understands that Marxism missed the moment of symbolic appropriation by confusing it with that of productive appropriation, or even by thinking that such productive appropriation must be self-producing and, thereby, move beyond itself into symbolic appropriation: the self-suppression of capital as the integral reappropriation of Being as communal existence. More specifically, they understand that it is this sort of self-surpassing that does indeed take place. But it does not take place by bringing about an appropriation of being-in-common understood as symbolic Being (taking *symbol* in the strong sense of being a bond of recognition, an ontological instance of the "in-common," like Marx's bond of "free labor" where everyone produces himself or herself as a subject *with* others and as a subject *of* being-with-one-another). Instead, this self-surpassing takes place as the symbolization of production itself, which allows for coexistence only in the form of the technical or economic co-ordination of the various commodity networks.

Situationism thus understands that the "human sciences" have come to constitute this self-symbolization of society, which is not, in fact, a symbolization but only a representation and, more precisely, the representation of a subject that has no subjectivity other than this representation itself. In fact, it turns out to be quite clear that the "human sciences" (even in their various critical capacities, where these capacities do not turn into an insidious form of "super-representation") are the real strength behind what is known as the generalized "spectacle." Here, the gravity of the question concerning the "media" comes to the fore. "Mediatization" does not depend on overblown hype, which is nothing new in itself; nor does it depend on technological or economic power as such. It depends primarily on the fact that a society gives itself its representation in the guise of symbolism. This is also why it has such a capacity for absorbing its own critique and its own rebellious, ironic, or distanced presentations. A sort of general psychosociology takes the place of the presupposition of a figure or identity of being-social.

In this respect, Situationism is not wrong to discern misery at the very heart of abundance, a symbolic misery that does not exclude sustained material misery and certain people's deprivation, in particular the misery of much of the southern hemisphere. . . . The misery of the "spectacle" names that coexistence where the *co-* ends up referring to nothing by which existence could symbolize itself according to itself. That is, at the very moment when it exposes itself and proves to be the entire property of Being, it is nothing by which existence says itself as such, nothing by which it makes sense of Being. At that very moment when the only other thing that is given along with existence is existence-with as the space for deployment and appropriation, the *co-* is nothing that can make sense. Being-together is defined by being-together-at-the-spectacle, and this being-together understands itself as an inversion of the representation of itself, which it believes to be capable of giving itself as originary (and lost): the Greek city assembled in community at the theater of its own myths. An example of today's response might be the following advertisement, which itself constitutes a spectacular and disturbing recuperation of the Situationist critique: "Football makes all other art forms insignificant."[50]

In any case, it is precisely this indefinite capacity for recuperating the Situationist critique that demands attention. The denunciation of mere appearance effortlessly moves within mere appearance, because it has no other way of designating what is proper—that is, nonappearance—except as the obscure opposite of the spectacle. Since the spectacle occupies all of space, its opposite can only make itself known as the inappropriable secret of an originary property hidden beneath appearances. This is why the opposite of deceitful "imagery" is creative "imagination," the model for which is still something like the Romantic genius. According to such a model, the artist plays the part of the productive-subject, but still according to the structure of an ontological presupposition that involves no specific interrogation of the "common" or "in-common" of Being, nor of the meaning of Being that is in question.

We must, therefore, understand how this version of Marxist critique, and all the versions of critical thinking inaugurated by Marx (whether they be the more "leftist" versions or the more "sociological" ones, those of Bataille or the Frankfurt School, and so on), in some way obscured, *in statu nascendi*, the correctness of its own intuition. This was the intuition of society exposed to itself, establishing its being-social under no other horizon than itself—that is, without a horizon of Meaning in which to relate being-together as such, without an instance of com-position as society's dis-position splayed open and laid bare. But this very intuition is interpreted only as the reign of appearance, as the substitution of the spectacle for authentic presence; appearance is understood, here, in the most classical way, namely, as "mere appearance" (surface, secondary exteriority, inessential shadow), and even as "false appearance" (semblance, deceptive imitation). In this respect, critique remains obedient to the most trenchant and "metaphysical" tradition of philosophy, "metaphysical" in the Nietzschean sense: the refusal to consider an order of "appearances," preferring, instead, authentic reality (deep, living, originary—and always on the order of the Other).

Within this tradition, it is over and against the demand of intelligible reality that sensible appearance has been constituted and disregarded all in the same gesture, just as plurality has been constituted and disregarded for the sake of the requirement of unity. Likewise, public appearance has been constituted and disregarded in favor of an interior and theoretical reality (think of Plato's Thales, who was inept in the affairs of the city), and when authentic reality was demanded in the political or communitarian order, it happened at the cost of relegating the political or the communitarian to interiority, and at the cost of simply disregarding "social" exteriority (the sphere of the exteriority of needs and exchanges, the sphere of worldly appearance, and so forth). The Situationist critique continued to refer essentially to something like an internal truth (designated, for example, by the name "desire" or "imagination"), the whole concept of which is that of a subjective appropriation of "true life," itself thought of as origin proper, as self-deployment and self-satisfaction. In this, Situationism demonstrates the nearly constant characteristic of the modern critique of exteriority, appearance, and social alienation—at least, since Rousseau.

I certainly do not want to suggest by this that the critique of alienation, illusion, or ideology is ineffectual. But we do have to wonder to what extent the critique of alienation is itself in danger of remaining subject to another, symmetrical alienation of the sort that I am trying to point out by referring to different species of the Other, which is still to say the Same or the Oneself of a unique, exclusive, and egoistic appropriation, however *ego* is to be understood (whether generic, communitarian, or individual). On another level, one could say that this is a more or less explicit reference to "nature": universal nature, human nature, natural to each person or natural to a people. The idea of nature retains within itself the dominant theme of self-sufficiency, of self-organization, and of a process oriented toward an end state. This sort of nature is at a remove from exteriority and contingency, which, in other places, are marks of a "nature" that is "outside" us, to which we are exposed and without which our exposition would not take *place*. Similarly, the *ego* is from the very start removed from that exteriority and contingency without which it is impossible to expose it *as ego*.

Both the theory and praxis of critique demonstrate that, from now on, critique absolutely needs to rest on some principle other than that of the ontology of the Other and the Same: it needs an ontology of being-with-one-another, and this ontology must support both the sphere of "nature" and sphere of "history," as well as both the "human" and the "nonhuman"; it must be an ontology for the world, for everyone—and if I can be so bold, it has to be

an ontology for each and every one and for the world "as a totality," and nothing short of the whole world, since this is all there is
(but, in this way, there is *all*).

As the last great form of radical critique, Situationism was no
stranger to this necessity. Despite everything, its critique worked
itself out while giving little play to [the practice of] referring society to a model of some sort. This is undoubtedly where its rupture
with various Marxisms was most decisive and where, with some
others and partly in Marx's name, it offered one of the first and
most virulent critiques of what was until just recently called "real"
socialism and also social-democracies. As a result, Situationism has
brought to light rather well, although not to its fullest extent, the
theme of referring society back to itself. The "society of the spectacle" is both a denunciation (of the generalized spectacle-market)
and an affirmation of society facing itself and, maybe even more
so, the affirmation of society *as* exposed to itself and only to itself.

We must, therefore, pose the following two questions at the same
time:

1. How can one know in what way and just how far critique—
both revolutionary critique, including its most recent manifesta-
tions, and also so-called reformist critique—remains paradoxically
and unconsciously subject to a classical model in which reality is
opposed to appearance and unity is opposed to plurality? (This
model assumes that a certain Nietzschean lesson is constantly misunderstood or avoided within the critical tradition and, at the same
time, that the whole question of what can be called "art" from the
point of view of social critique remains more or less untouched.)
In other words, to what extent do "critical" thinking and the "critical" attitude as such entail this subjection (if "critique" always presupposes the possibility of unveiling the intelligibility of the real),
and what other attitude is necessary, where an attitude of resignation is out of the question?

2. How can one know if the "spectacle" is, in one way or another,
a constitutive dimension of society? That is, how can one know if
what is called "social relation" can be thought of according to
something other than the symbolic order, and if the symbolic or-

der can, in turn, be thought of in some way other than according to the order of "imagination" or "figuration," all of which indicates the necessity of thinking all these terms in a new way? Once again, "art" would come into play, but only according to a thinking that is quite different from asking the trivial question about "art and society" and, at the same time, according to a wholly different thinking of "art" itself, and of what we might include under the heading "critical art."

These questions serve as the programmatic heading of some fuller inquiry. I will not take them both on at once, because each one is too enormous in itself. I will only attempt to open some different ways of approaching them.

At the very heart of the tradition, it must be said that "intelligible reality" can only be the reality of *the sensible* as such—and that the "intelligible reality" of the community can only be the reality *of being-in-common* as such. This is why reduction to or subsumption in intelligibility (Idea, Concept, Subject) regularly comes into tension with *its own* requirement that it provide an intelligibility of the sensible that occurs within sensibility, for it and right at [*à même*] it; this is often so forceful an opposition that it leads to a rupture, where sensible intelligibility either breaks apart or dissolves itself altogether.

What comes to us today is the demand to give the meaning of being-in-common according to what it is—*in-* common or *with*— and not according to a Being or an essence of the common. As such, it is the demand to give the meaning of being-with right at the with, and in a "making sense with" ["faire-sans-avec"] (a praxis of meaning-with [*sens-avec*]) where the opposition of a Meaning (horizon, history, community) and a simple "with" (spacing, exteriority, disparity) would dissolve or break apart. In short, it is becoming a matter of urgency to know whether social critique is to be made by virtue of a presupposition that is not at all social (an ontology of Being-*tout-court*, as it were) or by virtue of an ontology of being-in-common, that is, of the plural singular essence of Being. This is why the subject of "ontology" first of all entails the critical examination of the conditions of critique in general.

Co-appearing

It might be, then, that the current situation of "social Being" has to be understood in some other way than by starting from the schema of an immense, spectacular self-consumption, a schema where the truth of community is dissolved and engulfed—whether community [is understood] as subject or as occurring between subjects. If only we made the effort to decipher it in a new way, it might be that the phenomenon of the generalized "spectacle," along with what we call the "tele-global dimension," which accompanies it and is cosubstantial with it, would reveal something else altogether. What is of primary importance in this is to avoid presupposing that the subject of "social Being" or the subject of Being *tout court* is already established.

But this cannot simply be a matter of the classic gesture of wanting to begin without presuppositions (which always assumes that this desire [*volonté*] itself is not already the whole presupposition). It is a matter of rigorously thinking what Being-without-presuppositions-about-itself means, which is, once again, the "creation of the world." In a general way, indeed in an absolutely general way, the primordial requirement of ontology or first philosophy must now be that Being not be presupposed in any way or in any respect, and, more precisely, that *every presupposition of Being must consist in its nonpresupposition.*

Being cannot be pre-sup-posed [*pré-sup-posé*] if it is only the Being of what exists, and is not itself some other existence that is previous or subjacent to existence by which existence exists. For existence exists in the plural, singularly plural. As a result, the most formal and fundamental requirement [of ontology] is that "Being" cannot even be assumed to be the simple singular that the name seems to indicate. Its being singular is plural in its very Being. It follows, then, that *not only must being-with-one-another not be understood starting from the presupposition of being-one, but on the contrary, being-one* (Being as such, complete Being or *ens realissimum*) *can only be understood by starting from being-with-one-another.* That question which we still call a "question of social Being" must, in fact, constitute *the* ontological question.

If one really understands the necessity of this groundless presupposition, one would also have to try to say the following: if the situation of being-social is not that of a spectacular self-alienation that presupposes a lost or dissimulated "real presence," neither is it that of a general communicational arrangement, which presupposes a "rational subject" of communication. This does not mean that there is nothing to the illusions of spectacular self-alienation or to the rationality of a general communicational arrangement, but it does mean that "real presence" and "rationality" can only be thought or evaluated by beginning from something else; and they cannot themselves constitute the groundless presupposition. If left to itself, as a sort of grand, hermeneutical antinomy of the modern world (and one that is clearly at work everywhere), this contrary double form of the "[illusory] spectacle" and "[rational] communication" could even switch their predicates around, such that the "spectacle" would be nothing other than "communication" and vice versa. This chiasma or circle worries us in our confused and anxiety-ridden awareness that society just "turns round and around," without substance, without foundation, without end.

In fact, it might be that what is happening to us is just another sort of "Copernican revolution," not of the cosmological system, or of the relation of subject and object, but rather of "social Being" revolving [*tournant*] around itself or turning on itself, and no longer revolving around something else (Subject, Other, or Same).

What happens to us, then, is the stripping bare [*mis à nu*] of social reality, the very *reality* of being-social in, by, and as the symbolicity that constitutes it, where "spectacle," "communication," "commodity," and "technology" would be different figures of this symbolicity. These are, however, perverse figures that still have to be thought.

It is still necessary to understand what this word "symbolic" means. The proper value of symbolism is in making a *symbol*, that is, in making a connection or a joining,[51] and in giving a face [*fig-*

ure] to this liaison by making an *image*. Insofar as the relation is imagined [*se représente*], and because the relation as such is nothing other than its own representation, the symbolic is what is real in such a relation. By no means, however, is such a relation the representation of something that is real (in the secondary, mimetic sense of representation), but the relation is, and is nothing other than, what is real in the representation—its effectiveness and its efficacy. (The paradigm for this is "I love you" or, perhaps more originally, "I am addressing myself to you.")

In this respect, it is important to emphasize that the symbolic and the imaginary are far from opposites. But the way in which they are not opposites is even contrary to how the common way of speaking [*vulgate*] conflates the image (understood as manifestation and recognition) with the simulacrum (understood as a captivating and mystifying hypostasis). The simple, or simplistic, critique of "the image" (and of the "civilization of images"), which has become a sort of ideological trope in theories of the "spectacle" and in theories of "communication," is nothing but the mythic and mystifying effect of the frantic desire for a "pure" symbolization (and a symptomatic manifestation of the weakness of "critique" in general). The sole criterion of symbolization is not the exclusion or debasement of the image, but instead the capacity for allowing a certain play, in and by the image-symbol, with the joining, the distancing, the opened interval that articulates it as *sym-bol*: this word simply means "put with" (the Greek *sun* equals the Latin *cum*), so that the dimension, space, and nature of the "with" are in play here. Therefore, the "symbolic" is not simply an aspect of being-social: on the one hand, it is this Being itself; on the other hand, the symbolic does not take place without (re)presentation, the (re)presentation of one another [*des uns aux autres*] according to which they are with one another [*les-uns-avec-les-autres*].

If I speak of "social" reality's being stripped bare as its symbolicity, then I am talking about "society" uncovered, society no longer being the appearance of only itself, society no longer reduced to a sort of background "symbolizing" (in the ordinary sense) nothing (no community, no mystical body). I am talking about society making a symbol of itself, society making its appearance by facing [*face à*] itself in order to be all that it is and all that it has to be. In this way, being-social is not reduced to any assumption of an interior or superior unity. Its unity is wholly symbolic; it is wholly of the with. Being-social is Being that is by appearing in the face of itself, faced with itself: it is *co-appearing* [com-parution].

~

Co-appearing does not simply signify that subjects appear together. In that case (which is the "social contract"), it would still need to be asked from where it is that they "appear," from which remote depth do they come into being-social as such, from what origin. We must also wonder why they appear "together" ["ensemble"] and for what other depth they are destined, destined "all together" or "further-on [outre] together." Either the predicate "together" is only a qualification that is extrinsic to subjects, which does not belong to the appearance of each one as such, but designates a pure, indifferent juxtaposition, or it adds a particular quality, one granted a meaning of its own that must be worked out for all subjects "together" and as "together." These two questions lead straight to the dead ends of a metaphysics—and its politics—in which (1) social co-appearance is only ever thought of as a transitory epiphenomenon, and (2) society itself is thought of as a step in a process that always leads either to the hypostasis of togetherness or the common (community, communion), or to the hypostasis of the individual.

In either case, one comes to a dead end because being-social as such—or again, what might be called the *association* [sociation] *of Being*—is instrumentalized, related to something other than itself. On this account, the essence of the "social" is not itself "social." As a result, it is never presentable under the heading of the "social," but only under the heading of either a simple, extrinsic, and transitory "association," or of a transsocial presupposition, the unitary entelechy of common Being—which are both ways to repress and foreclose the problem of "association."

The very meaning of the word "together," just like the meaning

of the word "with," seems to oscillate indefinitely between two
meanings, without ever coming to a point of equilibrium: it is either the "together" of juxtaposition *partes extra partes*, isolated and
unrelated parts, or the "together" of gathering *totum intra totum*, a
unified totality [*unitotalité*] where the relation surpasses itself in
being pure. But it is clear from this that the resources found in the
term are situated precisely on the point of equilibrium between the
two meanings: "together" is neither *extra* nor *intra*. In fact, the pure
outside, like the pure inside, renders all sorts of togetherness impossible. They both suppose a unique and isolated pure substance,
but pure in such a way that one cannot even say "isolated," exactly
because one would be deprived of all relation with it. As such, then,
God is not together with anything or anyone, but is—at least in
Spinoza and Leibniz, although in different, but equally exemplary,
ways—the togetherness or being-together of all that is: God is not
"God."[52]

Togetherness and being-together are not equivalent. (On the contrary, the equivocation between the two makes the status of the
gods of onto-theology uncertain. [Whether it is a matter of] pan-
theism, panentheism, polytheism, monotheism, atheism, deism,
and so on, [are such gods] representable or unrepresentable? [Do
they] ground representation or remove it? Or [might they] even be
representation itself?) Togetherness, in the sense of being a substantive entity, is a collection (as in the theory of togethernesses [*ensembles*]). Collection assumes a regrouping that is exterior and indifferent to the being-together ("in common") of the objects of the
collection. In a general way, the themes and practices of the "collective" or of "collectivism" move in this register. It could be said,
then, that the ontological *togetherness* which we must think through
is never substantive; it is always the adverb of a *being-together*. But
this adverb is not a predicate of "Being"; it brings to it no particular and supplementary qualification. Like all adverbs, it modifies or
modalizes the verb, but here modalization is of the essence and of
the origin. Being is together, and it is not a togetherness.

"Together" means simultaneity (*in, simul*), "at the same time."
Being together is being at the same time (and in the same place,

which is itself the determination of "time" as "contemporary time"). "Same time / same place" assumes that "subjects," to call them that, share this space-time, but not in the extrinsic sense of "sharing"; they must share it between *themselves*; they must themselves "symbolize" it as the "same space-time" without which there would not be time or space. The space-time itself is first of all the possibility of the "with." Very long analyses are called for here. Cutting them far too short, let me say that time cannot be the pure moment [*instant*], or pure succession, without being simultaneity "at the same time." Time itself implies "at the same time." Simultaneity immediately opens space as the spacing of time itself. Starting from the simultaneity of "subjects," time is possible, but above all, it is necessary. For in order to be together and to communicate, a correlation of places *and* a transition of passages from one place to another is necessary. Sharing [*partage*] and passage control each other reciprocally. Husserl writes, "It is essentially necessary that the *togetherness* of monads, their mere *co*-existence, be a *temporal* co-existence. . . . "[53] In fact, simultaneity is not a matter of indistinction; on the contrary, it is the distinctness of places taken together. The passage from one place to another *needs time* [*D'un lieu à l'autre*, il faut le temps]. And moving in place [*du lieu à lui-même*] as such also needs time: the time for the place to open itself as place, the time to space itself. Reciprocally, originary time, appearing as such, *needs space* [il lui faut l'espace], the space of its own dis-tension, the space of the passage that divides [*partage*] it. Nothing and nobody can be born without being born to and with others who come into this encounter, who are born in their own turn. The "together," therefore, is an absolutely originary structure. What is not together is in the no-time-no-place of non-Being.

Co-appearance, then, must signify—because this is what is now at stake—that "appearing" (coming into the world and being in the world, or existence as such) is strictly inseparable, indiscernable from the *cum* or the *with*, which is not only its place and its taking place, but also—and this is the same thing—its fundamental ontological structure.

That Being is being-with, absolutely, this is what we must think.[54]

The *with* is the most basic feature of Being, the mark [*trait*] of the singular plurality of the origin or origins in it.

Undoubtedly, the *with* as such is not presentable. I have already said so, but I have to insist upon it. The *with* is not "unpresentable" like some remote or withdrawn presence, or like an Other. If there is a subject only with other subjects, the "with" itself is not a subject. The "with" is or constitutes the mark of unity/disunity, which in itself does not designate unity or disunity as that fixed substance which would undergird it; the "with" is not the sign of a reality, or even of an "intersubjective dimension." It really is, "in truth," a mark drawn out over the void, which crosses over it and underlines it at the same time, thereby constituting the drawing apart [*traction*] and drawing together [*tension*] of the void. As such, it also constitutes the traction and tension, repulsion/attraction, of the "between"-us. The "with" stays between us, and we stay between us: just us, but only [as] the interval between us.

In fact, one should not say the "with"; one should only say "with," which would be a preposition that has no position of its own and is available for every position. But if the unpresentability of "with" is not that of a hidden presence, then it is because "with" is the unpresentability of this pre-position, that is, the unpresentability of presentation itself. "With" does not add itself to Being, but rather creates the immanent and intrinsic condition of presentation in general.

Presence is impossible except as copresence. If I say that the Unique is present, I have already given it presence as a companion (even if such presence constitutes the Unique, and I have split it in two). The *co-* of copresence is the unpresentable par excellence, but it is nothing other than—and not the Other of—presentation, the existence which co-appears.

If we now have to think about social Being in some other way than according to its spectacular-market self-mockery or its communicational self-assurance, both of which take place on the basis of an unlikely and nostalgic inauthenticity, it is quite likely that there would be nothing else for us to meditate on, nothing to ruminate about or mull over between us. What is proper to community is neither a creativity nor a rationality laid down like some fundamental internal resource, readily available to be put into practice through critique. In this respect, we are definitely no longer in the age of Enlightenment or Romanticism. We are elsewhere, which does not mean we are opposed to them or beyond them, as if we had dialectically surpassed them. We are in a sort of simultaneous drawing together [*tension*] of these two epochs; they are contemporaries of ours and we see them wearing thin. One is worn thin to the point of being an extremely dull platitude; the other is stretched out toward the night of extermination. We are thus in a suspension of history where an enigma is gathering anew; we are contemporaries of ourselves, contemporaries of the stripping bare of being-in-common.

What is proper to community, then, is given to us in the following way: it has no other resource to appropriate except the "with" that constitutes it, the *cum* of "community," its interiority without an interior, and maybe even its *interior intimo sui*. As a result, this *cum* is the *cum* of a co-appearance, wherein we do nothing but appear together with one another, co-appearing before no other authority [*l'instance*][55] than this "with" itself, the meaning of which seems to us to instantly dissolve into insignificance, into exteriority, into the inorganic, empirical, and randomly contingent [*aléatoire*] inconsistency of the pure and simple "with."

So it appears to us that what is proper to community is nothing more than the generalized impropriety of banality, of anonymity, of the lonely crowd and gregarious isolation. The simplest solidarities, the most elementary proximities seem to be dislocated. As such, then, "communication" is only the laborious negotiation of a reasonable and disinterested image of community devoted to its own maintenance, which constantly reveals itself as nothing but the maintenance of the spectacular-market machine.

It must be said, however, that co-appearance might only be another name for capital. At the same time, it might be a name that runs the risk of once again masking what is at-issue, providing a consoling way of thinking that is secretly resigned. But this danger is not a sufficient reason to be satisfied with a critique of capital that is still held prisoner to the presupposition of an "other subject" of history, economics, and the appropriation of the proper in general. In pointing to "capital," Marx designated a general de-propriation [*dépropriation*] that does not allow for the presupposition or preservation of the other, or the Other, which would be the subject of the general reappropriation.

Or more precisely, the presupposition cannot take the form of presupposing a "subject"; rather, it must take the form of being-with-one-another, and must do so in a way that is much more problematic, but far more radical, than Marx could have suspected. It must also be said, then, that the classic critique of capital, even in its latest post-Marxist forms, is not sufficient for taking hold of what capital exposes. At the very least, a thinking of co-appearance must awaken this anxiety.

The intuition buried in Marx's work is undoubtedly located in the following ambivalence: at one and the same time, capital exposes the general alienation of the proper—which is the generalized disappropriation, or the appropriation of misery in every sense of the word—*and* it exposes the stripping bare of the *with* as a mark of Being, or as a mark of meaning. Our thinking is not yet adequate to this ambivalence. This is why, since Marx and up through Heidegger, such ambivalence constantly revives a great, undefined hesitation on the subject of "technology," the limit-object—and perhaps the screen [*l'objet-écran*]—of a thinking which projects onto it either the promise of a self-overcoming of capital or the assurance of the implacable character of its machinery carrying on uncontrolled—and, thereby, controlling everything thanks to this absence of control.

This is also why the truth of our time can only be expressed in Marxist or post-Marxist terms. This why it is a question of the market, of misery, of social-democratic ideology, or the substantial reappropriations that give a reply to it (nationalism, fundamentalism, and fascism in all their various forms). But this truth itself demands that it be thought starting from the *with* of co-appearance, so long as bringing it to life and stripping it bare signifies at least this—to put it in a formulaic way: what is at stake is not a reappropriation of the *with* (of the essence of a common Being), but rather a *with* of reappropriation (where the proper does not return, or returns only *with*).

(This is why we do not make an economy out of an ontology, but it is also why this ontology must be both an *ethos* and a *praxis,* identically. This will have to be developed later.[56] Let us hold the following in reserve: an ontology of being-with can only be located within the distinction of these terms: to be, to act, event, meaning, end, conduct, just as much as, and because, it must be located within the distinction of the "singular" and the "plural," the "in oneself" ["à soi"] and the "in several" ["à plusieurs"].)

The Spectacle of Society

If being-with is the sharing of a simultaneous space-time, then it involves a presentation of this space-time as such. In order to say "we," one must present the "here and now" of this "we." Or rather, saying "we" brings about the presentation of a "here and now," however it is determined: as a room, a region, a group of friends, an association, a "people." *We* can never simply be "the we," understood as a unique subject, or understood as an indistinct "we" that is like a diffuse generality. "We" always expresses a plurality, expresses "our" being divided and entangled: "one" is not "with" in some general sort of way, but each time according to determined modes that are themselves multiple and simultaneous (people, culture, language, lineage, network, group, couple, band, and so on). What is presented in this way, each time, is a stage [*scène*] on which several [people] can say "I," each on his own account, each in turn. But a "we" is not the adding together or juxtaposition of these "I's." A "we," even one that is not articulated, is the condition for the possibility of each "I." No "I" can designate itself without there being a space-time of "self-referentiality" in general. This "generality," however, does not have a "general" consistency; it only has the consistency of the singular at "each time" of each "I." "Each time" implies *at one and the same time* the discreteness of "one by one" *and* the simultaneity of "each one." After all, an "each one" that was not in any way simultaneous, that was not at-the-same-time-and-alongside-other "each ones," would be isolated in a way that would no longer even count as isolation. Rather, it would be the pure and simple impossibility of designating oneself and, therefore, of being a "self." The pure condition of being distributed [*distributivité*] would be transformed immediately into absolute autism. (But this is not to say that the "group," whatever it is, is of a higher order; it is a stage [that serves as] a place of identification. More generally, the question of the "with" can never be expressed in terms of identity, but rather always in terms of identifications.)

As I have already pointed out, not even Descartes can claim to be alone and worldless, precisely because he is not alone and worldless. Rather, his pretense makes it clear that anyone who feigns solitude thereby attests to the "self-referentiality" *of anyone* [de quiconque]. The *ego sum* counts as "evident," as a first truth, only because its certainty can be recognized *by anyone*. So, to articulate it completely would be to say: *I say that we, all of us and each one of us, say "ego sum, ego existo."* One is not obliged to read Descartes as Heidegger does, which is as someone who, in staying at the point of substance or *res cogitans*, does not go back as far as the absolutely primordial condition. In fact, one must read Descartes literally, as he himself invites us to: engaging *with* him and like him in the experience of the pretense [to solitude]. Only this thinking *with* achieves the status of evidence, which is not a proof [*une démonstration*]. From its very first moment, the methodological pretense is neither substantialist nor solipsistic: it uncovers the stage of the "at each time" as our stage, the stage of the "we."

This stage—this "theater of the world," as Descartes also liked to call it, using the persistent image of his time—is not a stage in the sense of an artificial space of mimetic representation. It is a stage in the sense of the opening of a space-time for the distribution of singularities, each of whom singularly plays the unique and plural role of the "self" or the "being-self." "Self" does not mean in itself, or by itself, or for itself, but rather "one of us": one that is each time at a remove from immanence or from the collective, but is also each time coessential to the coexistence of each one, of "each and every one." The stage is the space of a co-appearing without which there would be nothing but Being pure and simple, which is to say, all and nothing, all as nothing.

Being gives itself as singular plural and, in this way, organizes itself as its own stage. We present the "I" to ourselves, to one another, just as "I," each time, present the "we" to us, to one another. In this sense, there is no society without spectacle; or more precisely, there is no society without the spectacle of society. Although already a popular ethnological claim or, in the Western tradition, a claim about the theater, this proposition must be understood as ontologically radical. There is no society without the spectacle because society is the spectacle of itself.

But in a certain sense, this itself must be understood as a play of mirrors (at least insofar as "play" and "mirror" simply designate artifice and unreality). As a concept of being-together [*être-ensemble*], co-appearance consists in its appearing, that is, in its appearing to itself and to one another, all at once. There is no appearing to oneself except as appearing to one another. If this were put in classical terms, terms that presuppose a sphere of proper and isolated individuality as the starting point, then it would be rendered in the following way: one appears to oneself insofar as one is already an other for oneself.[57] But it is immediately clear that one could not even begin to be an other for oneself if one had not already started from the alterity with—or of the with—others in general. Others "in general" are neither other "me's" (since there is no "me" and "you" except on the basis of alterity in general), nor the non-me (for the same reason). Others "in general" are neither the Same nor the Other. They are one-another, or of-one-another, a primordial plurality that co-appears. Therefore, "appearing," and appearing to oneself as well as to one another, is not on the order of appearance, manifestation, phenomena, revealing, or some other concept of becoming-visible. This is because of what that order inevitably entails regarding the invisible origin of such appearance, and what it entails regarding the relation of appearance to this origin as either an expression or an illusion, as resemblance or semblance.[58] So co-appearing is not "appearing"; it is not a question of coming out from a being-in-itself in order to approach others, nor is it a question of coming into the world. It is to be in the simultaneity of being-with, where there is no "in itself" that is not already immediately "with."

But "immediately with" does not refer to an immediacy in the sense of an absence of exteriority. On the contrary, it is the instantaneous exteriority of space-time (the instant itself as exteriority: the simultaneous). And this is how co-appearance forms a stage that is not a play of mirrors—or rather, how the truth of the play of mirrors must be understood as the truth of the "with." In this sense, "society" *is* "spectacular."

$\sim$

Looking at it closely, one will find that the various critiques of "spectacular" alienation are, in the end, grounded on the distinction between a good spectacle and a bad spectacle—[this is true] whether they like it or not. Within the good spectacle, the social or communitarian being presents its proper interiority to itself, its origin (which is itself invisible), the foundation of its rights, the life of its body, and the splendor of its fulfillment. (For the Situationists, then, a certain idea of "art" almost always plays the role of the good spectacle, and it is no accident that the [bad] "spectacle" for them is first and foremost the falsification of art.) In the bad spectacle, the social being imagines [*se représente*] the exteriority of interests and appetites, of egotistic passions and the false glory of ostentation. At the most basic level, this Manichean division not only supposes a distinction between the represented objects, but it also supposes an opposition within the status of the representation: it is what is now in interiority (as manifestation, expression of the proper), now in exteriority (as image, reproduction). As such, the fact that these are intertwined is ignored: there is no "expression" that is not [already] given in an "image," no "presentation" not already [given] in "representation"; there is no "presence" that is not presence to one another.

It is, of course, well known that the distinction between these spectacles is drawn out explicitly by Rousseau, who stipulates that the best spectacle, and the only one that is necessary, is the spectacle of the people itself, assembled in order to dance around the tree they have planted as their own proper symbol. What Rousseau thus makes clear, even despite himself,[59] is the necessity of the spectacle. In modernity, society knows itself as that which takes place in the immanent nonpresence to oneself. That is, it takes place as a *subject*, not so much the "subject of representation" as *representation as subject*: it is presentation-to [*la présentation-à*], or what one could call a-presentation [*l'apprésentation*], the realm of coming into presence as coming conjoined, coincidental and concurrent, simultaneous and mutual. This a-presentation is that of a "we" that possesses *neither* the nature of a common "I" *nor* that of a geometric place, in the sense of an ensemble in which all the "I's" would be equidistant from one another. Rather, it is what opens the spacing of co-appearance on this side of every I-subject. "Association" ["Sociation"] does not disclose itself as a being, but rather as an act that, by definition, exposes itself: it is in exposing itself that it is what it is, or that it does what it does. Being-social must testify before itself to the act of association, the act that brings it to be—not in the sense that it produces it (as a result), but rather in the sense that "Being" remains wholly within the act and in the exposition of the act. In this sense, one could say that Rousseau's "social contract" is not in essence the conclusion of an agreement; it is the stage, the theater for the agreement.

∽

Even if being-social is not immediately "spectacular" in any of the accepted senses of the word, it is essentially a matter of being-exposed. It is as being-exposed; that is, it does not follow from the immanent consistency of a being-in-itself. The being-in-itself of "society" is the network and cross-referencing [*le renvoi mutuel*] of coexistence, that is, *of* coexistences. This is why every society gives itself its spectacle and gives itself as spectacle, in one form or another.[60]

To this extent, every society knows itself to be constituted in the nonimmanence of co-appearance, although society does not expose this as a "knowledge." It exposes what it knows as its own stage and through its own *praxis* of staging [praxis *scénographique*]; and what it knows is that, hidden behind being-together, there is not some other Being which would no longer or not yet be being-together; that is, what it knows is that there is not togetherness itself hidden behind being-together—in presence, in person, in body, or in essence. Therefore, it knows that "togetherness" is not a predicate of Being and that "togetherness" is the trace of Being itself. In other words, the togetherness of Being [*l'ensemble de l'être*] is not a being; it shares Being.

Thus, the spontaneous knowledge of society—its "preontological comprehension" of itself—is knowledge about Being itself, absolutely, and not about the particular and subordinate region of beings, which would be the "social" region of Being. Being-with is constitutive of Being, and it is [constitutive] for the totality of beings (I will return to this below); "social" co-appearance is itself the exposing of the general co-appearance of beings. This insight makes its way from Rousseau to Bataille, or from Marx to Heidegger, and it requires that we find a language that is *ours*.

Undoubtedly, we are still stuttering: philosophy always comes too late, and as a result, also too soon. But the stuttering itself betrays the form of the problem: we, "we," how are we to say "we"? Or rather, who is it that says "we," and what are we told about ourselves in the technological proliferation of the social spectacle and the social as spectacular, as well as in the proliferation of self-mediatized globalization and globalized mediatization? We are incapable of appropriating this proliferation because we do not know how to think this "spectacular" nature, which at best gets reduced to a discourse about the uncertain signs of the "screen" and of "culture." The same applies to "technological" nature, which we regard as an autonomous instrument. We do so without ever asking ourselves if it might not be "our" comprehension of "our-selves" that comes up with these techniques and invents itself in them, and without wondering if technology is in fact essentially in complete agreement with the "with."[61] We are not up to the level of the "we": we constantly refer ourselves back to a "sociology" that is itself only the learned form of the "spectacular-market." We have not even begun to think "ourselves" as "we."

This is not to say that such thinking can only occur to us to-morrow or at some later point, as if it depended on progress or some revelation. It may not be a matter of a new object of thinking that could be identified, defined, and exhibited as such. We do not have to identify ourselves as "we," as a "we." Rather, we have to dis-identify ourselves *from* every sort of "we" that would be the subject of its own representation, and we have to do this *insofar as* "we" co-appear. Anterior to all thought—and, in fact, the very condition of thinking—the "thought" of "us" is not a representational thought (not an idea, or notion, or concept). It is, instead, a *praxis* and an *ethos*: the staging of co-appearance, the staging which is co-appear-ing. We are always already there at each instant. This is not an in-novation—but the stage must be reinvented; *we* must reinvent it each time, each time making our entrance anew.

~

A major sign of the difficulty we have regarding the spectacle is indicated by the paradigmatic character that the Athenian theater has for us. There is certainly nothing accidental in the fact that our modern way of grounding the so-called Western tradition involves a triple reference: to philosophy as the shared exercise of *logos*, to politics as the opening of the city, and to the theater as the place of the symbolic-imaginary appropriation of collective existence. The Athenian theater, both the institution itself and its content, appears to us as the political (civil) presentation of the philosophical (the self-knowledge of the logical animal) and, reciprocally, as the philo-sophical presentation of the political. That is, it appears to us as the "one" presentation of being-together, yet as a presentation where the condition for its possibility is the irreducible and institutive dis-tance [*l'écart*] of representation. Moreover, this distance defines the theater, insofar as it is *neither* political *nor* philosophical at the same time—and neither of these in a rather specific way. The Athenian theater appears to us as the conjunction of *logos* and *mimesis*, but when we see it in this way, we systematically efface the moment of *mimesis* in favor of the moment of *logos*.

We efface it in our imagining [*réprésentant*] that there could be

—and especially that there was, once upon a time—a "good" *mimesis* (the sort Plato wanted), a *mimesis* of *logos*, and a "bad" *mimesis* (that of the "sophist," the prototype of the spectacular merchant who sells the simulacra of *logos*). But we never pursue this logic to its end, for doing so would require that we recognize the following: if there is a necessity to *mimesis*, then it is because *logos* does not present itself of its own accord—and maybe because it does not present itself at all, because its logic is not the logic of presence.[62]

This amounts to recognizing that "social *logos*," the logic of "association," and "association" itself as the *logos* all require *mimesis*. Has there ever been a *logos* that was not "social"? Whatever *logos* means—whether a word or number, a gathering or welcoming in which Being is manifest, reason that is rendered or constructed—it always implies sharing, and it always implies itself as sharing.

By effacing the intrinsic moment or dimension of *mimesis*, we efface this sharing. We give ourselves the representation of a presence that is immanent and enclosed, self-constitutive and self-sufficient, the integrally self-referential order of what we call a "logic" in the most general and basic sense. In this sense, "logic" represents self-referentiality held to its ontological condition, which is the originary—and, as such, existential—plurality or sharing of *logos* itself.

Against this good conjunction of the logical and the mimetic, we now oppose the "bad" one: that where logic remains within its immanent order, cold and faceless (which today, for us, is the "logic of capital"), all the while outwardly producing a *mimesis* that dissimulates it according to its inverted simulacrum, the self-consuming "spectacle." The self-referentiality of the "image" stands in opposition to the self-referentiality of the process or the force, as its product and truth. As over and against the "Greek" paradigm, this is the way in which our tradition has for a long time set up the "Roman" paradigm: the site of circus games, burlesque theater, and the theater of cruelty; without "civil" identification; the Empire and the reason for Empire [*raison d'Empire*]; the forum emptied of its meaning. . . . [63]

Aeschylus or Nero . . . our referring to things in this way, which sets the Greek stage in such violent contrast to the Roman circus (and which also divides—this is a remarkable example—the Christian traditions of Protestantism and Catholicism, or divides the several different forms of the profane theatrical tradition), reveals a consciousness that is itself conflicted, as is demonstrated by its unease with regard to the spectacle: "good" (re)presentation is represented as lost; "bad" (re)presentation is represented as both popular and generalized. But, in fact, both of them are our representations; they compose the double spectacle that we give to ourselves, the double spectacle of the double unpresentability of social Being and its truth. There is one unpresentability because of a certain retreat, and another unpresentability on account of a certain vulgarity. Maybe we have to begin by taking some distance from this double spectacle, by no longer wishing to be Greeks, by no longer fearing that we are Romans, and by simply understanding ourselves as moderns, where being modern means the following: taking note of an exposed "unpresentability" as such, but which is nothing other than the very presentation of our co-appearing, of "us" co-appearing, and whose "secret" exposes itself and exposes us to ourselves without our even beginning to penetrate it—if it is a matter of "penetrating" it at all.

The Measure of the "With"

The bare exposition of co-appearance is the exposition[64] of capital. Capital is something like the reverse side of co-appearance *and* that which reveals co-appearance. Capital's violent inhumanity displays [*étale*] nothing other than the simultaneity of the singular (but the singular posing as the indifferent and interchangeable particularity of the unit of production) and the plural (itself posing as the system of commodity circulation). The "extortion of surplus-value" presupposes this concomitance between the "atomization" of producers (of "subjects" reduced to being-productive) and a "reticulation" of profit (not as an equal redistribution, but as a concentration that is itself more and more complex and delocalized).

One could say that capital is the alienation of being singular plural as such. This would be quite accurate so long as one did not understand being singular plural as a primitive, authentic subject, a subject to which capital happened as its other and purely by accident. (Nothing could be more foreign to Marx's thinking.) Capital is the "alienation" of Being in its being-social to the extent that it puts this being in play as such. It is not the negative dialectic of some prior community that occurs within a continuous historical process; instead, it exposes a singular-plural constitution or configuration that is neither the "community" nor the "individual." Incalculable "surplus-value"—"value" as indefinite, circulatory, and autotelic growth—exposes the inaccessibility of a primordial or final "value." In a paradoxical and violent way, it immediately poses the question of an "outside-value" or "absolute value"—which would be immeasurable, priceless (what Kant called a "dignity"). There is, then, a certain concomitance between the globalization of the market and that of "human rights": these rights represent the supposed absolute value that capital claims to exchange for . . . itself.

However, this is also why there is the stripping bare [*mise à nu*] of being-social and, at the same time, its being brought to life [*mise à vif*], exactly because the "rights-bearing" "human" is "valuable" in itself. In fact, he is nothing other than the idea of a "value in itself" or a "dignity." If "humanity" must be worth something, or if Being in general must "be worth something" under the heading "humanity," this can only be by "being valuable" *singularly* and, simultaneously, in "being valuable" by and for and with the *plural* that such singularity implies, just as it implies the fact of the "value" itself. Indeed, who could be [more] valuable for oneself than oneself? "Being valuable" is worth something only within the context of being-with, that is, only insofar as it concerns *commerce* in every sense of the word. But it is precisely the sharing of these senses—the commerce of goods/the commerce of being-together—that capital exposes: the sharing of the senses of *exchange*, the sharing of the sharing itself. Capital exposes it as a certain violence, where being-together becomes being-of-market-value [*l'être-marchand*] and haggled over [*marchandé*]. The being-with that is thus exposed vanishes at the same time that it is exposed, stripped bare.

To say that this violence exposes being singular plural as an absolute of existence is not to justify it. For this violence violates what it exposes. This, however, does not amount to declaring that the "secret" of capital has been revealed, along with the means of converting it into its opposite. Instead, the violence of capital gives the measure of what is exposed, of what comes to "us" to expose itself: singular plural being-with is the only absolute measure of Being itself, or of existence. But this is an incommensurable measure if it is equal to the "at each time" of each "one" and, *at the same time*, to the indefinite plurality of coexistences *against* which each one *is measured* in turn—according to the indefinite commensuration of the coincidences of commerce, combat, competition, comparison, communication, concurrence, concupiscence, compassion, *co-jouissance*. . . .

There is a common measure, which is not some one unique standard applied to everyone and everything. It is the commensurability of incommensurable singularities, the equality of all the *origins-of-the-world*, which, as origins, are strictly unexchangeable [*insubstituable*]. In this sense, they are perfectly unequal, but they are unexchangeable only insofar as they are equally with one another. Such is the sort of measurement that it is left up to us to take.

∿

"Society" is neither Greek nor Roman—nor Judeo-Christian, to which we will return later. Society knows itself and sees itself as bared, exposed to this common excess [*démesure*]. At one and the same time, it sees itself as something quite evident and transparent, whose necessity eclipses that of every *ego sum*, and as an opacity that denies itself every subjective appropriation. At that moment when we clearly come [to stand] before ourselves, as the lone addresser(s) facing the lone addressee(s), we cannot truly say "we."

But it is through this that we now have to attain to a knowledge of the "we"—attain to a knowledge and/or a praxis of the "we." The "we" is not a subject in the sense of egoistic self-identification and self-grounding (even if this itself never takes place outside of a "we"); neither is the "we" "composed" of subjects (the law of such composition is the aporia of all "intersubjectivity"). However, the "we" is not nothing; it is "someone" each time, just as "each one" is someone. Moreover, this is why there is no universal "we": on the one hand, "we" is said each time of some configuration, group, or network, however small or large; on the other hand, "we" say "we" for "everyone," for the coexistence of the entire universe of things, animals, and people that is mute and without "us." "We" neither says the "One" nor does it say the adding together of "ones" and "others"; rather, "we" says "one" in a way that is singular plural, one by one and one with one.

Nothing can really be thought about this situation unless the one, in general, is first thought in terms of with-one-another. Yet, it is here that our ontology fails, since we are "amongst us" ["*entre nous*"] and since "Being" comes down to just that—if I can say it like this.

(It is as if Being has come back to this "between," which is its true place, as though it had been a matter of a "forgetting the between" rather than "forgetting Being." Or rather, it is as if the invention of Being, throughout the whole tradition, were nothing but the invention of our existence as such—as the existence *of us* and *as us*, us in the world, we-the-world. "We" would be, then, the most remote, absolute priority of every ontology; as a result, "we" would also be the most belated, most difficult, and least appropriable effect of the ontological demand.)

The *with* constitutes a sort of permanent end point of the tradition. It is a minor category; in fact, even up until today, including Heidegger in certain regards, it is barely a category at all insofar as "Being" has been represented as being alone with itself, and as having no coexistence or coincidence. So, when Husserl declares "the intrinsically first being, the being that precedes and bears every worldly Objectivity, is transcendental intersubjectivity: the universe of monads, which effects its communion in various forms,"[65] this Being constitutes for him nothing less than an ultimate horizon, freed from contingency and the exteriority of coexistents. It corresponds to a transcendental solidarity rather than an empirico-transcendental simultaneity. As a result, it again becomes something like a substratum rather than something open or dis-posed in itself through its coconstitution. Generally speaking, then, the

Being of philosophical ontology cannot have coessence, since it only has non-Being as its correlate. But what if Being itself *is* the coessentiality of existence?

Since being-social appears to us to lie beyond our reach, whether as community (subsumption under the Subject, pure Being without relations) or as association (accommodation of subjects, relation without essentiality), it is the category of the "other" that crosses through much contemporary thinking. It would be necessary to show how this category, and the obsession [*la hantise*] that it ends up constituting for a good portion of our thinking, both represents the incommensurability of Being as being-with-one-another *and* runs the risk of covering over or deferring this Being's realm, insofar as it is the realm of the *with*, that is, insofar as it is the measure of this incommensurability.

The other is presented as the *alter ego* or as the other of the ego, as the other outside of the self or as the other within the self, as "others" or the "Other"; all these ways of looking at it, all these aspects, all these faces, and all of "those whom we cannot look in the face" ["ces indévisageables"]—whose necessity is, in every case, incontestable—always bring us back to the very heart of the matter, to an alterity or alteration where the "self" is at stake. The other is thinkable, and must be thought, beginning from that moment when the self appears and appears to itself as a "self."

Yet, this identification of the self as such—its subjectivization in the deepest and richest philosophical sense of the term, the one that reaches its extreme limit in Hegel—can only take place once the subject finds itself or poses itself originarily as other than itself, doing so in the infinite presupposition of the self that constitutes it as a subject and according to the necessary law of such presupposition. This would be a self that is older and more originary than itself, a self in itself that is other than the self for itself. This is really not much more than a transcription of Hegel.

Therefore, the self knows itself principally as other than itself: such is the constitution of "self-consciousness." And yet, the logic of this constitution is paradoxical, since it involves simultaneously the opening of the self to the other *and* its closure. In fact, the alterity of the other is such that to recognize it is to be denied access to it; there can be access only on the condition of a radical alteration or, more precisely, a radical alienation. A dialectic of the same and the other, of the same in the other, of the same as other, undoes this aporia, but this undoing comes at a price, the price of the dialectic in general. It reveals that the power of the negative which holds the self to the other, the dis-alienating and reappropriative power of alienation itself as the alienation of the same, will always be presupposed as the power of the self, or the Self as this very power. The Self remains alone in itself even as it emerges out of itself. What is properly lacking or passed over in this false emergence is the moment of the *with*.

Open to the other and occurring as other, the self has its originarity in the loss of self. Birth and death become the marks of a point of origin [*provenance*] and destination within the other: an origin/destination as a loss, as the memorial mourning of the immemorial, and as the reconquering or reappropriation of an inappropriable aseity in all its irreducible alterity. This other is not "with"; it is no longer and not yet "with"; it is nearer and further away than every being-together. It does not accompany identity; it crosses through it, and transgresses it; it transfixes it. Within the discourse about alterity, a general mode of *trans-* (transport, transaction, transcription, transfer, transmission, transformation, transparency, transubstantiation, transcendence) continually runs alongside the mode of *cum-*, but it will never be able to eclipse it or replace it.

In and of itself transcendent, the subject is born into its *intimacy* ("interior intimo neo"), and its intimacy wanders away from it *in statu nascendi* ("interfeces et urinam nascimur"). "To exist" is no longer "to be" (for itself, in itself), to-already-no-longer-be and to-not-yet-be, or even to-be-lacking, that is, to-be-in-debt-to-being. To exist is a matter of going into exile. The fact that the intimate, the absolutely proper, consists in the absolutely other is what alters the origin in itself, in a relation to itself that is "originarily plunged into mourning."[66] The other is in an originary relation to death and in a relation to originary death.

In this way, then, "solitude" appears. This is the Christian event, which does not mean that it was not prepared for well in advance, or that it was not, in its own way, contemporary to our whole tradition. Solitude par excellence is solitude of the self insofar as it relates to itself, outside of itself *in extremis* and *in principis,* outside of the world, ex-isting existence. Consciousness of self is solitude. The other is this very solitude exposed as such: as a self-consciousness that is infinitely withdrawn in itself, into itself—in itself as into itself.

As such, the coexistent—the other person, but also the other creature in general—appears as that which is in itself infinitely withdrawn. It appears inaccessible to "me" because it is withdrawn from the "self" in general, and because it is as the self-outside-itself: it is the other in general, the other that has its moment of identity in the divine Other, which is also the moment of the identity of everything, of the universal *corpus mysticum.* The Other is the place of *community* as *communion,* that is, the place of a being-self-in-other [*être-soi-en-l'autre*] that would no longer be altered or where such alteration would be identification. In this world, the mystery of communion announces itself in the form of the *nearby* [prochaine].

Proximity is the correlate of *intimacy*: it is the "nearest," the "closest," which is also to say "the most approximate" or "infinitely approximate" to me, but it is not me because it is withdrawn in itself, into the self in general. The proximity of the nearest is a minute, intimate distance and, therefore, an infinite distance whose resolution is in the Other. The nearest is that which is utterly removed, and this is why the relation to it presents itself (1) as an imperative, (2) as the imperative of a love, and (3) as a love that is "like the love of myself."[67] The love of self, here, is not egoism in the sense of preferring oneself over others (which would contradict the commandment); it is an egoism in the sense of privileging oneself, one's own-self [*le soi-propre*], as a model, the imitation of which would provide the love of others. It is necessary to love one's own-self in the other, but reciprocally, one's own-self in me is the other of the ego. It is its hidden intimacy.

This is why it is a matter of "love": this love is not some possible

mode of relation; it designates relation itself at the heart of Being—in lieu of and in the place of Being[68]—and designates this
relation, of one to another, as the infinite relation of the same to
the same as originarily other than itself. "Love" is the abyss of the
self in itself; it is the "delectation" ["dilection"] or "taking care" of
what originarily escapes or is lacking; it consists in taking care of
this retreat and in this retreat. As a result, this love is "charity": it is
the consideration of the *caritas*, of the cost or the extreme, absolute,
and, therefore, inestimable value of the other as other, that is, the
other as the self-withdrawn-in-itself. This love speaks of the infinite cost of what is infinitely withdrawn: the incommensurability
of the other. As a result, the commandment of this love lays out
this incommensurability for what it is: access to the inaccessible.
Yet, it is not sufficient to discredit such love as belonging to some
intemperate idealism or religious hypocrisy. Rather, it is a matter
of deconstructing the Christianity and sentimentality of an imperative the openly excessive and clearly exorbitant character of which
must be read as a warning to us; I would even go so far as to say
that it just is a warning to us. It is a matter of wondering about the
"meaning" (or "desire") of a thinking or culture that gives itself a
foundation the very expression of which denotes impossibility, and
of wondering how and to what extent the "madness" of this love
could expose the incommensurability of the very constitution of
the "self" and the "other," of the "self" in the "other."

    With regard to this constitution, then, and at the heart of Judeo-
Christianity and its exact opposite, it would be a matter of understanding how the dimension of the *with* both appears and disappears all at once. On the one hand, the proximity of what is nearby
[*prochain*] points to the "nearby" ["l'auprès"] of the "with" (the
apud hoc of its etymology). One could even add that it encircles
this "nearby" and makes it stand out on its own, as a contiguity
and simultaneity of being-near-to as such, without any further determination. That is, what is "nearby" is no longer the "nearness"
of the family or the tribe, which may be what the primary meaning
of the Biblical precept refers to; it is not the nearness of the *people*
or the *philia*, or the brotherhood; it is what underlies every logic of

the group or ensemble, every logic of community that is based on nature, blood, source, principle, and origin.[69] The measure of such "nearness" is no longer given, and the "nearby," the "very near" is exhibited as stripped bare, without measure. As such, everyday milling around [*le côtoiement*], the crowd, the mass all become possible—right up until the piling-up of bodies in the anonymous mass grave or the pulverization of collective ashes. The proximity of what is nearby, as pure dis-tance, as pure dis-position, can contract and expand this dis-position to its extreme limit, both at the same time. In universal being-with-one-another, the *in* of the in-common is made purely extensive and distributive.

On the other hand, this is why the "nearby" of the *with*, the simultaneity of distance and close contact, the most proper constitution of the *cum-*, exposes itself as indeterminantness and as a problem. According to this logic, there is no measure that is proper to the *with*, and the *other* holds it there, within the dialectic of the incommensurable and common intimacy, or within an alternative to it. In an extreme paradox, the other turns out to be *the other of the with*.

〜

As a result, there are two different measures of the incommensurable to be found within the very depths of our tradition, two measures that are superimposed, intertwined, and contrasted. One is calibrated according to the Other; the other is calibrated according to the with. Because the intimate and the proximate, the same and the other, refer to one another, they designate a "not being with" and, in this way, a "not being in society." They designate an Other of the social where the social itself—*the* common as *Being* or as a common *subject*—would be in itself, by itself, and for itself: it would be the very sameness of the other and sameness as Other. In contrast, being-with designates the other that never comes back to the same, the plurality of origins. The just measure of the with or, more exactly, the with or being-with as just measure, as justness and justice, is the measure of dis-position as such: the measure of the distance from one origin to another.

In his analytic of *Mitsein*, Heidegger does not do this measure justice. On the one hand, he deals with the indifference of an "un-circumspective tarrying alongside" and, on the other, an "authentic understanding of others"[70]—the status of which remains indeter-minate as long as what is in question is anything other than the negative understanding of the inappropriability of the death of oth-ers or the codestination of a people. Between this indifference and this understanding, the theme of existential "distantiality"[71] imme-diately reverts back to competition and domination, in order to open onto the indistinct domination of the "one" [*"Das Man"*]. The "one" is produced as nothing other than that conversion which levels out the general attempt by everyone to outdistance everyone else, which ends in the domination of mediocrity, of the common and average measure, common as average. It ends with the "com-mon-mediocre" concealing the essential "common-with." But, as such, it remains to be said just how being-with is essential, seeing as it codetermines the essence of existence.

Heidegger himself writes that: . . . as Being-with, Dasein "is" es-sentially for the sake of [*umwillen*] Others. . . . In being-with, as the existential "for-the-sake-of" of Others, these have already been disclosed [*erschlossen*] in their *Dasein*."[72] The *with*, therefore, des-ignates being-with-regard-to-one-another, such that each one is "disclosed" ["ouvert"][73] then and there, that is, constituted as ex-isting: being the *there*, that is, the disclosure of Being, being an "each time" of this disclosure, in such a way that no disclosure would take place (no Being) if the one "disclosed" did not disclose itself with regard to an other "disclosed." Disclosure itself consists only in the coincidence of disclosures. To-be-the-there is not to dis-close a place to Being as Other: it is to disclose/be disclosed to/ through the plurality of singular disclosures.

Since it is neither "love," nor even "relation" in general, nor the juxta-position of in-differences, the "with" is the proper realm of the plurality of origins insofar as they originate, not from one another or for one another, *but in view of one another or with regard to one an-other.* An origin is not an origin for itself; nor is it an origin in order to retain itself in itself (that would be the origin of nothing); nor is it an origin in order to hover over some derivative succession in which its being as origin would be lost. An origin is something other than a starting point; it is both a principle and an appearing; as such, it repeats itself at each moment of what it originates. It is "continual creation."

If the world does not "have" an origin "outside of itself," if the world is its own origin or the origin "itself," then the origin of the world occurs at each moment of the world. It is the *each time* of Being, and its realm is the *being-with* of each time with every [other] time. The origin is for and by way of the singular plural of every possible origin. The "with" is the measure of an origin-of-the-world *as such*, or even of an origin-of-meaning as such. To-be-with is to make sense mutually, and only mutually. Meaning is the fullest measure of the incommensurable "with." The "with" is the fullest measure of (the) incommensurable meaning (of Being).

Body, Language

The plurality of origins essentially disseminates the Origin of the world. The world springs forth[74] everywhere and in each instant, simultaneously. This is how it comes to appear *out of nothing* and "is created." From now on, however, this being created must be understood differently: it is not an effect of some particular operation of production; instead, it is, insofar as it is, as created, as having arisen, come, or grown (*cresco, creo*); it has always already sprung from all sides, or more exactly, it is itself the springing forth and the coming of the "always already" and the "everywhere." As such, each being belongs to the (authentic) origin, each is originary (the springing forth of the springing forth itself), and each is original (incomparable, underivable). Nevertheless, all of them share originarity and originality; this sharing *is itself* the origin.

What is shared is nothing like a unique substance in which each being would participate; what is shared is also what shares, what is structurally constituted by sharing, and what we call "matter." The ontology of being-with can only be "materialist," in the sense that "matter" does not designate a substance or a subject (or an antisubject), but literally designates what is divided of itself, what is only as distinct from itself, *partes extra partes*, originarily impenetrable to the combining and sublimating penetration of a "spirit" [or "mind"], understood as a dimensionless, indivisible point beyond the world. The ontology of being-with is an ontology of bodies, of every body, whether they be inanimate, animate, sentient, speaking, thinking, having weight, and so on. Above all else, "body" really means what is outside, insofar as it is outside, next to, against, nearby, with a(n) (other) body, from body to body, in the dis-position. Not only does a body go from one "self" to an "other," it is *as itself* from the very first; it goes from itself to itself; whether made of stone, wood, plastic, or flesh, a body is the sharing of and the departure from self, the departure toward self, the nearby-to-self without which the "self" would not even be "on its own" ["à part soi"].[75]

Language is the incorporeal (as the Stoics said). Either as an audible voice or a visible mark, saying is corporeal, but what is said is incorporeal; it is everything that is incorporeal about the world. Language is not in the world or inside the world, as though the world were its body: it is the outside of the world in the world. It is the whole of the outside of the world; it is not the eruption of an Other, which would clear away or sublimate the world, which would transcribe it into something else; instead, it is the exposition of the world-of-bodies as such, that is, as originarily singular plural. The incorporeal exposes bodies according to their being-with-one-another; they are neither isolated nor mixed together. They are *amongst themselves* [entre eux], as origins. The relation of singular origins among themselves, then, is the relation of *meaning*. (That relation in which one unique Origin would be related to everything else as having been originated would be a relation of saturated meaning: not really a relation, then, but a pure consistency; not really a meaning, but its sealing off, the *annulment* of meaning and the end of the origin.)

Language is the exposing of plural singularity. In it, the all of being is exposed as its meaning, which is to say, as the originary sharing according to which a being relates to a being, the circulation of a meaning of the world that has no beginning or end. This is the meaning of the world as being-with, the simultaneity of all presences that *are* with regard to one another, where no one is for oneself without being for others. This is also why the essential dialogue or polylogue of language is both the one in which we speak to one another and, *identically*, the one in which I speak to "myself," being an entire "society" onto myself—being, in fact, in and as language, *always simultaneously "us" and "me" and "me" as "us," as well as "us" as "me."* For I would say nothing about myself if I were not with myself *as* I am with numerous others, if this *with* were not "in" me, right at me, at the same time as "me," and, more precisely, *as the* at-the-same-time according to which, solely, I am.

At this exact point, then, one becomes most aware of the essence of singularity: it is not individuality; it is, each time, the punctuality of a "with" that establishes a certain origin of meaning and connects it to an infinity of other possible origins. Therefore, it is, at one and the same time, infra-/intraindividual and transindividual, and always the two together. The individual is an intersection of singularities, the discrete exposition of their simultaneity, an exposition that is both discrete and transitory.

This is why there is no ultimate language, but instead languages, words, voices, an originarily singular sharing of voices without which there would be no voice. In the incorporeal exposition of languages, all beings pass through humanity.[76] But this exposition exposes humanity itself to what is outside the human, to the meaning of the world, to the meaning of Being as the being-meaning of the world. Within language, "humanity" is not the subject of the world; it does not represent the world; it is not its origin or end. It is not its meaning; it does not give it meaning. It is the exponent, but what it thus exposes is not itself, is not "humanity"; rather, it exposes the world and its proper being-with-all-beings in the world, exposes it as the world. Moreover, this is why it is also what is exposed by meaning; exposed as "gifted" with language, humanity is, above all, essentially ex-posed in its Being. It is ex-posed to and as this incorporeal outside of the world that is at the heart of the world, that which makes the world "hold" or "consist" in its proper singular plurality.

It is not enough to say that the "rose grows without reason." For if the rose were alone, its growth without reason would enclose within itself, by itself, all the reason of the world. But the rose grows without reason because it grows along with the reseda, the eglantine, and the thistle—as well as with crystals, seahorses, humans, and their inventions. And the whole of being, nature, and history do not constitute an ensemble the totality of which would or would not be without reason. The whole of being is its own reason; it has no other reason, which does not mean that it itself is its own principle and end, exactly because it is not "itself." It *is* its own dis-position in the plurality of singularities. This *Being* ex-poses itself, then, as the *between* and the *with* of singulars. *Being, between,* and *with* say the same thing; they say exactly *what can only be said* (which is called the "ineffable" elsewhere), what cannot be presented as a being among [*parmi*] others, since it is the "among" of all beings (*among*: inside, in the middle of, with), which are each and every time among one another. *Being* says nothing else; as a result, if saying always says Being in one way or another, then Being is exposed only in the incorporeality of the saying.

This does not signify that Being "is only a word," but rather that Being is all that is and all that goes into making a word: being-with in every regard. For a word is what it is only among all words, and a spoken word is what it is only in the "with" of all speaking. Language is essentially in the with. Every spoken word is the simultaneity of at least two different modes of that spoken word; even when I am by myself, there is the one that is said and the one that is heard, that is, the one that is resaid. As soon as a word is spoken, it is resaid. As such, meaning does not consist in the transmission from a speaker to a receiver, but in the simultaneity of (at least) two origins of meaning: that of the saying and that of its resaying.

As far as meaning is concerned, what I say is not simply "said," for meaning must return to me resaid in order to be said. But in returning to me in this way, that is, from the other, what comes back also becomes another origin of meaning. Meaning is the passing back and forth [*passage*] and sharing of the origin at the origin, singular plural. Meaning is the exhibition of the foundation without foundation, which is not an abyss but simply the *with* of things that are, insofar as they are. *Logos* is *dialogue*, but the end [or purpose] of dialogue is not to overcome itself in "consensus"; its reason is to offer, and only to offer (giving it tone and intensity), the *cum-*, the *with* of meaning, the plurality of its springing forth.

It is not enough, then, to set idle chatter in opposition to the authenticity of the spoken word, understood as being replete with meaning. On the contrary, it is necessary to discern the conversation (and sustaining) of being-with as such within chatter: it is in "conversing," in the sense of discussion, that being-with "sustains itself," in the sense of the perseverance in Being. Speaking-with exposes the *conatus* of being-with, or better, it exposes being-with as *conatus*, exposes it as the effort and desire to maintain oneself as "with" and, as a consequence, to maintain something which, in itself, is not a stable and permanent substance, but rather a sharing and a crossing through. In this conversation (and sustaining) of being-with, one must discern how language, at each moment, with each signification, from the highest to the lowest—right down to those "phantic," insignificant remarks ("hello," "hi," "good" . . .) which only sustain the conversation itself—exposes the with, exposes itself as the with, inscribes and *ex-scribes* itself in the with until it is exhausted, emptied of signification.

"Emptied of signification": that is, returning all signification to the circulation of meaning, into the carrying over [*transport*] that is not a "translation" in the sense of the conservation of one signification (however modified), but "trans-lation" in the sense of a stretching or spreading out [*tension*] from one origin-of-meaning to another. This is why this always imminent exhaustion of signification—always imminent and always immanent to meaning itself, its truth—goes in two directions: that of common chatter and that of absolute poetic distinction. It is exhausted through the inexhaustible exchangeability of "phantic" insignificance, or exhausted by the pure "apophantic" significance, declaration, or manifestation ("apophansis") of this very thing as an unexchangeable spoken word, unalterable as this very thing, but there as the thing *as* such. From one to the other, it is the same *conatus*: the "with" according to which we expose ourselves to one another, *as* "ones" and *as* "others," exposing the world *as* world.

Language constitutes itself and articulates itself from out of the "as." No matter what is said, to say is to present the "as" of whatever is said. From the point of view of signification, it is to present one thing as another thing (for example, its essence, principle, origin, or its end, its value, its signification), but from the point of view of meaning and truth; it is to present the "as" *as such*. That is, it is to present the exteriority of the thing, its being-before, its being-with-all-things (and not its being-within or being-elsewhere).

Mallarmé's phrase "I say 'a flower' . . . " expresses [the fact] that the word says "the flower" as "flower" and as nothing else, a "flower" that is "absent from all bouquets" only because its "as" is also the presence *as such* of every flower in every bouquet. Giorgio Agamben writes, "The thinking that tries to grasp being *as* beings retreats toward the entity without adding to it any further determination . . . comprehending it in its being-such, in the midst of its *as*, it grasps its pure non-latency, its pure exteriority. It no longer says *some thing* as '*some thing*' but brings to speech this *as* itself."[77] Every spoken word brings to speech this "as itself," that is, the mutual exposition and disposition of the singularities of the world (of a world of singularities, of singular worlds, of world-singularities). Language is the element of the with *as such*: it is the space of its declaration. In turn, this declaration as such refers to everyone and to no one, refers to the world and to its coexistence.

∼

Although he was certainly not the first to do so, La Bruyere put it in the following way: "Everything is said, and one comes to it too late. . . . " Certainly, everything is said, for everything has always already been said; yet, everything remains to be said, for the whole as such is always to be said anew. Death presents the interruption of a saying of the whole and of a totality of saying: it presents the fact that the saying-of-everything is at each time an "everything is said," a discrete and transitory completeness. This is why death does not take place "for the subject," but only for its representation. But this is also why "my death" is not swallowed up with "me" in pure disappearance. As Heidegger says, insofar as it is the utmost possibility of existence, it exposes existence *as such*. Death takes place essentially as language; reciprocally, language always says death: it always says the interruption of meaning as its truth. Death as such, [like] birth as such, takes place as language: it takes place in and through being-with-one-another. Death is the very signature of the "with": the dead are those who are no longer "with" and are, at the same time, those who take their places according to an exact measure, the appropriate measure, of the incommensurable "with." Death is the "as" without quality, without complement: it is the incorporeal as such and, therefore, the exposition of the body. One is born; one dies—not as this one or that one, but as an absolute "as such," that is, as an origin of meaning that is both absolute and, as is necessary, absolutely cut off (and consequently, immortal).

It follows that one is never born alone, and one never dies alone; or rather, it follows that the solitude of birth/death, this solitude which is no longer even solitude, is the exact reverse of its sharing. If it is true, as Heidegger says, that I cannot die in place of the other, then it is also true, and true in the same way, that the other dies insofar as the other is with me and that we are born and die to one another, exposing ourselves to one another and, each time, exposing the inexposable singularity of the origin. We say in French "mourir à" ["dead to"]—to the world, to life—as well as "naître à" ["born to"]. Death is *to* life, which is something other than being the negativity through which life would pass in order to be resuscitated. To put it very precisely: death as fertile negativity is that of a single subject (either individual or generic). Death *to* life, exposition *as such* (the ex-posed as ex-posed = that which turns toward the world, in the world, the very *nihil* of its creation) can only be being-with, singular plural.

In this sense, language is exactly what Bataille calls "the practice of joy before death." Language is not a diversion, not an arrangement with the intolerability of death. In one sense, it is the tragic itself. But it is joy as the destitution of meaning, which lays bare the origin: the singular plural as such. It is the *with* as such, which is also to say the being-such as such: perfectly and simply—and immortally—equal to itself and to every other, equal to itself *because* and *as* it is equal to every other; it is, therefore, essentially *with* every other equally. As is often said, this is a "common fate": we have nothing in common except our telling ourselves so (and I have nothing in common with myself except in telling myself so); we exchange, and we do not exchange; we un-exchange [*in-échangons*] this extreme limit of the saying in every spoken word, as speaking itself. Language exposes death: it neither denies it nor affirms it; it brings it to language, and death is nothing but that, that which is essentially brought to language—and that which brings it there.

"Death speaks in me. My speech is a warning that at this very moment death is loose in the world, that it has suddenly appeared between me, as I speak, and the being I address: it is there between us at the distance that separates us, but this distance is also what prevents us from being separated, because it contains the condition for all understanding."[78] As such, then, "literature" is language stretched out [*en tension*] toward birth and death, exactly because it is, and insofar *as* it is, striving toward address, understanding [*entente*], and conversation. And it is stretched like this since it occurs as recitation, discourse, or singing. (Each of these, in turn, forms the dis-position of language itself, language's exteriority to/in itself; each forms language's sharing, not only the sharing of languages, but that of voices, genres, or tones; it is a multiple sharing without which there would be no "as" in general.) "Literature" means the being-in-common of what has no common origin, but is originarily in-common or with.

If, as Heidegger says, this is why the relation to one's own death consists in "taking over from [one]self [one's] ownmost Being," this taking over does not imply, contrary to what Heidegger himself says, that "all Being-with Others, will fail us when our ownmost potentiality-for-Being is the issue."[79] If being-with is indeed coessential to Being *tout court*, or rather is to Being itself, this ownmost possibility is coessentially a possibility of the with and as the with. My death is one "ownmost" co-possibility of the other existences' own possibility. It is, or it "will be," my death that says "he is dead" in their speaking; in this way, my death is not, it will not be, anywhere else. It is "my" possibility insofar as it withdraws the possibility of the "mine" into itself: *that is to say,* insofar as this "mineness" is returned to the singular plural of the always-other-mineness. In "he *is* dead," it is indeed Being that is in question—and as being-with.

"Death," therefore, is not negativity, and language does not know or practice negativity (or logic). Negativity is the operation that wants to depose Being in order to make it be: the sacrifice, the absent object of desire, the eclipse of consciousness, alienation—and, as a result, it is never death or birth, but only the assumption of an infinite supposition. As such, then, Being is infinitely pre-supposed by itself, and its process is the reappropriation of this pre-supposition, always on this side of itself and always beyond itself; it is negativity at work. But things work out completely differently if Being is singular plural dis-position. The distancing of disposition is *nothing*; this "nothing," however, is not the negative of anything. It is the incorporeal by which, according to which, bodies are with one another, close to one another, side by side, in contact and (therefore) distanced from one another. This *nothing* is the *res ipsa*, the thing itself: the thing as being-itself, that is, the being-such of every being, the mutual exposition of beings that exist only in and through this exposition. *Such* is a demonstrative; being-such is the demonstrative essence of Being, the being who shows itself to an-other being and in the midst of beings.

Moreover, whether they are aware of it or not, all the different ways of thinking negativity lead to the same point (they at least pass through it, even if they refuse to stop there). It is that point where the negative itself, in order to be the negative (in order to be the *nihil negativum* and not just the *nihil privatum*) must avoid its own operation and be affirmed in itself, with no remainder; or else, on the contrary, it must be affirmed as the absolute remain-der that cannot be captured in a concatenation of procedure or op-eration. (It is the critical, suspended, inoperative point at the heart of the dialectic). Self-presupposition interrupts itself; there is a syn-

copation in the process and in its thinking, a syncopation and instant conversion of supposition into dis-position. Dis-position is
the same thing as supposition: in one sense, it is absolute an-
tecedence, where the "with" is always already given; in another
sense, it does not "underlie" or preexist the different positions; it is
their simultaneity.

The non-Being of Being, its meaning, is its dis-position. The *nihil negativum* is the *quid positivum* as singular plural, where no
quid, no being, is posed *without with*. It is *without* (at a distance)
precisely to the extent that it is *with*; it is shown and demonstrated
in being-with, [which is] the evidence of existence.

In addition, evil is only ever [found] in an operation that fulfills
the *with*. One can fulfill the *with* either by filling it up or by emptying it out; it can be given a foundation of plenitude and continuity or an abyss of intransitivity. In the first case, the singular becomes a particular within a totality, where it is no longer either
singular or plural; in the second case, the singular exists only on its
own and, therefore, as a totality—and there too it is neither singular nor plural. In either case, murder is on the horizon, that is,
death as the operative negativity of the One, death as the *work* of
the One-All or the One-Me. This is exactly why death is [actually]
the opposite of murder: it is the inoperative, but existing, "with"
(such that murder inevitably lacks death).

The "with" is neither a foundation nor is it without foundation.
It is nothing except for being-with, the incorporeal *with* of the be-
ing-body *as such*. Before being spoken, before being a particular
language or signification, before being verbal, "language" is the following: the extension and simultaneity of the "with" insofar as it is
the *ownmost power* of a body, the propriety of its *touching* another
body (or of touching *itself*), which is nothing other than its definition as body. It finishes itself there, where it is-with; that is, it
comes to a stop and accomplishes itself in a single gesture.

In this sense, "to speak with" is not so much speaking to oneself
or to one another, nor is it "saying" (declaring, naming), nor is it
proffering (bringing forth meaning or bringing meaning to light).
Rather, "to speak with" is the conversation (and sustaining) and

conatus of a being-exposed, which exposes only the secret of its own exposition. Saying "to speak with" is like saying "to sleep with," "to go out with" (*co-ire*), or "to live with": it is a (eu)phemism for (not) saying nothing less than what "wanting to say" means [*le* "vouloir-dire" *veut dire*] in many different ways; *that is to say*, it says Being itself *as* communication and thinking: the *co-agitatio* of Being. "Language" is not an instrument of communication, and communication is not an instrument of Being; communication *is* Being, and Being *is*, as a consequence, nothing but the incorporeal by which bodies express themselves to one another *as such*.

Coexistential Analytic

The existential analytic of *Being and Time* is the project from which all subsequent thinking follows, whether this is Heidegger's own latter thinking or our various ways of thinking against or beyond Heidegger himself. This affirmation[80] is in no way an admission of "Heideggerianism"; it completely escapes the impoverished proclamations of "schools." It does not signify that this analytic is definitive, only that it is responsible for registering the seismic tremor of a more decisive rupture in the constitution or consideration of meaning (analogous, for example, to those of the "cogito" or "Critique"). This is why the existential analytic is not complete, and why we continue to feel its shock waves.

The analytic of *Mitsein* that appears within the existential analytic remains nothing more than a sketch; that is, even though *Mitsein* is coessential with *Dasein*, it remains in a subordinate position. As such, the whole existential analytic still harbors some principle by which what it opens up is immediately closed off. It is necessary, then, to forcibly reopen a passage somewhere beyond that obstruction which decided the terms of being-with's fulfillment, and its withdrawal, by replacing it with the "people" and their "destiny." This is not a matter of saying that it is necessary "to complete" the merely sketched-out analysis of *Mitsein*, nor is it a matter of setting up *Mitsein* as a "principle" like it deserves. "In principle," being-with escapes completion and always evades occupying the place of a principle. What is necessary is that we retrace the outline of its analysis and push it to the point where it becomes apparent that the coessentiality of being-with is nothing less than a matter of the co-originarity of meaning—and that the "meaning of Being" is only what it is (either "meaning" or, primarily, its own "precomprehension" as the constitution of existence) when it is *given as with.*

There is no "meaning" except by virtue of a "self," of some form or another. (The subjective formula of the ideality of meaning says that "meaning" takes place for and through a "self.") But there is no "self" except by virtue of a "with," which, in fact, structures it. This would have to be the axiom of any analytic that is to be called coexistential.

"Self" is not the relation of a "me" to "itself."[81] "Self" is more originary than "me" and "you." "Self" is primarily nothing other than the "as such" of Being in general. Being is only its own "as Being." The "as" does not happen to Being; it does not add itself to Being; it does not intensify Being: it is Being, constitutively. Therefore, Being is directly and immediately mediated *by itself*; it is itself mediation; it is mediation without any instrument, and it is nondialectic: dia-lectic without dialectic. It is negativity without use, the *nothing* of the with and the *nothing* as the with. The with as with is nothing but the exposition of Being-as-such, each time singularly such and, therefore, always plurally such.

Prior to "me" and "you," the "self" is like a "we" that is neither a collective subject nor "intersubjectivity," but rather the immediate mediation of Being in "(it)self," the plural fold of the origin.

(Is mediation itself the "with"? Certainly, it is. The "with" is the permutation of what remains in its place, each one and each time. The "with" is the permutation without an Other. An Other is always the Mediator; its prototype is Christ. Here, on the contrary, it is a matter of mediation without a mediator, that is, without the "power of the negative" and its remarkable power to retain within itself its own contradiction, which always defines and fills in [*plombe*] the subject. Mediation without a mediator mediates nothing: it is the mid-point [*mi-lieu*], the place of sharing and crossing through [passage]; *that is, it is place* tout court *and absolutely.* Not Christ, but only such a mid-point; and this itself would no longer even be the cross, but only the coming across [*l'croisement*] and the passing though, the intersection and the dispersal [*l'écartement*],[82] radiating out [*étoilment*] from within the very di-mension of the world. This would be both the summit and the abyss of a deconstruction of Christianity: the dis-location of the West.)

"Self" defines the element in which "me" and "you," and "we," and "they," can take place. "Self" determines the "as" of Being: if it is, it is *as* [en tant que] it is. It is "in itself" prior to any "ego," prior to any presentable "property." It is the "as" of all that is. This is not a presentable property, since it is presentation itself. Presentation is neither a propriety nor a state, but rather an event, the coming of something: of its coming *into the world,* where the "world" itself is the plane [*la géométral*] or the exposing of every coming.

In its coming, that which exists appropriates itself; that is, it is not appropriated, neither by nor into a "self" (which could only preexist what exists by removing and neutralizing the coming in itself). What is born has its "self" *before* self: it has it *there* (which is the meaning of Heidegger's "Dasein"). *There* means *over-there,* the distance of space-time (it is the body, the world of bodies, the body-world). Its appropriation is its moving [*transport*] and being-moved through [*transpropriation*] this dispersal of the *there*; such is the appropriating-event ("Ereignis"). But its being determined as such does not signify that there is some event in which the "proper self" would spring forth, like a jack-in-the-box, but that the coming is in itself and by itself appropriative as such. (As a result, differencing [*différant*] is in itself the propriety that it opens.) This is why "self" does not preexist (itself). "Self" equals what ex-ists as such.

Thus, insofar as "self," or "ipseity," means "by itself," relation to itself, returning into itself, presence to itself as presence to the "same" (to the sameness of the "as such"), ipseity occurs or happens to itself as coming; and such coming is anticipation, which is neither preexistence nor providence, but instead the unexpected arrival [*sur-venance*], the surprise and the being-placed back [*remise*] into the "to come" as such, *back into what is to come.* "Self" is neither a past given nor a future given; it is the present of the coming, the presenting present, the coming-*to*-be and, in this way, coming into Being. But *there where* it comes is not "into itself," as though into the interior of an determined domain; it is "beside itself."[83] *Beside itself* means into the dispersal of the dis-position, into the general element of proximity and distance, where such proximity and distance *are measured against nothing*, since there is nothing that is given as a fixed point of ipseity (before, after, outside the world). Therefore, they are measured according to the dis-position itself.

From the very start, the structure of the "Self," even considered as a kind of unique and solitary "self," is the structure of the "with." Solipsism, if one wants to use this category, is singular plural. Each one is beside-himself insofar as and because he is beside-others. From the very beginning, then, "we" are with one another, not as points gathered together, or as a togetherness that is divided up, but as a being-with-one-another. Being-with is exactly this: that Being, or rather that *to be* neither gathers itself as a resultant *commune* of beings nor shares itself out as their common substance. *To be* is nothing that is in-common, but *nothing* as the dispersal where what is in-common is dis-posed and measured, the in-common as the with, the beside-itself of *to be* as such, *to be* transfixed by its own transitivity: *to be* being all beings, not as their individual and/or common "self," but as *the proximity that disperses* [écarte] *them*.

Beings touch; they are in con-tact with one another; they arrange themselves and distinguish themselves in this way. Any being that one might like to imagine as not distinguished, not dis-posed, would really be indeterminate and unavailable: an absolute vacancy of Being. This is why the ontological moment or the very order of ontology is necessary. "*To be*" *is not the noun of consistency; it is the verb of dis-position.* Nothing consists, neither "matter" nor "subject." In fact, "matter" and "subject" are nothing but two names that are correlates of one another; in their mode of consistency, they indicate the originary spacing of the general ontological dis-position.

As such, then, "being-there" (*Dasein*) is *to be* according to this transitive verbal value of the dis-position. Being-there is [the] disposing [of] Being itself as distance/proximity; it is "to make" or "to let" be the coming of all with all *as such*. *Dasein* (that is, humanity as the index of Being) thus exposes *Being-as-to-be*.

Someone enters a room; before being the eventual subject of a representation of this room, he disposes himself in it and to it. In crossing through it, living in it, visiting it, and so forth, he thereby exposes the disposition—the correlation, combination, contact, distance, relation—of all that is (in) the room and, therefore, of the room itself. He exposes the simultaneity in which he himself participates at that instant, the simultaneity in which he exposes himself just as much as he exposes it and as much as he is exposed in it. He exposes himself. It is in this way that he is [a] "self," that he is it, or that he becomes it as many times as he enters into the disposition and each time that he does. This "at each time" is not the renewal of the experiences or occurrences of one self-same subject: so long as "I" am "the same," there will still always need to be an *other* time where I dis-pose myself according to this "sameness." This, in turn, implies that another time in general—that is, other times, indefinitely—are not only possible, they are real: the "each" of the "each time," the taking place of the *there* and as *there*, does not involve primarily the succession of the identical; it involves the simultaneity of the different. Even when I am alone, the room is at the same time the room where I am close to, next to, alongside of all its other dispositions (the way it is occupied, how it is passed-through, and so on). One is not in the disposition without being with the other-disposition, which is the very essence of dis-position. These "times" are discontinuous, but they are their being-with-one-another in this discontinuity. "Each time" is the singular-plural structure of the disposition. Therefore, "each time mine" signifies primarily "each time his or hers," that is, "each time *with*": *"mineness" is itself only a possibility that occurs in the concurrent reality of being-each-time-with.*

The world, however, is not a room into which one enters. It is also impossible to start from the fiction of someone who is alone and finds him- or herself in the world: in both cases, the very concept of the world is destroyed. This concept is that of being-with as originary. That is, if the meaning (of Being) is dis-position as such, then this is being-with as meaning: the structure of *with* is the structure of the *there*. Being-with is not added on to being-there; instead, to be there is to be with, and to be with makes sense—by itself, with nothing more, with no subsumption of this meaning under any other truth than that of the with.

In being-with and as being-with, *we* have always already begun to understand meaning, to understand ourselves and the world as meaning. And this understanding is always already completed, full, whole, and infinite. We understand ourselves infinitely—ourselves and the world—and nothing else.

~

"With" is neither mediate nor immediate. The meaning that we understand, insofar as we understand it, is not the product of a negation of Being, a negation destined to represent itself to us as meaning, nor is it the pure and simple ecstatic affirmation of its presence. "With" neither goes from the same to the other, nor from the same to the same, nor from the other to the other. In a certain sense, the "with" does not "go" anywhere; it does not constitute a process. But it is the closeness, the brushing up against or the coming across, the almost-there [*l'à-peu-près*] of distanced proximity.

When we try to evaluate this closeness (as if in a marketplace or railway station, or in a cemetery, we were to ask what are the meanings and values of these hundreds of people, of their restlessness and passivity), it comes out as frantic or distraught. But the meaning of the "with," or the "with" of meaning, can be evaluated only in and by the "with" itself, an experience from which—in its plural singularity—nothing can be taken away.

In understanding ourselves, we understand that there is nothing to understand; more precisely, this means that there is no appropriation of meaning, because "meaning" is the sharing of Being. There is no appropriation; therefore, there is no meaning. This is itself our understanding. This is not a dialectical operation (according to which "to understand nothing" would be "to understand everything"), nor is it a matter of turning it into the abyss (to understand the nothing of this same understanding), nor is it a reflexivity (to understand, for all understanding, that we understand ourselves); instead, it is all these replayed together in another way: as *ethos* and *praxis*.

To put it in Kantian terms, if pure reason is practical *by itself* (and not by reference to and according to any reverence for some transcendental norm), this is because it is essentially "common reason," which means the "with" *as* reason, as foundation. There is no difference between the ethical and the ontological: the "ethical" exposes what the "ontological" disposes.

Our understanding (of the meaning of Being) is an understanding *that* we share understanding between us and, at the same time, *because* we share understanding between us: between us all, simultaneously—all the dead and the living, and all beings.

§ War, Right, Sovereignty—Technē

What follows is a response to a request that came from the United States for some reflections on "war and technology."[1] In the midst of war (it is worth noting that I am beginning to write on 26 February 1991; the ground attack has begun; its future is still uncertain) undertaking this sort of reflection might be incongruous, even indecent. On the one hand, what counts today is what is now at stake, the deaths, the suffering of all sorts, and the great sympathy that accompanies all wars. (I hope some of it adheres here, stuck to these lines.) On the other hand, what also counts are the political determinations, the approbation and criticism, the motives and reasons that can still, if possible, engage everyone's responsibility. Yet, we are already responsible in still another way: we have the responsibility to think. As far as moral, political, and affective considerations are concerned, "war," as it reappears today, is a whole new reality in virtue of its very archaism. In other words, the return of "war," not as the reality of military operations but as a figure (War) in our symbolic space, is undeniably a new and singular phenomenon, because it produces itself in a world where this symbol seems to have been all but effaced. This is certainly worth thinking. And it might be that thinking about this is urgent. It is perhaps no longer a question of the degree to which war is a more or less necessary evil, or a more or less troublesome good. It is a question—and it is a question for the world—of knowing to which symbolic space we can entrust what is known as liberty, humanity.

War, in Spite of It All

Of course, what appeared to be the effacing of symbolic War concerned only the group of nations that make up the planet's core of "order," "law,"[2] and "development." The "third" world has never stopped being ravaged by armed conflicts: they all did happen, even if they did not fit into the strict category of war, or even if their local character prevented them from reaching full symbolic dignity. Since 1914, it has seemed that, in one way or another, "War" demanded a "global" dimension. I will come back to what this adjective implies. First, let us take up the point that this "globalization" is determined less by the spreading-out of the areas of conflict (again, there are conflicts throughout the world) than by the global role—economic, technical, and symbolic—of certain states whose sovereignty is involved in the war. For war is necessarily the war of sovereigns; that is, there is no war without Warlords: this is what I want to deal with here.

It might seem that this is hardly the way to open the question of "war and technology." It will soon become clear, however, that rather than concerning military technology (about which there is nothing special to be thought), attention devoted to the *sovereign* of and in war reveals war as *technē*, as *art*, the execution or putting to work of sovereignty itself. Yet, war is also an imperious, decisive interruption [*ponctuation*], exemplary of all our Western symbolism.

The war of States and coalitions of States, the "great war" (the war which is, by all rights, only a part—but an important, exemplary part—of the exercise of the state/national sovereignties it presupposes, war properly speaking as it has been defined since the beginnings of our history—I will come back to this), that war, insofar as it is easily distinguishable from others, is the [sort of] war we thought had been circumscribed, if not suspended, in the figure of the "cold" war and nuclear deterrence.

This war makes its return, or at least all of its signs are returning. Or rather, what is happening, whatever its exact name should be, will have to be accompanied, sustained, illustrated, and decorated with the signs, significations, and insignia of war. This will have been irresistible, and it will not have been the result of a simple negligence in the use of words.

As far as the last forty-five years are concerned, and in order to hold up the most identifiable figures of war (from a formal point of view), those in the Malvinas and Grenada have most clearly prefigured such a return. (I am indebted to Robert Fraisse for pointing out the decisive indication of this "return" and, as he put it, of the "wild contentment" that came along with the Malvinas War.) Other armed operations officially concerned our "world" only as police interventions in conflicts that operated on the order of revolt, subversion, or "civil war" (a name that, like the Greek *stasis* or the Roman *seditio,* indicates that it is not a war between sovereigns, a "warriors' war"), or even an intervention in the confrontation of sovereigns who are far away from us, and often more or less questionable. (Every detail of the uses, claims, manipulations, aporias of sovereignty in the postcolonial world ought to be exposed, as they are being exposed today in the post-Soviet world. And the details of *our* relations to all this sovereignty, the concept of which is ours, should also be added.)

But now there is *war,* "global" war in this new sense, in which many of the Sovereigns—whose titles we interpret in complex and contradictory ways—are implicated. Even if the conflict is not a question of North versus South, their presence globalizes global war again (if we can say such a thing). Therefore, there is war; for three months, the world has had nothing but this word on its lips. But *what is* War, really? What is it *today*? This is a question worth posing. What is most surprising is not that there is (*if indeed there is*) this war. It is not that there is this combat, or that battle, whatever their origin and their modalities. What is surprising is that in our eyes the very idea of war has again taken hold of us as the right of the city (there is no better way of putting it). In other words, it is highly remarkable that the idea of legitimate state/national violence, for so long regarded as suspect and suffering a tendentious delegitimation, could have regained (or almost regained) its full legitimacy, which means the legitimacy of the sovereign, absolutely.

According to good politico-juridical semantics, it is said and written that it is neither correct nor legitimate to use the word "war" for the present situation. I will come back to this. But this remark is still quite rare, confined as it is to juridical purism and the good, moral soul; general discourse, quite to the contrary, has thrown itself into the semantics, logic, and symbolism of war.

These, of course, have never really been annulled. But still, war appeared to be held within the shadows into which it had been plunged by the two previous "world" wars. In contrast to earlier centuries, the spirit of the time has not claimed the right to wage war above all the other prerogatives of the State; for example, only up until the First World War was it common to refer to States as "Powers."

On the other hand, the favor enjoyed by the idea of a "State of law" drew attention to that element in sovereignty regarded as exempt from violence and its force. It drew attention to the point where such violence, which would have presided in the institution of power, had to be effaced, sublimated, or curbed. War seemed to be at rest in the peace of now-defunct or obsolete feudalisms and nationalisms. And the aura of sovereignty grew dim there as well. Moreover, there was no more talk of "ideologies" and the "withering of the State." In decline with regard to the global complex of techno-economics, the State seems to have entered into the age of *self-control* by offering itself as a counterpoint in the barely sovereign role of regulative, juridical, and social administration.

But now one finds that there is nationalism springing up on all sides (and sometimes feudalism as well). These figures are heroic or ridiculous, pathetic or arrogant, dignified or questionable, but they are always shadowy either by vocation or according to their intended purpose. Certainly, a globalized recognition of "value" or of the democratic norm tends to regulate these affirmations of identity (and) of sovereignty. As such, these state/national figures are not marked [*tracée*] by a violent gesture, [which is] both somber and glorious; they are spontaneously modeled from within a wholly available, general legitimacy.

It is well known, however, that there is (still?) no such thing as supranational or prenational law—but, of course, it is exactly this war that revives the debate on the subject. There is no ready-made "democracy," no foundation for a law that is above nations or peoples. There is really only a supposed law that borders nation-states, a law that is only vaguely sure of being founded on universality, and fairly certain of being devoid of sovereignty. So-called international law, where this "inter," this "between," causes all the problems, is only graspable as that common space devoid of law, devoid of every sort of "setting in common" ["mise en commun"] (without which there is no law), and is structured *by* the techno-economic network and the supervision of Sovereigns.

Within this context, war makes its looming [*grande*] figure known. In a certain sense, whether it is "war" or "police action," whether it takes place as "war" or not, is unimportant. It has been granted and even "required" (as is said of it) that this not be war. Given this, we would have, while we even had a claim to the allegories of Mars or Bellone, allegories of need tempered by a beautiful—that is, arrogant—demand for "justice" and "morality."

Of course (I add this on returning to this text after the ceasefire), we are told about victory parades, after which the entire world will enthusiastically adopt the proud formula "The Mother of all Battles," which will even be the sovereign motto of those who were vanquished. But in order to unfold what another sovereign way of speaking [*une autre parole souverain*] has named "the logic of war," the possible return of this figure had to be perceptible, if only in a furtive (indeed fleeting) way. The States concerned knew how to tap into the virtualities that flourished in "public opinion": war could again be required or desired. Pacifism was now only routine or accidental, disregarded by the rest for having failed to recognize the fascist threat not so long ago, and for representing, since the beginning of this century, nothing but the exact and impotent [*impuissant*] reverse of the very "globalization" of war.

But, in this way, just as pacifism today limits itself to a *habitus* without substance, the moral of which is articulated neither in terms of law nor in terms of politics (the only respectable dimension is pity; and although the tragedy of the warrior is not the only one in this world, it alone seems to have grandeur . . .) so, on quite a different level, the reaffirmation of war springs forth from a rediscovered *habitus*, redeployed in a new context. A *habitus* is a way of being, a disposition of mores, an *ethos*.

~

Which way of being is it? What is it made up of? My first reply will be simple: it is the *ethos* of war itself; it is this disposition of mores, civilization, and thinking that affirms war not only as the means of a politics but also as an end cosubstantial with the exercise of sovereignty, which alone holds the exceptional right to it.

This response presupposes the convention of calling the use of State force, with respect to its own right, "a police action" and calling the exercise of a sovereign right to decide to attack another sovereign State a "war." It is precisely this convention that has just been reactivated, whether we want to recognize it or not. (For example, in terms of its constitution, France is not at war—and really, who is, and according to which constitution?)

Nothing is superior to a sovereign right (*superaneus* means that above which there is nothing). The right to wage war is the most sovereign of all rights because it allows a sovereign to decide that another sovereign is its enemy and to try to subjugate it, indeed to destroy it, that is, to relieve it of its sovereignty (here, life comes into the bargain [*la vie vient par-dessus le marché*]). It is the sovereign's right to confront his *alter ego ad mortem*; this is not only an effect of sovereignty but also its supreme manifestation—just as our whole tradition has wanted it.

Within the sovereign context of war, nothing is valid if not some supposed conventions upheld in order to keep it within a certain moral (in former times, sacred) order. But this order is not exactly superior to war; it is the very order of which war is a sovereign extremity, the sharpest edge [*le fer de lance*] and the point of exception. (This is why Rousseau, against the whole tradition, did not want to see a special act of sovereignty in the right to war, but "only an application of the law"; Rousseau's sovereignty is an intimate debate with the exception, and with the force which cannot not haunt it. . . .)

War, then, is itself susceptible to creating a new law, a new distribution of sovereignties. And such is the origin of the majority of our national and state sovereignties, or legitimacies. This is also the point through which revolutionary war was able to inherit what is essential to the concept of State war, although at the cost of certain displacements. (This began with the wars of the French Revolution, a mixture of State wars and wars waged in the name of a universal principle, against enemies of a human sort. From that moment on, the question of knowing if one could present a universal sovereignty was put forward. . . .)

The right to wage war excepts itself from law at the very point where it belongs to it both as an origin and as an end; this point is a point of foundation, insofar as we are incapable of thinking of foundation without sovereignty, or of sovereignty itself without thinking in terms of exception and excess. The right to wage war excepts itself from law at a point replete with sovereign brilliance [*un éclat souverain*]. Law does not possess this brilliance, but it needs its light, and its founding event. (This is why War is also the Event par excellence; it is not an event in some "history of events" that consists in reciting, one by one, the dates of wars, victories, and treaties, but the Event that suspends and reopens the course of history, the sovereign-event. Our kings, generals, and philosophers have only ever thought of it in this way.)

This mode of instituting law becomes unacceptable, however, in a world that represents law itself as its own "origin" or its own "foundation," whether this falls under the heading of a "natural right" of humanity or under the heading of an irreversible sedimentation of the experiences [*les acquis*] of a positive law which, little by little, has become the law of all (whereas the soldiers of the year II [*l'An II*] could still represent this foundation as a conquest yet to be made or remade). This is where the anxiety and confusion that seize us when faced with the idea of war comes from, particularly as regards "just war," an expression which might, at one and the same time, subject war to law and law to war. (For all that, and for the entire tradition—I will come back to this—this expression is redundant, as redundant as the expression "dirty war". . . .)

Our anxiety testifies to the fact that our world, the world of "globalization," displaces the concept of war, along with all the politico-juridical concepts of sovereignty. In fact, the "return" of war only appears at the heart of these displacements. This is why some have dared to say that it does not appear at all. But our anxiety also testifies (and occasionally in the same people as above), not to a regret, or to a nostalgia (although . . .), but rather to a difficulty in doing without sovereign authority [*l'instance souveraine*], even down to its most terrible brilliance (seeing as it is also the most brilliant). This persistence of sovereignty in us is what I would like to examine before trying to understand where we could go or toward which "other" of sovereignty. We will see how that happens through "technology."

I am not unaware of the precautions one must take to avoid having this very simple project fall into the trap of simplification, that is, the coarseness [*la grossièreté*] of thinking. I take these precautions to be the following:

First, my intention is not to reduce the history of the Gulf War to a pure and simple sovereign decision for war, the action of one or more actors. In a general context involving [*mêlé*] endemic war, the proliferation of seditions, contested sovereignties, and multiple and conflicting police forces (economic, religious, and international rights and interests, as well as those of the state, of minorities, and so forth), a process is produced that is a mixture of war and police action, in which the one constantly comes down to the other. I do not claim, here, to completely disentangle the role that each plays; in fact, that would be impossible. Yet again, everything is displaced and the pair—that is, war/police action—no longer allows itself to be easily manipulated, as if that had ever been possible. But in this pair, I do want to interrogate what seems, at the limit of law itself, to obstinately, or even fiercely, maintain the demand for war that carries the sovereign exception within itself and also exposes it.

Because of this logic of the exception, the logic of the "sovereign" as being "without law," it is not immediately obvious that any of the lines of thinking available to us will suit our purposes. The style of neo-Kantian humanism dominant today does no more than re-new the promise of moralizing politics, all the while offering law the weapons of a politics that has yet to be moralized. The revolutionary style faded out along with all the pretensions of designating the sub-ject by means of another law, and appearance [*le surgissement*] by means of another history. As for the "decisionist" style, it has been relegated to the heart of the "totalitarian" style. None of them yield a possibility either for thinking sovereignty *hic et nunc* or for think-ing beyond it. Ever since the first global conflict gave ample testi-mony to this general difficulty, ours has been a history of the doc-trines and problems of international law, sovereignty, and war.

For the moment, we can only draw out the strict consequences of this list [of the available lines of thinking]. I am not interpret-ing the Gulf War according to any of these schemes. I am only sug-gesting that an empty space stretches between the always weak and troubled schema of the "war of law (police action)" and a reacti-vated (warmed over?) schema of "sovereign war." Moreover, this space is not the space of a "peoples' war" ["guerre des peuples"]: for the moment, the people are in the museums of the Revolution, or in the folklore museums. Indeed, this space is a desert. It is not only pitted with oil wells and bomb craters; it is also the desert of our thinking, as well as that of "Europe," and that of the desola-tion that crosses through rights and war in the Gulf and elsewhere; it is that increasingly worse desolation defined by economic and cultural injustice. In the end, then, it is true that the desert is grow-ing. I have long detested the morose relish with which some have rehashed this sentence. But I do admit that the desert is growing. And, although no longer militant, the sterility of the dominant hu-manism, arrogant with the arrogance of the weak, reveals its glaring irresponsibility in the end.

I am not claiming to have invented another [way of] thinking; I only want to situate its demand, its extreme urgency. For we are already at another [way of] thinking; it precedes us, and the war shows us that we must catch up with it.

Second, if it is clear that my preference (which, at this point, I hold in reserve) was not, in this war, for war, I am nonetheless keenly aware that the great majority of those who supported the war wanted to be partisans of a law superior or exterior to state sovereignties. What is more, many have testified to a refined sense of the responsibilities of all the parties involved in the conflict; I am setting aside all notions of intention here; I am not claiming that the war was only passed off under the guise [*manteau*] of law. Some did as much, but that is so clear as to be no longer interesting. What is interesting is that it was possible to affirm the war, and the manner in which this was possible was more or less simple or war-like, restrained or complicated.

But at the same time, it is not a question of embarking on another round of the sort of simplification so fashionable today, thereby suspending the consideration of the interests and calculations that set the economic stakes of the war on an East-West axis, as well as a North-South one. Besides, the denial of this was transparent; everyone knows what was going on, and it is no longer necessary to be a member of the Party in order to share, despite oneself, certain truths that come from Marx. It is not a question of simple "economic determination." Instead, it is a question of the following: although there may be casualties, the economy is in the process of exhausting perspectives, hopes, and ends. Whatever is not governed by economics belongs to a timid, juridical projection (where it is no longer a question of creating or founding a new law) or to the realm of fantastical compensations (that is, religions, sometimes art, and also, from now on, politics). The return of the figure of War corresponds to an exasperated desire for legitimation and/or finality, at exactly a time when no one can believe that economics has its own, universally legitimated finality anymore. (In this regard, what remains of the distinction between liberal and planned economies is hardly important.) In fact, at the very moment when the supposed "death" of Marx was being celebrated, his *political economy* (it could also be called *economic war*) cordoned off [*verrouille*] our whole horizon. It is not sovereign, but it is dominant, and this is a different thing. All at once, politics commits suicide in that juridical-moralism that is without sovereignty—or rather, in order to better serve domination, it tries to regild its sovereign shield: thus we have War, the ambiguous sovereign-slave of economics. I will came back to a consideration of world without end. Its critique, however, must be no less radical than Marx's. But there is no doubt that radicality no longer involves the founding of a new End, or the restoration of Sovereignty in general. On the contrary, this logic seems to be the one in which economic war constantly radiates sovereign War, and vice versa.

Third, it is true that in interpreting facts and discourses under the heading of the return of a dimension of war, or of a warlike pose or postulation, which one might have believed to be completely forgotten (or repressed), I seem to jettison [*faire fi des*] the reserve and prudence that has been used in dealing with a war that has been thought of as "well-tempered." It is true that there has been little discourse that is properly or directly warmongering; (instead, talk of "going to war" reignited the polemics of the pacifists, while *at the same time*, some remarkable figures [of speech] came up in private discourse; I will certainly not be the only one to have heard "how good it will be for the West to have rediscovered its balls.")

Taking up this text again after the cease-fire, I would like to add the following: given that the contest was so unequal, how can we avoid thinking that we needed a discourse of war, without quite wanting a war—but, all the while, wanting its result? The "fourth army in the world" could not and did not want to fight. And the "first" fought principally in order to smother the very possibility of battle under the weight of its bombs, running the risk of restraining its heroism by limiting its own losses. This, of course, did not prevent there being death and destruction; moreover, it did not prevent the enormous difference in the amount of suffering on each side. But these amounts count for nothing (first of all . . .) in the symbolic dimension of war; this dimension is expressed only in terms of victory or defeat, of sovereignty affirmed, conquered, or reconquered. (Even according to this very standard, this war—both certain and uncertain—had a certain and uncertain result. At the moment, Iraq is minting coins carrying the claim "Victory is ours," while military parades are being organized in the United States,

England, and France. It is true that all of this is pure facade and that, for the most part, the period after the war has propagated civil war, at least in Iraq and Kuwait, and set economic war in motion again. It remains the case, however, that "the facade" plays a role in the constructions of the political and collectivity in general.)

It is true, in fact, that I am presupposing the interpretation of a number of details, from the approval of the war by national parliaments (which is a supererogatory measure in a police operation, as well as in genuinely exceptional cases of distinct military urgency) to all the indices provided by the semantics, style, and emphases of many of the discourses devoted to urgency, peril, sacrifice, national duty, military virility, the sublimity of great commanders, the unleashing of primal force, and so on. (For instance, I read the following in a prominent French newspaper: "but how can one fight efficiently without freeing one's primitive instincts?"; to stay with this point for a moment, this sentence, taken as such and in the ordinary context of our culture, is undoubtedly irreproachable; although it does testify to the "ordinary" context of a state which tends toward the vulgar.) To those listed above, one must add the discourse of the holy mission: both sides had God on their side (*monotheos* versus *monotheos*), as well as calls for the "foundation" of a new order or regime.

I have no interest in collecting public and private documents. There are a great many of them. Interpretive violence is hardly called for in order to decipher in them the presence of a symbolism and warlike fantasy that is more or less unobtrusively mixed together with reasons that have to do with law and the need for police actions. This does not mean the latter are disqualified, but the former must be brought to light.

In addition, it is impossible to forget the role played on both sides by the political desire and need to recuperate military defeats (Vietnam on the American side, and Sinai on the Arabic, even though the two cases are very different). In the case of the United States, the most powerful of today's adversaries, what needed to be washed away was not only the humiliation that attaches to all defeats, but also a war that had made war shameful.

Indeed, the taste for the spectacle of epic beauty and heroic virtue, which was so clearly laid out during the buildup to war and in its first phases, will not be easily forgotten. After all, these images are not the slightest bit different from those of war films. However, I do not so much want to join forces with the critics of the "spectacular society" who have made a point of qualifying this as a "spectacular" war (the denial of which is directly symmetrical to what is at work in the discourse of law). Yet, the images of war did form a part of the war—and perhaps war itself is like a film, even before a film imitates war. In the face of horror and pity, which is where it necessarily ends up, there would be no war without a war-like momentum of the imaginary. Its spectacle is inextricably bound up with the sometimes stupefying, mechanical constraint that makes the soldier march on. The psychologists of the American army took pleasure in explaining (on television) that the *boys* do not march for a cause, for right or democracy, but only so as not to give up in front of their companions. That is, what drives honor and glory already belongs to the order of the "spectacle," and it cannot be dismantled by the simple denunciation of a modern age in which simulation is generalized and commodified. (In addition, and as always happens with this sort of discourse, there were good reasons for wondering, on reading certain critiques of the "war-spectacle," about the nostalgia revealed there, nostalgia for the good old wars of yesteryear.) What is at play in the "spectacle" of war goes much further back than that, extending out to the very limits of a whole culture (of which Islam is a part)—and undoubtedly even beyond that.

I am not claiming that the epic is on its way back—neither the Homeric epic, nor the Napoleonic, nor even those that can still be associated with the battles of Rommel, Montgomery, Leclerc, or Guderian, for example. (All the same, there was talk of the "legendary past" of various units or vehicles of war that had carried the aura of their deeds from the last world war into the Gulf.) A great deal is needed for the epic to make a comeback, but this "great deal" is not enough to ensure that no aspect of the affirmation or celebration of war would remain. At the very least, the facets of a brilliant [*éclat*] sovereignty would remain. In war, a brilliant, incandescent, fascinating sovereignty is celebrated (for an instant, for a split second, in a flash of light). But is this not an essential part of what we think we are deprived of in general: the brilliant flash, the figures of the Sun? Even now, our world does not represent itself as lacking in power or intelligence, or even completely lacking in grace. But the lack of Sovereignty surely structures an essential part of our world's representation of itself, and therefore of its desire.

Sovereign Ends

What has returned with war, or remains of it, has nothing obviously to do with military technologies. For these technologies have never stopped being used during the course of all quasi-wars, guerrilla wars of liberation and their repression, or in all the political, economic, or judicial police operations. What is achieved primarily by the technologies regarded as properly military can be just as well, if not better, achieved by the use of so-called civil technologies put to military purposes. In fact, it is almost impossible to distinguish between these two. For example, psychology is also a weapon, and, in turn, the progress which military research has made regarding civil technologies (for example, in the field of sleeping medication) is not often taken into account. Perhaps a specific difference between them only truly begins to emerge, on the one hand, at the level of the finalities of massive destruction (but one wonders to what extent even this criterion can be used with delicacy, at least as regards material destruction that can interfere with civil activities) and, on the other hand and above all, on the order of symbolic marks (for instance, the uniforms and insignia of armies). There are uniforms outside of the army, but where there are uniforms, there is also an army, as a principle or a more or less latent model. Short of [elaborating upon] this dividing line, all the technologies in play, from the manufacture and use of a rifle or dagger to the logistical and strategic manipulation of whole armies, provide no means of making the idea of war as such distinct.

In one sense, this is why there is no specific question concerning the technologies of war, except technical questions, which here, as elsewhere, do not allow for the questioning or thinking of "technology"—but this is the case with all technical fields. During the first days of this war, the way certain technologies were allocated starring roles [*la mise en vedette*] made it possible to observe how discourses that were favorable and unfavorable to technology had nothing to do with thinking through [the question of] technology; instead, they espoused all the established prejudices, problems, or aporias of the war itself. (The English word "technology" is well placed to suggest a logic proper to [the French word] *la technique*, with which the discourses about "meaning" or "value" almost never engage.) Technological fire power was celebrated, that is, the power of the electronic, chemical, and mechanical complex that produced the missiles (among other things), a new addition to the series of warlike emblems that stretches to time immemorial, including the sword, helmet, or cannon. There was self-congratulation on the self-limiting possibilities of this very power, and it emerged in a discourse of "surgical" war that corresponded to the thesis of law: flaunting limits that are stricter than the limits set by international convention serves to make more credible an interpretation that operates according to the notion of "police action." The terrible possibilities offered by new technologies were deplored (for example, the possibility of "vitrification" offered by these new bombs, whereas the possibilities of shrapnel bombs, or bombs with phosphorus or napalm, were already well known by this point . . .). In the end, there was a fear that recourse would be made to technologies banned by those conventions that set the rules of war; the effective use of that now-forbidden group of biochemical weapons in the past, with all their catastrophic potential, obviously plays a strategic role. In this regard, conventions regarding the means of war constantly demonstrate the fragility of the law that upholds them: not only is it infinitely difficult to legitimate the distinction between different sorts of weapons on the basis of humanitarian principles, but it also remains the case that the collision—indeed, the contradiction—between such humanitarian principles and the principles of war is constantly perceptible and consistently brings the "right to war" back down to its foundation in the sovereign exception. For example, it is clearly not from the right to—or logic of—war that one can infer the interdiction against including genetic patrimonies within the ambit of warlike destruction. But this is also why, up to a certain point in this war, one could see a particular progress being made by the idea of deploying tactical nuclear weapons in response to the chemical threat posed by Iraq. (It could very well be that the nuclear weapon was, far more than admitted, a major stake in this conflict: this particular weapon, its possession, and its use in the next war. . . .) One could develop parallel considerations regarding the protection of civilians. But all this is already well known, which really means, and rightly so, that no one wants to know anything about it.

Thus, there is no "question of technology" proper to war, any more than there is a "question of technology" in general, that is, a question put to technology or its subject and involving the application of criteria that do not belong to it. War-with-missiles is neither better nor worse than war-with-catapults; it is still a question of war. And communication is neither better nor worse when it is carried by fiber-optics, instead of messengers on foot: it is rather a question of knowing what "communication" means. If "technical" civilization displaces the concepts of war or communication (or health, or life, and so on), then it must be a question of the concepts themselves, of their "becoming-technology" ["devenir-technique"] in a generalized space of the world's becoming-technology. But this is not a question of evaluating new instruments for the unchanged ends of a world that is still the world as it used to be.

War is undoubtedly a privileged terrain for bringing to light the inaneness of all the considerations of technology that do not proceed from this preliminary consideration (and it must be admitted that these former sorts of discourse are, in fact, more numerous). It is clear that technologies are not responsible for war, any more than war is responsible for the technologies that are not proper to it—even though technologies give war its means, and war generates technical progress. The ethical, juridical, and cultural problems posed by civil technology (nuclear or biological, for example) are no less acute than those posed by certain armaments. It is quite likely that the disparity between the two sets of problems has been very much reduced, for example, since the invention of artillery (which testifies to this "becoming-technology" of the world, which is what we have to take into account). In the end, the interminable celebratory or execratory discourses on technology, all of them founded on "values" that are obstinately foreign to this becoming-technology, can only mask what there is of "war," as well as what there is now of "medicine" or "the family," and so forth.

There is no such thing as the "question of technology," properly speaking, so long as technology is considered as a means to an end. Except for technical problems as such, all such "questions," are posed according to the order of ends: practical, ethical, political, aesthetic, and so on. Insofar as war is itself considered as a means to an end (whether political, economic, juridical, religious, and so forth), it falls under this logic. This is what is really at stake in Clausewitz's formulation that "war is the continuation of politics by other means." It indicates a modern mutation of the thinking of war, a mutation which implies that the "classical" way of thinking about war as the exercise, setting to work, or extreme expression of sovereignty is now set at a distance and denied in a more or less confused manner. As I have already said, such thinking is still the only rigorous thinking of war. The displacement that took hold with Clausewitz still remains to be brought to term: it may be the end of war.

For that thinking of war which is still ours, war is sovereignty's technology par excellence; it is its setting to work and its supreme execution (end). In this sense, a "technology" is not a means; instead, it is a mode of execution, manifestation, and effectuation in general. To be more precise, it is the mode of accomplishment that distinguishes itself from the "natural" mode as that mode's double, and its rival in perfection. When one has recourse to the Greek terms *physis* and *technē*, which in their contemporary use refer to Heidegger (and more discretely to Nietzsche, if not to the German Romantics), it is in order to give specific names to these "modes of accomplishment," taking care to distinguish them, on the one hand, from "nature" as a collection of materials and forces, possessed of its own laws and, on the other, from "technology" as an "artificial" means of reaching its ends. *Phusis* and *technē*—one could say "birth" ["éclosion"] and "art"—are two modes of accomplishment and are, in this respect, the same (but not identical) in their difference: the same as concerns accomplishment in general, as putting to work or carrying out [*l'exécution*]. As a result, they are doubly the "same" with regard to the end; they are not two different finalities, but two finishes [*deux finitions*] (like a "hand" finish and a "machine" finish—a comparison that also serves to recall the hierarchy which we "quite naturally" set up between these two sorts of finishes . . .). Furthermore, ever since Plato and Aristotle, these two modes have constantly referred to one another in a double relationship that has come to be known as *mimesis*: it is not that one "copies" the other ("copying" is quite impossible in this case), but that each replays the play of the end or ends [of the other], [as] the art or birth of the finish.

The finish consists in executing (*ex-sequor* means to follow though to the end), in carrying out something to the limit of its own logic and its own good, that is, to the extremity of its own Being. In our thinking, Being in general, or rather, Being proper or plainly Being [*l'être propre ou l'être en propre*], in each of its singular effectuations or existences, has its substance, end, and truth in the finish of its Being. For us, it is so evident that this trait belongs to "Being" in general (or to "reality," or to "effectivity") that it seems odd to insist on expressing such a redundancy.

We think that to be is not to half-be [*être-à-demi*], but to be fully present, perfect, complete, finished, and, every single time, final, terminal, done. The whole problem, if there is a problem, is of knowing if the execution, the finish, is finite or infinite, and in what sense of these words. As we will see, questions of technology and war come down to this troublesome articulation in every last instance.

Physis and *technē* are, in this way, the Being of Being, the same that plays itself out twice, with a difference to which I will have to return. For the moment, let me just add that *history* is that general realm of twisting or displacement that affects this difference.

If there is a "question of technology," then it only begins at that moment when technology is taken into account as the finish of Being, and not as a means to some other end (science, mastery, happiness, and so on). It only begins when technology is taken into account as an end in itself, *sui generis*. Technology is the "finality without end" (= without an extrinsic end) of a genre that perhaps remains to be discovered. It is to such a discovery that we expose our history, as a technological-becoming of Being or its finish.

What, in principle, falsifies so many considerations of technology is the desire to locate its principles and ends outside of itself—for example, in a "nature" that itself constantly enters into a becoming-technology. . . . Just as, in the past, we never stopped relating "nature" to some sovereign Power—as the creation and glory of a Power named God, Atom, Life, Chance, or Humanity—so we have never stopped securing from technology, and for technology, a *Deus ex machina*, which is yet another sovereign Power that the most habitual tendencies of our ways of representing leads us to designate as a *Diabolus ex machina* (this is the story of Faust). With regard to the *ex machina*, the *Deus* becomes *diabolicus* because it is no longer the "technician of nature" or the Natural Technician, that is, the one who relates all things to one End, or to one absolute, transcendental, transcendent, and sovereign Finish. For we deny "technology" access to the realm of ends and, to an even greater extent, to the realm of the Infinite End, in this sense.

As a result, Leibniz may have been the closest to expressing the first clear consciousness of technology in his looking to put the *machina ex Deo* into play—we can say as much unless, of course, it is not also advisable to combine this formulation with that of Spinoza's, the *Deus sive natura sive machina*: after which the "death of God" signifies the rigorous carrying out of the program formulated as the *machina ex machina* (*ex natura*), that which does not finish finishing [*celle qui n'en finit pas de finir*] and about which it remains for us to think its law and to discover just what is at stake in it.

It is necessary, here, to include a consideration of the extremely pronounced position in which our thinking puts war, between "nature" and "technology." (Also note the "wholly natural" ambiguity of our understanding of such a sentence: is it a matter of war considered as an intermediary position between nature and technology, or is it a matter of war which takes place between nature and technology? Precisely speaking, we are ready to think these two things together.) War is what there is that is most and/or least "natural." It arises from the most brutal instincts and/or from the coldest calculation, and so on. This position is not without certain connections to that place between "art" and "nature" that we give to "beauty." This position, which is both problematic and privileged—and is itself replayed twice between two orders, that of art and war, considered in some way to be opposed to one another—is not without importance. We will return to this below.

∼

Every consideration about ends leads back to sovereignty. The power of ends, as the power of the ultimate or extreme, resides in a sovereignty. And every end, as such, is necessarily ordered by a sovereign end (a "sovereign good"). For the whole of our thinking, the End is in Sovereignty, and Sovereignty is in the End. The absolute transcendence, or the abyss, or the mystery of supreme ends that is found all throughout the tradition—for example, the impossibility of determining the "content" of the Platonic Good or the Kantian Law—is held firmly within this circle: that which is sovereign is final, that which is final is sovereign.

Sovereignty is the power of execution or the power of finishing as such, absolutely so and without any further subordination to something else (to another end). Divine creation and the royal decision compose its double image: to make or unmake a world, to submit to a will, to designate an enemy. Although anticipated by the legislative power and controlled by the judicial power, this is why the executive power attains to an exceptional state [of power] in war; in spite of everything, however, this occurrence touches upon (de jure and de facto) the very extremity of decision making and power (powerful decision and decisive power) where it accomplishes its "executive" essence most properly, the sovereign essence of Being—

where this is "power" (as the prince, State, nation, people, father-land, and so on).

This is why accusing a sovereign power of wanting war so obvi-ously falls short of the mark. The execution of this desire [*vouloir*] for war is not only one of the proper ends of the executive organ; it also represents the extreme mode of these ends. So that it is no longer an organ with regard to the execution of such desire; in-stead, it is sovereignty itself in its finishing—insofar as we think sovereignty according to the only concept that is at our disposal. In war, there is something that immediately goes beyond all the possible goals of war, whether they be defensive or offensive: the accomplishment of the Sovereign as such in a relation of absolute opposition with another Sovereign. War is indissociably the *physis* and *technē* of sovereignty. Its law, the exception of its law, has as its counterpoint the law of grace: but with the latter, the Sovereign never identifies itself nor executes itself vis-à-vis the *other*.

If it were necessary, one could find a certain confirmation [of this] in the very peculiar symbolic or fantastical weight of the in-struments and machinery of war. It is difficult to deny that even if the Gulf War gave rise to an explicit discourse of sovereignty only in an awkward and cursory manner, that is, in the form of a denial, it certainly aroused an exceptional deployment of the images of tanks, jets, missiles, and helmeted soldiers, images saturated with symbolic weight. It even deployed images of symbolic saturation itself, which could well constitute a trait of sovereign finishing.

Objects lose their symbolic character to the extent that their technicity grows, at least that technicity posited in terms of func-tionality (in terms of means); but this does not prevent the object from being symbolically (or fantastically) invested again. With re-gard to this, think of a sickle, a hammer, a set of gears, and even a circuit board. But today (and in the past, for that matter), there is no better place for such symbolism to adhere to function in such an immediately obvious manner as in the images of the weapons of war. Such adherence undoubtedly comes from the fact that this image does not present a tool of destruction, but rather the affir-mation of the sovereign right of the sovereign power to execute a

sovereign destruction, or to execute itself in destruction, *as* Destruction (of the other sovereign). This is not really a function; it is
a destination: to give and receive collective death, death sublimated
into the destiny of the community, the community identified in a
sovereign exposition to death. (Is Death the true Sovereign in this
whole affair? We will come back to this.)

Thus, war borders on art. This is not to say that it borders on the
art of war, the technology of the strategist; it is to say, rather, that it
borders on art understood absolutely in its modern sense, *technē* as
a mode of the execution of Being, as its mode of finishing in the
explosive brilliance [*éclat*] of the beautiful and sublime, that dou-
bled rivalry for sovereignty that occurs within the blossoming [*éclosion*] of *physis*. (Moreover, *physis* no longer takes place except as mediated through *technē*, or one could say that it never takes place "in
itself," or in any other way, except as the image of the sovereignty of
technē.) Undoubtedly, the aestheticization of the warlike spectacle
also comes from denial [*dénégation*] or dissimulation. But this manipulation does not exhaust an aesthetic (a sensible presentation)
of the destiny of community: the death of individuals is immediately recuperated within the figure of the Sovereign Leader or Nation where the community finds its finishing. War is the monu-
ment, the festival, the somber and pure sign of the community in
its sovereignty.

～

In essence, war is collective, and the collectivity that is endowed
with sovereignty (the Kingdom, State, or Empire) is by definition
endowed with the right to war (as Thomas Aquinas writes, "*bellum
particulare non proprie dicitur*"). The entire history of the concept
of war demonstrates that its determination is located within the
constant play between its relation with the *res publica* (the commonwealth as *good* and *end* in itself) and its relation with the *Prin-
ceps* (the principle and principate of sovereign authority). Not only
is the latter in charge of the former, not only is the Prince in possession of the armed forces necessary to the [maintenance of the]
Republic, but the commonwealth as such must also present and

represent his absolute and final character, his sovereignty, and its armed forces must carry the flag of his glory.

It is at this very point that the law of the republic—of any kind of republic, even today's republics—inevitably comes up against [*touche*] the exception of the prince, whatever the form of government might be. Even today, democracy has not profoundly displaced this schema; it has only suppressed or repressed it, back into the shadow of its own uncertainties (that is, the uncertainty concerning its own sovereignty, an uncertainty that even today remains cosubstantial with it). Like what is repressed, then, the schema of the sovereign exception never stops returning, and it returns as the perversion of democracy, whether this return happens in the innumerable coups d'etat of its history or in becoming totalitarian (where the exception transforms itself into a doubling of the structure of the State by another [structure] which incarnates true sovereignty).

Since World War I, however, it is democracy as such—such as it has ended up presenting itself as the general principle of humanity, if not humanity's End—that has been supposedly endowed with the right to war, thereby transforming war into the defense of the *res publica* of humanity. This presupposes that a neutral country (the United States—when one thinks about it, as long as there are several sovereigns, neutrality is a strange form of sovereignty) decides to take leave of its neutral position in the name of human rights, and that it explicitly designate as its enemy, not a people or a nation, but governments judged to be dangerous to the good of all peoples ("civilized" . . .). In world war, democracy does not go to war against a sovereign (Germany and the countries of the Alliance), but against bad leaders.

(Note added 6 April 1991: today, in the face of the suppression of the Kurds by the same sovereign leader on whom was inflicted the "police action" of law, the Powers hesitate between respect for his sovereignty within his own borders and an affirmation by the "international community" of a right to interfere in the matters of certain countries. . . . Today, there is no better way to illustrate the inconsistencies and aporias that belong to the coupling of "international law" and "sovereignty." This said, however, it is evidently not these conceptual difficulties that motivate the various different judgments and hesitations. . . . These difficulties do express the actual state of a world encumbered by sovereignty, but it is a world that does not know how to displace or go beyond sovereignty.)

In order for the decision to go to war—against Germany, against Iraq—in the name of human rights to become a decision (and not a wish), it was necessary that this decision take form and force in and by way of the sovereignty of a State—and/or an alliance of States. When one or several States speak in the name of the rights of man, and, under this name, put to use the prerogatives of the *jus belli*, this continues to operate as a sovereign decision (or an alliance of such decisions). In a sense, this is even an increase of sovereignty in comparison with that of the prince. This is why, in the Gulf War, the tug of war [*le va-et-vient*] between the authority of the United Nations and the United States (and, if one considers it carefully, the authority of some other States as well) has been so complex and so simple at the same time, so delicate and so indelicate. The legitimacy without sovereignty of "international law" needed a sovereign *technē*—and not just a means of execution, as we have been made to believe. But this sovereign, in turn, needed the legitimacy of human rights in order to establish its decisions and pretensions, which could only be of global dimensions, just like the principles and promises of the law (which itself still remains without foundation, that is, without sovereignty and without "finishing").

$\sim$

Here, as everywhere else, it is solely a question of the public Good and of Peace. From Plato and Aristotle to Christian and Republican doctrines, the whole history of our thinking about war testifies to this. Not that long ago, Henry Kissinger declared "the goal of all wars is to ensure a durable peace," and his judgment offered there was upheld (or weakened?) by twenty-five centuries of philosophical, theological, ethical, and juridical repetition. Western [*occidentale*] war always has peace as its *end*, even to such a extent that it is necessary to "battle peacefully," as was put forth from

Augustine to Boniface. Sparta was that state which gave itself war as *the* end of its structure and formation, and Plato subjected it to a severe critique. What constitutes the principle of final peace has undoubtedly shifted more than once, not only in fact—which is more than evident, but in theory itself (for example, by mixing the logic of "peace" together with a logic of religious conversion, or with a logic of the occupation of a territory claimed as an inheritance). Nonetheless, the general theoretical regulation of Western war remains that of pacificatory war (a motif that has been extended so far as to include the exportation of certain colonialist forms of "peace"). Western war denies itself as sovereign end, and its denial, of course, constitutes its admission.

It would be necessary here to take the time to analyze the complex play between the three great monotheisms "of the Book," which are also the three monotheisms "of community" and, therefore, of sovereignty. Although each of them has its own particular complexity, both Israelite (at least until the destruction the Temple) and Islamic monotheism reserve a place for a principle of war that does go together [*se confond*] with the peace of the peoples. Christian monotheism presents another complexity, which mixes the model of the *pax romana* together with the model of the war against the Infidels. Even as a religion of love, it does not simply go together with a principle of peace: for there are enemies of love, where divine love is of another essence than human love. In the process of its becoming-modern, a process it has been engaged in from the very start, Christian love recuperates within itself the irenic principle of Greek philosophy (which presupposes the breakdown of the Epic and imitates this breakdown in the installation of *logos*) and becomes entirely a principle of peace, and peace in terms of universal human rights. It is here that the god of love loses his divinity little by little, and love in peace loses its sovereignty. The peace of humanism is without force or grandeur; it is nothing other than the enervation of war.

Deprived of the Temple and of any place for sovereignty, State, and soil, Jewish monotheism needs to be annihilated, somewhere beyond war itself [*dans un au-delà de la guerre même*], precisely because of this lack of sovereignty. On the other side, taken up in the service of Western statism and nationalism, the Islamic *jihad* reignites the flame of the Crusades in the face of peace and the rule [police] of law. In each instance, however, Jewish monotheism can identify and summon [*assigner*] anew the sublime Sovereignty it puts into play; while at every moment, Islam can take the absolute Sovereignty that seals its community and plunge into contemplation and abandonment. In this way, then, triple monotheism is positioned within a double regime that is constituted, on the one hand, by the war of Sovereignties and, on the other, by the tension between its execution and its retreat—a tension that occurs in each one of them, and between them.

But as such, the symbiosis of this triple monotheism, and its other/same philosophical monologism, presents itself under a sign of the war of principles: sovereign war (that of three gods at war with the triple god) versus pacificatory war—or again, the confrontation between sovereign war and sovereign peace. This confrontation is present in philosophy itself, between an absolute appeal for peace (that demanded by the *logos*) and incessantly resorting to the schema of the *polemos* (also demanded by the *logos*, through which it mediates itself). But the sovereignty of peace remains a promised and/or ideal sovereignty, while the sovereignty of war is already given. It leaves intact the trace of divine refulgence found within the *polemos*, the trace of the epic song, and of royal privilege. It is in this way that even today, in philosophy and in all the nerve centers of our culture, war undertaken for peace can never stop being war for war's sake, and against peace. This is true no matter what course such war may take. Technology in the service of peace cannot avoid being taken up again into the *techné* of sovereignty, that is, into Sovereignty as *techné*, the execution and finishing of the community, where community allegedly has nothing to do with *physis* and does not desire its "nature" from *techné politike*. (In this regard, it would be necessary to show how, with the Greeks, *techné politike* in principle splits itself into sovereign *techné* and the *techné* of justice or law, thereby making the project of suturing them together impossible).

It follows from this that, when a claim to it is made, the sovereignty of peace is not perfectly symmetrical with the sovereignty of war. Instead, peace would be the "supreme" good, where its supremacy could not manifest itself as such, either in glory, power, or collective identification. The white dove remains. . . . Peace would be the supremacy of the absence of any supreme distinction, the absence of exception at the heart of any rule, everywhere indefinitely and equally closed in on itself. But, in this way, peace cannot fail to have, for the whole of our culture, some aspect of renunciation within it. This is because, in the end, anything that is properly to be called Sovereignty requires the incandescence of the exception and the identifiable distinction of its finishing. (In fact, do we ever identify *a* peace, presented in person, except under the name and insignia of an empire—*pax romana, pax americana?*)

The sovereignty of law, which would necessarily structure peace, is inevitably, and to however small an extent, sovereignty by default—whereas true sovereignty takes place not only in plenitude but in excess and as excess. Even now, this fundamental disposition prevents war from ever simply becoming a technique destined to enlist force into the service of right, without it also always being the *technē* of sovereign affirmation.

~

It is not sufficient, therefore, to keep returning to the final exigency of peace, any more than it is sufficient to denounce the illusion of such an aim and rely on the realism of force. In essence, these two different faces of the same attitude have regulated our comportment to the recent war, by means of the total or partial repression of what I have attempted to lay out here. To remain at this point, however, is to prepare the way for the wars to come—and without even bothering to know if the restraint that has been shown in certain aspects of conducting this war (to such an extent that there was not "truly" a war, although there has been all the desirable destruction) does not, in fact, represent a small step toward a complete "relegitimation" of war, where the conditions of such a possibility would not be as far away as one would have liked to believe or been led to believe.

At this point, one might object that the emphasis placed on the symbolic order of sovereignty denies, either at the same time or in turn, the authenticity of the need for law and the play of economic forces. Not at all, as we will see. Rather, a symbolic order so widely and deeply woven into the whole culture produces all its effects in the real (and thus, for example, in economy and law; in truth, however, none of these "orders" simply comes from the symbolic or the real . . .). It is important not to misunderstand these effects. Just as much as art, anything that is properly to be called war is absolutely archaic in its symbolic character, which indicates that it escapes from being a part of "history" understood as the progress of a linear and/or cumulative time. But it returns to this when it is a matter of opening anew a certain space within this time: the space of the presentation of Sovereignty. This "archaism" (again, like that of art) thus obeys laws that are more deeply set within our civilization, in such a way as to indicate that it is something more than a regrettable holdover [*fâcheuse survivance*]. But it is precisely because it is not consistent to treat war like a regrettable holdover from a bygone age, always tendentiously effaced in the progress and project of a global humanity, that it is all the more important and urgent to think what is at stake in its "archaism," and to think this for ourselves today.

(A thorough examination of this space of sovereignty and war obviously would require something quite different from what I have just outlined above. This would be an enormous project, in particular as regards offering different analyses of the "sacred." Sovereignty has always been mixed up with the "sacred" through the mechanism of exception and excess, but the implications of sovereignty have still not been as clearly thought out as those of the "sacred" itself (as though this is the effect of an obscure interest in not knowing too much about the sovereignty that is always at work). But there would also need to be a lot of work done with regard to a psychoanalysis that could manage, in a way different from what has always been done, to treat collectivity or community as such (which Freud always seems to submit, *volens nolens*, to the schema of the Sovereign), not to mention the sexual difference that is always put into play via war . . .).

Ecotechnics [*Écotechnie*]

All that said, it still remains that the persistence [*rémanence*] or reinvention of war does not occur outside history, even if our epoch appears to be the great suspension of the historicity by which we have been carried along. The conflict between the police and the *bellum proprie dictum* is also the effect of a historical displacement of great importance, and of great consequence, for war.

The first "worldwide" war corresponds to the emergence of a schema of worldwide proportions, which imposes itself on the sovereigns themselves. Thus, war/police action [*la guerre-police*] is delocalized; for example, it has less to do with the borders of the sovereign States themselves than with the multiple forms of the "presence" of these States that span the world (interests, zones of influence, and so on). As such, war/police action also becomes a confrontation of "worldviews": a "worldview" is never the attribute of sovereignty; by definition, sovereignty is higher than any "view," and the "world" is the imprint of its decision. The powers have the world as the space given for the play of their sovereignties. But when this space is saturated and the play closed off, the world as such becomes a problem. It is no longer certain that the finish of this world can be envisaged in the same way that the world of sovereigns was. The world, that is, man or global humanity, is not the sum total of humanity or the installation of a new sovereignty (contrary to what humanism sought and desired, even to the point of exhaustion). The war/police action of global humanity puts the ends of "man" directly into play, whereas sovereign war exposes the end itself. And just as war—and art—composed the *technai* of sovereignty, so global humanity has no *technē* of its own: however thoroughly "technological" our culture may be, it is only *technē* in suspension. It is not surprising that war haunts us. . . .

As a corollary to the development of a world market, one can see in the invention of world war the result of all the wars that accompanied the creation of the contemporary world: on the one hand, there are the American Revolutionary War and Civil War, wars in the tradition of sovereign war and bearing the self-affirmation of a new and distinct Sovereignty (during the nineteenth century, these served as the model for the wars and/or founding of nations, principally the new Germany; even later, this model was inherited by various colonies); on the other hand, there is the war of liberation in the name of humankind, in the name of its "natural" rights and fraternity, such as it was invented in the French Revolution. It is this second model that no longer corresponds strictly to the sovereign schema: it oscillates between a general revolt against the very order of sovereigns (who are called *tyrants*, a term that makes an appeal for a possible legitimacy of rebellion within the ethico-juridical tradition) and a policed administration of humankind, which restrains itself from abusing its governance.

As such, then, the global state of war expresses a simple need, as either its cause or its effect: it needs an authority that goes beyond that of Sovereigns endowed with the right to war. Strictly speaking, there is no place for this need within the space and logic of sovereignty. More precisely, it can be analyzed in one of the following ways: either this authority would have to be a global sovereignty, which could not be in a state of war with anyone on earth (but only with all the galactic empires of science fiction, which demonstrates that we really only have one model at our disposal from which to extrapolate. . . .); or this authority is of another nature, and of another origin (and end), than that of sovereignty.

∿

From the League of Nations to the United Nations, there has been an incessant putting into play of the aporias of such "suprasovereignty," both from the standpoint of its legitimate foundation and from the standpoint of its capacity to endow itself with an effective force. To different degrees, analogous problems are posed by the various transnational organizations of African or Asian States. In yet another way, Europe itself is coming up against the problem of *inter-*, *trans-*, or *supra*national sovereignty; in this case, it is not principally a problem that pertains to war, except as regards the transformations of the two great military alliances already underway.

One can see that the problem is radical. It is not solely a matter of combining the needs of coordination, that is, to see how international cooperation goes together with the respect for the sovereign rights of States. It is also not solely a matter of inventing new politico-juridical forms (whether one goes in the direction of the deliberative Assembly or in the direction of a global Federation, there is no leaving these aporias behind). Such forms hold fast to the ground, and to grounding per se. Moreover, it is one of the tasks of law and its formalism to bring to light the work of grounding that goes on in the purifying of concepts. But clearly, law itself does not have a form for what would need to be its own sovereignty.

The problem is put forward clearly, and in a decisive manner, at the very place of sovereignty—or of the End.

The problem is not a matter of fixing up [*aménager*] sovereignty: in essence, sovereignty is untreatable, but the untreatable essence of sovereignty, in fact, no longer belongs to a world that is "global." Thus, the problem is indeed one of grounding something in an entirely new way, something for which there are neither reasons (why? for what? for whom is there or must there be a *global* world?) nor any applicable models. Global humanity, or man after humanism, is exposed to a limit or an abyss of grounding, of end and exemplarity.

However relative it may be, however mixed up it is with the rise and fall of many unconvincing and particularist claims to "sovereignty," the "return of war" expresses essentially a need or impulse for sovereignty. Not only do we have nothing other than models of sovereignty, but Sovereignty in itself is also a principal model or schema of "civilization" where "globalization" is at work. It is on the model or schema of "that which has nothing above itself," of the unsurpassable, the unconditional, or the nonsubordinable. It is the model of all this *quo magis non dici potest* where origin, principle, end, finishing, leader, and brilliance [*éclat*] come together again for us. . . . But global humanity is another sort of extremity, another *quo magis . . .* , to which this model no longer pertains.

Although the dominion of this model is maintained by default, only law appears to elude it. This is because, right away, law sets itself up between first principles and final ends (the sovereign space is the figure; the juridical space is the interval). Law consents to let principles and ends fall under an authority other than its own, and this consent belongs to its structure. It thus escapes from the model only in order to designate anew the places where the model applies: at each of the two extremities, principles and ends. Sovereignty cannot stop haunting us, since it is at these extremities that law, of its own accord, locates authority [*l'instance*] as the exception and the excess, which is also the authority of exemplarity.

Within such exemplarity, there is always an exception that provides, or gives, the rule. (Thus, the sovereign warrior was able to provide a model that did not simply lead to battle. In the end, however, the history of sovereignties is a history of devastation. . . .) But within the dissolution of exemplarity there are two elements: on the one hand, the exception into which the rule is reabsorbed; on the other, a rule without example (the law), that is, without finish.

Ever since the invention of "natural" man (an expression where "natural" really signifies "technological"), we have insisted on closing our eyes to the absence of the foundation of law—and, along with this, we have insisted on ignoring the foundational role sovereignty plays in the schema of the exception (divine creation, originary violence, the founding hero, the royal race, imperial glory, the soldier's sacrifice, the genius at work, the subject of one's own law, the subject without faith or law . . .). In this way, we have ignored what is truly at stake in war. By way of the judgment that war is "evil," even as an evil which is sometimes "necessary," we repress the truth that war is the model of executive and finitive [*finitrice*] *technē*, as long as the end is thought as sovereign end; in a parallel manner, beneath the judgment that the law is a "good," but a formal good without any force, we repress the truth that the law which is wholly without any model or foundation, when it is not governed by sovereignty, represents a *technē* without end. This is what our thinking does not know how to deal with (except to confine it in "art," for better or worse) and what in every technology creates fear in our thinking. We will not have responded to the question of war, except by means of ever more war, until we have crossed through this problematic field.

How [is one] to think without end, without finishing, without sovereignty—and, in this, without resigning oneself to a weak, instrumental, and slavishly humanist thinking of the law (and/or "communication," "justice," the "individual," the "community"— all of which are concepts that are debilitated insofar as there has been no response to this question)?

~

It is not sufficient, however, to ask the question in this way. Even it if is without reason, end, or figure, it is clearly the case that the "global (dis)order" has behind it all the effectiveness of what we call "planetary technology" and "world economy": the double sign of a single network of the reciprocity of causes and effects, of the circularity of ends and means. In fact, this network or order is what is without-end [*sans-fin*], but without-end in terms of millions of dollars and yen, in terms of millions of therms, kilowatts, optical fibers, megabytes. If the world is a world today, then it is primarily a world according to this double sign. Let us call this *ecotechnics*.

It is remarkable that the country which has thus far been the symbol of triumphant ecotechnics also concentrates within itself the figure of the sovereign State (supported by the arche-law of its foundation and by the hegemony of its domination) and the figure of the law (present in its foundation, and thought to structure "civil society"). The Soviet world was supposed to have represented the revolution that both reverses and goes beyond this triple determination, restoring a social-human *whole* in itself as end. In fact, this world was not the world of the State, or law, or ecotechnics, but a painfully contorted imitation of the three and their various relations, put to the service of the pure appropriation of power. But it is no less remarkable that these two entities shared, in their difference and opposition (in the "Cold War" of two Sovereigns fixed or frozen in different ways), as a kind of asymptote or common line of flight, something that one would have to call sovereignty without sovereignty, to the extent that this word and its schema remain inevitable: that is, the supreme domination of what would neither have the brilliance [*éclat*] of origin nor the glory of accomplishment in a sovereign presence; although there was no God, no hero, no genius, there remained the logic of the subject of exception, the subject without the law of its own law, and there remained an execution, an indefinite and unending finishing of this logic. Ecotechnics might be the last figure without figure of the world's slow drift into sovereignty without sovereignty, into finishing without end.

In this way, then, the recent war might have been a powerful resurgence of sovereignty (while perhaps warning us to expect others) and, at the same time, the opening of a passage that leads to the regime (or reign?) of sovereignty without sovereignty, a passage that opens up from inside war itself. But just as there has been an attempt to skirt the issue of war by making it into a police action, there has been an attempt to avoid the necessary coupling of victory and defeat by making it a matter of negotiation, where what is at stake is "international law" as the guarantor of ecotechnics. At the same time, all sides have refused to count the dead in a clear way (to say nothing of the distinction between dead soldiers and dead civilians): given the plausible report of at least one dead (in the North, in the West . . .) for every five hundred dead (in the South, in the East . . .), it seems that victory and defeat are growing closer together, terms which themselves are as untenable as they are insignificant. Finally, as everyone knows perfectly well, the true realm of this war has revealed itself to be that of ecotechnical war, or confrontation, a destructive and appropriative maneuvering without sovereign brilliance. Such war yields nothing to real war as far as power and the technologies of ruination and conquest are concerned.

The class struggle was supposed to be the other of both sovereign war and ecotechnical war. If one claims that this struggle is no longer taking place, or that it no longer has a place in which to take place, then one is also saying that there is no conflict outside of sovereign war (called a "police [action]," in order to be denied at the very point of its return) and ecotechnical war (which is called "competition"). Nowhere, then, is there war, and everywhere there is tearing apart, trampling down, civilized violence, and the brutalities that are mere caricatures of ancient, sacred violence. War is nowhere and everywhere, related to any end without any longer being related to itself as supreme end. In a sense, then, ecotechnics is also pure *technē*, the pure *technē* of nonsovereignty: but because the empty place of sovereignty remains occupied, encumbered by this very void, ecotechnics does not attain toward another thinking of the end without end. By way of the administration and control of "competition," ecotechnics substitutes crushing blows for sovereignty.

∽

From now on, then, ecotechnics is the name for "political economy," because according to our thinking, if there is no sovereignty, then there can be no politics. There is no longer any *polis* since the *oikos* is everywhere: the housekeeping of the world as a single household, with "humanity" for a mother, "law" for a father.

But it is clearly the case that this big family does not have a father or a mother, and that, in the end, it is no more *oikos* than *polis*. (*Eco*logy: What semantics, what space, what world can it offer?) This situation can be summarized in three points:

1. It implies a triple division that is in no way a sharing of sovereignties: the division of the rich from the poor; the division of the integrated from the excluded; and the division of the North from the South. These three dimensions do not overlap as easily as is sometimes presented, but this is not the place to speak to that. It is solely a matter, here, of emphasizing that these divisions imply struggles and conflicts of great violence, where every consideration of sovereignty is in vain and always borrowed. In addition, if the schema of "class struggle" hides itself (and undoubtedly, it is no longer even admissible, at least in a certain historical dimension), then nothing remains to prevent violence from being camouflaged as ecotechnical competition. Or rather, nothing remains except for bare justice: But what is a justice that would not be the *telos* of a history, or the privilege of a sovereignty? It is necessary, then, to learn how to think this empty place. . . .

2. Ecotechnics damages, weakens, and upsets the functioning of

all sovereignties, except for those that in reality coincide with ecotechnical power. Nationalisms, whether they be of an ancient lineage or of recent extraction, deliver themselves up to the painful imitations of a mummified sovereignty. The current space of sovereignty, which cannot be recuperated by any cosmopolitanism (because cosmopolitanism is always the dreamlike opposite of the sovereign order), which is also the space of the finishing of identity in general, is solely a distended space full of holes, where nothing can come to presence.

3. By way of hypocrisy and denial, but not without significance for all that, ecotechnics gives value to a primacy of the combinatory over the discriminating, of the contractual over the hierarchical, of the network over the organism, and more generally, of the spatial over the historical. And within the spatial, it gives priority to a multiple and delocalized spatiality over a unitary and concentrated spatiality. These motifs compose an epochal necessity (the effects of this mode are secondary, and do not in any way invalidate this necessity). Today, thought passes through these motifs, insofar as such thinking is of this world, that is, of this global world without sovereignty. But this is indeed why the entire difficulty of this thinking is concentrated here. One might give a general formulation of it in the following way: How [do we] not confuse this spacing of the world with either the spreading out of significations or a gaping open of meaning [*sens*]?

Either significations are spread out and diluted to the point of insignificance in the ideologies of consensus, dialogue, communication, or values (where sovereignty is thought to be nothing but a useless memory), or a surgery without sutures holds open the gaping wound of meaning, in the style of a nihilism or aestheticizing minimalism (where the gaping wound itself emits a black glow of lost sovereignty)—this not any less ideological. There are no improvements made either with regard to justice or identity.

⌒

In order to think the *spacing* of the world (of ecotechnics), the end of sovereignty must be faced head-on, without reserve, instead of making it seem as though it has been disposed of or sublimated. This spacing of the world *is itself the empty place* of sovereignty. That is, it is the empty place of the end, the empty place of the common good, and the empty place of the common as a good. Or if you like, it is *the empty place of justice* (at the foundation of the law). When the place of sovereignty is empty, neither the essence of the "good," nor that of the "common," nor the common essence of the good can be assigned any longer. Moreover, no essence at all can be assigned any longer, no finishing at all: only existences are finite [or finished]; this is also what the spacing of the world means.

How to think without a sovereign End? This is the challenge of ecotechnics, a challenge that up until now has not been taken up, but which this war is perhaps finally beginning to make absolutely urgent. In order to begin to respond, it is necessary to begin again with the following: ecotechnics washes out or dissolves sovereignty (or rather, the latter implodes in the former). The problem concerns the empty place *as such*, and is not about waiting for some return or substitution. There will be no more sovereignty; this is what history means today. The war, along with ecotechnics, lets us see the place of the sovereign State as empty from now on.

This is also why ecotechnics itself can summon the figure of sovereignty into this empty place. Thus the gaping open of the foundation of law, and all the questions revolving around exception and excess, can be forgotten in the sovereign brilliance that the power properly without power, which polices the world order and watches over the price of primary resources, borrows in the time of war. Or else, to put it in another way, the empty place of the one who recites an epic tale is now occupied by the sovereign figure of the prophet of the moral Law (who can, at the same time, make himself into the narrator of smaller, more familiar epics, like "our boys from Texas"). Over and against this, another figure attempted to reignite the Arab epic, with the sole aim of taking part in the ecotechnical power of the masters of the world. . . . In both cases, it was necessary that the models, the identifiable examples of the sovereign allure, guarantee the best presumption of justice, or of people [*ou de peuple*].

The empty place of Sovereignty will give rise to more or less successful substitutions of this type, that is, until this place *as such* is submitted to questioning and deconstruction, that is, until we have asked the question about the end without reserve, the question about the extreme-limit of finishing and identity, which is from now on the question of a *nonsovereign meaning* as *the very sense of the humanity of humans and the globalness of the world.*

The relation of a nonsovereign meaning, which *we are* to invent, to the archaism of Sovereignty is undoubtedly still more complex than this. The very spacing of the world, the opening of the discontinuous, polymorphous, dispersed, dislocated spatio-temporality presents something of itself in Sovereignty: just this side of its figures and their urgent [*impérieuses*], eager presences. It has also always, and maybe from the very start, exposed itself as spacing, that is, as the amplitude (of a brilliance), as the elevation (of a power), as the distancing (of an example), as the place (of an appearing). In turn, this is why these same motifs can serve the ardent and nostalgic recalling of sovereign figures, war primary among them, or access, to the spaciousness of the spacing, to the (dis)locality of the place, an access we must invent. (For example, and to be quite brief: the same process calls on America and Arabia, and exposes the pieces of a diverse and mixed-up reality, none of which is simply "Arab" or "American," and which compose an errant, strange "globalness.")

With a certain obscurity and ambivalence, the global world of ecotechnics itself definitively proposes the thoroughgoing execution of sovereignty. "Thoroughgoing" here means: going to the extreme, of its logic and movement. Until our own times (but this could continue . . .), this extreme limit always finished itself by means of war, in one way or another. But from now on, it appears —this is our history—that the extreme point of sovereignty situates itself still further out, and that the disruption of the world signifies for us that it is not possible not to go any further. War itself, which supposes that we can detach the appropriation of wealth and power from it, does not go any further than the brilliance of death and destruction (and after everything else, the voracious appropriation that war is—always already—may not be so extrinsic to the sovereign work of death as it appears). (Or else, if it is necessary to go further with the same logic, in continuing war beyond itself, and death beyond death, there is the night and fog of extermination.) Death, or identification in a figure of (the) death (which is the entirety of what we call *sacrifice*, of which war is a supreme form), provides the aim of sovereignty, which appropriates itself in order to come to an end.

In doing this, however, it has not gone far enough. Being-exposed-*to*-death, if this is indeed the "human condition" (finite existence), is not a "being-*for*-death" as destiny, decision, and supreme finishing off. The finishing of finite existence is an unfinishing [*infinition*], which everywhere overflows the death that contains it. The in-finite meaning of finite existence implies an exposition without brilliance: discreet, reserved, discontinuous, and spacious, accordingly such existence *does not even reach the point of the sovereign extremity*.

"*Sovereignty is NOTHING*": Bataille exhausted himself in trying to say this, but anyone would exhaust themselves in (not) saying this. What this sentence "means" cuts off one's breath (I do not really want to go into it further here), but it most certainly does not mean that sovereignty is death—quite to the contrary.

I will only say the following: the sovereign extremity signifies that there is nothing to "attain"; there is no "accomplishment" or "achievement"; there is no "finishing"; or rather, *for a finite finishing, the execution is without end*. The global world is also the finite world, the world of finitude. Finitude is spacing. Spacing "executes" itself infinitely. Not that this means endlessly beginning again, but that *meaning* no longer occurs in a totalization and presentation (of a finite and accomplished infinite). Meaning is in not finishing with meaning.

Within this "nothing," there is no repression or sublimation of the violent burst of sovereignty: never to be finished with, there is an explosion and violence [that comes] from beyond war, the lightning of peace. (Jean-Christophe Bailly suggested to me that I finally render the eagles of war as peaceful.)

In a sense, this is *technology* itself. What is called "technology," or again what I have called ecotechnics (in itself, which would be liberated from capital), is the *technē* of finitude or spacing. This is no longer the technical means to an End, but *technē* itself as in-finite end, *technē* as the existence of finite existence in all its brilliance and violence. It is "technology" itself, but it is a technology that, of itself, raises the necessity of appropriating its meaning against the appropriative logic of capital and against the sovereign logic of war.

In the end, the question is not whether war is "bad." War is "bad," and it is absolutely so, especially when the space where it deploys itself no longer permits the glorious and powerful presentation of its figure (as the figure of the death of all figures). When this space . . . constitutes spacing, the intersection of singularities, and not the confrontation of faces or masks.

∿

It is here that our history comes upon its greatest danger and its greatest opportunity. It is here in the still poorly perceived imperative of a world that is in the process of creating its global conditions, in order to render untenable and catastrophic the sharing of riches and poverty, of integration and exclusion, of every North and South. Because this world is the world of spacing, not of finishing; because it is the world of the intersection of singularities, not of the identification of figures (of individuals or of masses); because it is the world in which, in short, sovereignty is exhausting itself (and, at the same time, resisting this with gestures that are both terrifying and pathetic)—for all of these reasons, and from within the very heart of the appropriative power of capital (which itself started sovereignty's decline), ecotechnics obscurely indicates the *technē* of a world where sovereignty is nothing. This would be a world where spacing could not be confused with spreading out or with gaping open, but only with "intersection."

This is not given as a destiny; it is offered as a history. As *technē*, ecotechnics is still to be liberated from "technology," "economy," and "sovereignty." At least we are beginning to learn what the combined lesson of war, law, and "technological civilization" is after all; we have learned that the orientation, theme, and motive of this liberation are all contained in the following (provisional) statement: sovereignty is nothing. As a consequence of having learned this much, the multiplicity of "peoples" might be able to avoid being engulfed in the hegemony of one sole people, or in the turbulence of the desire to claim the sovereign distinction for everyone. As such, it might become possible to think what has not been thinkable to this point: a political articulation of the world that escapes from these two dangers (and for which the model of the "Federation" is not available). Therefore, law could expose itself to the nothing of its own foundation.

It would be a matter, therefore, of going to the extreme without an example, which belongs to the "nothing" of sovereignty. How to think, how to act, how to do without a model? This is the question that is avoided, and yet posed, by the entire tradition of sovereignty. Once "revolution" has also been exposed to the *nothing* of sovereignty, one has to take seriously how the execution without model or end may be the essence of *technē* as a *revolutionary* essence.

What if each *people* (this would be the revolutionary word), each *singular intersection* (this would be the ecotechnical word), substituted a wholly other logic for the logic of the sovereign (and always sacrificial) model, not the invention or the multiplication of models—from which wars would immediately follow—but a logic where singularity was absolute and without an example at the same time? Where each one would be "one" only in not being identifiable in a figure, but in-finitely distinct through spacing, *and* in-finitely substitutable through the intersection that doubles spacing. To parody Hegel, this could be called global [or world] singularity, which would have the right without right to say the law of the world. *Peace* comes at the price of abandoned sovereignty, the price of that which goes beyond war, instead of always remaining within it.

I am well aware of the fact that all of this does not let itself be conceived of easily. It is not for us, not for our thinking, modeled as it is on the sovereign model; it is not for our warlike thinking. But this is certain: there is nothing on the horizon except for an unheard-of, inconceivable task—or war. All thinking that still wants to conceive of an "order," a "world," a "communication," a "peace" is absolutely naive—when it is not simply hypocritical. To appropriate one's own time has always been unheard of. But everyone can clearly see that it is time: the disaster of sovereignty is sufficiently spread out, and sufficiently common, to steal anyone's innocence.

Postscript, May 1991

In the midst of the general climate of "humanitarian aid" set up as the perverse game that is being played by war's protagonists, "sovereignty" is more present than ever. (Does Saddam have the right to it? Who grants it to him? What is he doing with it? And what about the Kurds? And the Turks? And what is a border? What is police force? Or else, a little further away, what about nuclear capacity as Algeria's sovereign concern? Or the accord between the USSR and the eight republics to regulate the tense play of their sovereignties, in spite of everything else? Or what about Kuwait returned to sovereignty for purposes of a brutal settling of accounts *and* for the shameless recruitment of Filipino and Egyptian manpower? What is the character of Bangladesh's sovereignty, where a cyclone has just made five million people homeless? and so forth.) The proliferation of these ambiguities—which are, in fact, those of the *end* of sovereignty—makes me afraid of being misunderstood if I say that we should go (or that we already are) beyond its model and its order. By saying this, I do not mean for a instant to demand that a Kurd, an Algerian, a Georgian, or, for that matter, an American should abandon the identity and independence for which these proper names function as a sign. But what will always cause a problem is the question of exactly which *sign* is of concern here. If sovereignty has exhausted its meaning, and if it is everywhere acknowledged that it is in doubt, underhanded—or empty —then it is necessary to reconsider the nature and function of such a sign. For example, what is a *people*? The Iraqui "people," the Corsican "people," the Chicano "people," the Zulu "people," the Serbian "people," the Japanese "people": Is it always the same concept? If there is a "concept," then does it imply "sovereignty"? And what about the "people" of Harlem, or those of the shanty towns in

Mexico, *or* the populations of India or China? What is an "ethnicity"? What is a religious community? Are the Shiites a people? And the Hebrews and/or Israelis and/or Jews? And the "ex-East Germans"? What are the relations of a "sovereign" people to a "popular" people? Where to place tribes, clans, brotherhoods? And I have to insist on this, where to place classes, levels, margins, milieus, social networks? The almost-monstrous multiplication of these questions is the mark of the problem about which I am speaking. Neither the sovereign model, nor the authority of the law addresses this problem; they only deny it. Instead, what is of concern here is *globalness* as a proliferation of "identity" without end or model—and it may even be a matter of *"technology" as the technē of a new horizon of unheard-of identities.*

§ Eulogy for the Mêlée

(For Sarajevo, March 1993)

"Sarajevo" has become *the* expression of a complete system for the reduction to identity.[1] It is no longer a sign on the way, or a sign in history; it is no longer a possible destination for business trips or illicit rendezvous, or the uncertain space for a fortuitous meeting or distracted wandering. It is a dimension-less point on a diagram of sovereignty, an ortho-normative gauge on a ballistic and political computer, a target frozen in a telescopic sight, and it is the very figure of the exactitude of taking aim, the pure taking aim of an essence. Somewhere, a pure Subject declares that it is the People, the Law, the State, the Identity in the name of which "Sarajevo" must be identified purely and simply as a target.

Sarajevo is simply a name or a sign that grabs our attention [*même plus un nom, un écriteau qu'on nous cloue sur les yeux*], so that there will no longer be a Sarajevan landscape, or trips to Sarajevo, but only a pure and naked identity. It is such so that nothing else will get mixed in with it, and so that we do not get mixed up in it, that is, we other cosmopolitan Europeans.

~

A city does not have to be identified by anything other than a name, which indicates a place, the place of a *mêlée*[2], a crossing and a stop, a knot and an exchange, a gathering, a disjunction, a circulation, a radiating [*un étoilement*]. The name of a city, like that of a country, like that of a people and a person, must always be the name of *no one*; it must never be the name of anyone who might be presented *in person* or *in her own right* [en propre]. The "proper name" has no significance [*signification*], or what there is to it is nothing more than a sketch of a description that is, by all rights and in fact, indefinite. Inchoate and stochastic meaning: it is a mixture of syllables stirred on the brink of a semantic identity that is both gently and obstinately deferred. As soon as the proper name points to [*arraisonne*] a presence in person, a sovereign Subject, this sovereign is threatened; it is encircled, besieged. In order to live in Sarajevo, there was no need to identify Sarajevo. But now, those who die in Sarajevo die from the death of Sarajevo *itself*; they die from the possibility—imposed by gunfire—of identifying some substance or presence by this name, a presence measured by the yardstick of the "national" or the "state," a body-symbol set up precisely in order to create body and symbol where there had only been place and passage. Those who are exiled from Sarajevo are exiled from this place, expelled by this body. They are exiled from the mix, from the that *mêlée* that made up Sarajevo, but which, as a result, *made* nothing, engendered no *ego*. The "proper" name must always serve to dissolve the *ego*: the latter opens up a meaning, a pure source of meaning; the former indicates a *mêlée*, raises up a melody: *Sarajevo*.

～

I have been asked for a "eulogy of the mélange."[3] And I would like to give a eulogy that is itself "mixed" [*mélangé*]. This is not to say that it will be a mixture of eulogy and blame, so as to end in a balanced account of profits and losses. Nor is the idea to deliver a "mitigated" eulogy that would evoke an extreme form of half-heartedness, which is a curious concept. In the end, it is a matter (everyone understands that it is there; it is right there before our eyes; for the moment, it is will suffice to know how to gather what it is a question of and how to welcome it) of coming up against all sorts of winds and tides—and it is quite clear in what direction these are moving. It is solely a matter of not giving anything away, either regarding identity *or* regarding what mixes identity up in, or entangles it with, its own origin and principle. What is called for, then, is a eulogy mixed with reserve, a reserve that is appropriate if one wants to avoid giving a eulogy that itself goes so far as to betray its object by identifying it too well. This is what must be avoided.

In fact, it has to be said right away that the most just and beautiful eulogy of the *mélange* would be *to not have to give it,* exactly because the notion [of the *mélange*] itself could not even be discerned or identified. This very notion presupposes the isolation of pure substances, and the work of mixing them. It is an idea that is at home in the laboratory. But does this same way of thinking do justice to the idea of a painting as a eulogy for a *mélange* of colors? Painting never has anything to do with the spectrum of colors; it only has to do with the infinity mixed in with and derived from their nuances.

It is exactly because it was possible for there to be the ignoble talk of "ethnic cleansing" that it is necessary to respond. But this response will not be just another, symmetrical way of talking. This is why conferring too much identity on the *mélange* itself must be avoided; in order to ensure this, the emphasis will be displaced, and an attempt will be made to move from the *mélange* to the *mêlée*.

～

The whole task, here, is to do right by identities, but without ceding anything to their frenzy, to their presuming to be substantial identities ("subjects," in this sense). This task is enormous, and it is very simple. It is the task of a culture remaking itself, or the recasting of thinking such that it would not be crude or obscene like every thought of purity. It means mixing together again the various lines, trails, and skins, while at the same time describing their heterogeneous trajectories and their webs, both those that are tangled and those that are distinct. It is the task of never believing in the simple, homogenous, present "man." Or woman. Or Croat or Serb or Bosnian. It is the task of knowing (but of what knowledge?) that the subject of knowledge is now only some*one,* and like every some*one,* someone of *mixed blood.*

～

A *mélange* is a delicate and fragile thing, both subtle and volatile, which is often made thick [*épaisse*] and obscure these days. In fact, there does exist—and I am not the first one to point it out—a eulogy for the *mélange* that resonates with a conventional sort of political correctness, that is, with the normative stiffening of the most well-founded demands. Such a eulogy wholeheartedly celebrates generalized multiculturalism, hybridization, exchange, sharing, and a sort of transcendental variegation.

Although we know things are not so simple, we now feel that having such whirlwinds, mixtures, wanderings, and interferences are not enough, that is, *as they are*. Or rather, and first of all: we know that they do not allow themselves to be thought as they are. This is the whole question.

But we also know, only too well, that there still remains a discourse that takes advantage of the simplifications of the other in order to go one better than distinction, identity, property, or purity, and in order to be able to use the word "cosmopolitan," for example, with an obvious overtone of mistrust, even disgust (sometimes clearly associated with anti-Semitism).

In the end, and rightly so, there are those who place these two *correctnesses* back to back, and who recite an interminable catechism of unity in diversity, complementarity, and well-tempered differences. This well-intentioned discourse, sometimes welcome in moral and political emergencies, remains a discourse of intentions and exhortations. It does not reach as far as the very things with which it deals.

∼

First of all, let us be clear: the simplistic eulogy of the *mélange* has and is capable of producing errors, but the simplistic eulogy of purity has supported and still supports crimes. As such, there is no symmetry in this regard, no equilibrium to hold to, no fair medium. There is nothing to be discussed. The least bit of discussion, the smallest deferral to racism or to purification, in whatever form, already participates in such crime. Moreover, this crime is always a double crime, both moral and intellectual. All racism is stupid, obtuse, and fearful. I always hold my peace in the face of long discourses and great colloquia on the subject of racism. It seems to me that too much honor is paid to this trash. For similar reasons, this is why I am embarrassed by the idea of a "eulogy for the mélange": as if *the* mélange would have to be some sort of value or authenticity to be uncovered, even though it is only a piece of evidence, or, if one looks at it more closely, even though it does not exist if there is never anything "pure" that can be and must be "mixed" together [*mélanger*] with some other "purity."

Therefore, what is at question, here, is in no way a matter of sticking to a fair mean [*juste milieu*] held between two opposing theses, exactly because there are these two theses only to the extent that there is, first of all, the simplification and distortion of what is at stake.

∼

By definition, the *mélange* is not a simple substance to which place and nature could be assigned, to which one could lay claim as such, and which, as a result, one could plainly eulogize. Identity is by definition not an absolute distinction, removed from everything and, therefore, distinct from nothing: it is always the other of another identity. "He is different—like everyone" (Bertolucci's *Last Tango in Paris*). Difference *as such* is indiscernible. Neither *mélange* nor identity can be pinned down. They have always already taken place, are always already gone, or always already still to come. And they are *in common*, shared by all, between all, through one another.

∼

Precisely because the *mélange* is mixed (it is *mixed* [mêlé], and it is a *mêlée*), it is not a substance. Nor is it possible to replace the nonsubstantiality of its contents with a supposed consistency of that in which it is contained. This is exactly the problem with ideologies of the *melting pot*, where the *pot* is supposed to contain, in all senses of the word, the enigmas of the *mélange*, as well as its disruptive forces, all by virtue of its own identity.

Hybridization is not "some thing." And if the hybrid, which

each one of us is in his or her own way, is some*one*, it is not by virtue of any essence of hybridization (a contradictory notion), but rather insofar as it provides a punctuation, or a singular configuration, for the essencelessness of hybridization. To essentialize the *mélange* is to have already dissolved it, melted it down into something other than itself. Therefore, one must not say "the" *mélange* and, above all, one must not deliver its eulogy.

The *mélange* as such can take on, or seem to take on, two different identities: that of a fusion or a thoroughgoing osmosis, or that of an accomplished state of disorder [*mise en désorder achevée*]. These two fantastical extremities are alchemy and entropy, extremities that, in the end, come together and identify with one another in an apocalypse or a black hole. But the *mélange* is, in fact, neither the one nor the other, nor is it the fair mean between the two. It is something else, or again, it "is" in another way, in quite another way.

∼

It would be better, then, to speak of *mêlée*: an action rather than a substance. There are at least two sorts of *mêlée*, even though there may never be a *mêlée* "pure and simple." There is the *mêlée* of a fight, and the *mêlée* of love. The *mêlée* of Ares, and the *mêlée* of Aphrodite. They are mixed with one another, not identified. It is not a matter of entropy or alchemy. It is a contest that can never take place without desire and without attacks of jealousy, without the appeal to the other as always other.

(But the *mêlée* of Ares is not modern war, which, more often than ever before, involves no *mêlée* at all: modern war begins by exterminating hand-to-hand combat; it aims to crush and suppress combat, rather than attempting to set it aside; in fact, it has no space for combat. Instead, it spreads everywhere and kills, violates, irradiates, gasses, and infects the whole "civil" space. Today, war is an unlimited and *pure mélange*. It is not the *mêlée*. With regard to orgies and porn films, the same can be said of the *mêlée* of Aphrodite.)

The *mélange*, therefore, *is* not. It happens; it takes place. There is *mêlée*, crisscrossing, weaving, exchange, sharing, and it is never a single thing, nor is it ever the same. On the one hand, the *mélange* is an "it happens," rather than an "it is": displacements, chances, migrations, clinamens, meetings, luck, and risks. On the other hand, it is not "one": in a *mêlée* there are meetings and encounters; there are those who come together and those who spread out, those who come into contact and those who enter into contracts, those who concentrate and those who disseminate, those who identify and those who modify—just like the two sexes in each one of us.

The *mélange* is not simply "rich" in the diversity it mixes together. In fact, this diversity constantly escapes it, as long as it is nothing *itself.* There is a quantitative discourse of "mutual enrichment," a discourse that is at bottom capitalist and profiteering. But this is not a question of wealth or poverty. Cultures, or what are known as cultures, do not mix. They encounter each another, mingle, modify each other, reconfigure each other. They cultivate one another; they irrigate or drain each other; they work over and plough through each other, or graft one onto the other.

To begin with—but where is there an absolute beginning?—each one of them is a configuration, already a *mêlée*. The first culture constituted a *mêlée* of races or species, *erectus, faber, sapiens.* The West, which is so proud of the "Greek miracle" of its founding, should always meditate on the ethnic and cultural diversity, on the movements of peoples, the transfers and transformations of practices, the twists and turns of language or mores, which went to make up or configure the "Hellenics." The history of this *mêlée* should be reread:

> Thus, at the beginning of the second millennium, a phenomenon of extraordinary novelty was created; a cosmopolitan culture was put into place in which one could recognize the contributions of those diverse civilizations that were built on the edge of the sea, or in the middle of it. Some of these civilizations were those that became empires: Egypt, Mesopotamia, Asia Minor of the Hittites; still others of these set to sea and were supported by certain cities: the Syro-Lebanese coast, Crete, and much later, Myceanea. But they all communicated with one another. All of them, even Egypt, ordinarily so closed in on itself, turned

toward the outside with a passionate curiosity. This is the epoch of voyages, of exchanges of presents, diplomatic correspondence, and princesses who were given as spouses to foreign kings as proof of new "international" relations. It is the epoch where, in Egyptian tomb paintings, there appeared, in their native dress, all the peoples of the Near East and the Aegean: Cretans, Myceans, Palestinians, Nubians, Canaanites. . . . [4]

Every culture is in itself "multicultural," not only because there has always been a previous acculturation, and because there is no pure and simple origin [*provenance*], but at a deeper level, because the gesture of culture is itself a mixed gesture: it is to affront, confront, transform, divert, develop, recompose, combine, rechannel.

~

It is not that there is no "identity." A culture is single and unique. (If this is what one must settle for in the word "culture," which seems to identify already that with which it is concerned. But this word identifies precisely nothing. It is to settle for short-circuiting all the difficulties that bear down en masse if one tries to say "people," "nation," "civilization," "spirit," "personality.") A "culture" is a certain "one." The fact and law of this "one" cannot be neglected; even less can it be denied in the name of an essentialization of the "mélange."

But the more this "one" is clearly distinct and distinguished, the less it may be its own or pure foundation. Undoubtedly, the task is wholly a matter of not confusing distinction and foundation; in fact, this point contains everything that is at stake philosophically, ethically, and politically in what is brewing [*se trame*] around "identities" and "subjects" of all sorts. Thus, the absolute distinction of the *ego existo*, provided by Descartes, must not be confused with foundation in the purity of a *res cogitans*, with which it is joined together. For example, the "French" identity today no longer needs to found itself in Vercingétorix or Joan of Arc in order to exist.

The unity and uniqueness of *a* culture are unique precisely on account of a *mélange*, or a *mêlée*. It is a "mêlée" that defines the style or tone of a "culture," as well as the various different voices and aptitudes [*portées*] for interpreting this tone. There is such a thing as a French culture, but it itself has various voices, and nowhere is it presented in person—except for those who confuse it with the *coq sportif* or with Dupond-la-Joie. Voltaire's voice is not that of Proust, which is not Pasteur's, which is not Rita Mitsouko's. It is perhaps never *purely and simply* French. What is French, and what is not, in Stendhal, Hugo, Picasso, Lévinas, Godard, Johnny Hallyday, Kat'Onoma, Chamoiseau, Dib? Once again, however, this does not mean that there is no "French identity": it means that this sort of identity is never simply identical in the sense that a pencil is identically the same yesterday and today (assuming that this is not materially inexact . . .). The identity of the pencil leaves *this* pencil far less identifiable as "this one here," which, up to certain point, remains any pencil at all. This is exactly *not* the case with the identity of a culture or a person. To indicate the difference, this latter identity can be called an *ipseity*, a "being-its-self" ["être-soi-même"].

An ipseity is not [founded on] the pure inertia of the same, which would remain quite plainly the same in the sense of being the self-same [*posé çà même soi-même*]: one could imagine this as forming the being of a stone or a God. An ipseity leaves off exactly where it is identified. Because of this, a network of exchanges is required, a network of recognition, of references from one ipseity to another, from difference to difference. An ipseity is valued by the other and for the other, in consideration of the other, these others to whom it gives and from whom it takes a certain identifiable tone—all by way of its singular touch. *That is to say, insofar as it is unidentifiable*, it is both inimitable and impossible to assign identity to any *one*. In a very precise way, *ipseity* names what, for an identity, is always and necessarily impossible to identify.

In fact, a pure identity would not only be inert, empty, colorless, and flavorless (as those who lay claim to a pure identity so often are), it would be an absurdity. A pure identity cancels itself out; it can no longer identify itself. Only what is identical to itself is identical to itself. As such, it turns in a circle and never makes it into existence.

With all due rigor, who was ever *pure* enough to be an Aryan worthy of the name? We know that this question could drive a true Nazi, a Nazi absolutely identified with his cause or with his own concerns, to sterilization or even suicide. Purity is a crystalline chasm where the identical, the proper, the authentic is engulfed by itself; it is nothing at all, and it drags the other along in order to carry it into the abyss. The absolute and vertiginous law of the *proper* is that in appropriating its own purity [*s'appropriant sa propre pureté*], it alienates itself *purely* and simply. Another form of the *mélange* is the *mélange-with-itself*: self-mixing, autism, auto-eroticism.

∼

A language is always a *mêlée* of languages, something half-way in-between Babel as the form of total confusion and glossolalia [or speaking in tongues] as the form of immediate transparency. A style is always a crisscrossing of tones, borrowed elements, dispersions, and developments, to which it gives a new twist or turn. Of course, each style seems to tend toward making an ultimate or sovereign turn, the turn toward an absolutely proper language, an absolute idiolect. But an absolute idiolect or idiom would no longer be a language, and could no longer mix with others in order to be the language that it is: *being no longer translatable exactly in order to be the untranslatable that it is*. A pure idiolect would be *idiotic*, utterly *deprived* of relations and, therefore, of identity. A pure culture, a pure property, would be idiotic.

∼

What is a community? It is not a macroorganism, or a big family (which is to assume that we know what an organism or a family is . . .). The *common*, having-in-common or being-in-common, excludes interior unity, subsistence, and presence in and for itself. Being with, being together and even being "united" are precisely not a matter of being "one." Within *unitary* community [*communauté une*] there is nothing but death, and not the sort of death found in the cemetery, which is a place of spacing or distinctness, but the

death found in the ashes of crematorium ovens or in the accumu-
lations of charnel-houses.

To put it another way: in a paradigmatic manner, the systematic
rape of Bosnian women deployed all the various figures of this
delirious affirmation of "unitary" community: rape in order to beget
"bastards" regarded as unacceptable, excluded a priori from the assumed unity; rape in order, therefore, to make obligatory the abor-
tion of these bastards; rape in order to then kill these bastards and,
thus, to destroy the possibility of there being a bastard; and rape so
that this repeated act assigns its victims to the fantasy unity of their
"community." In the end, it is rape in order to show in every possible way that there *do not have to be relations* between communities.
Rape is the zero act; it is the negation of sex itself, the negation of all
relation, the negation of the child, the negation of the woman. It is
the pure affirmation of the rapist in whom a "pure identity" (a
"racial" identity . . .) finds nothing better than the submission to
the ignoble mimicry of what it denies: relation and being-together.
(In a general sort of way, what is undoubtedly paradigmatic in rape
is that it operates by way of that *relation* of which it is also the negation. It sinks its teeth into relation, into the *mêlée*.)

What we have in common is also what always distinguishes and
differentiates us. What I have in common with another Frenchman
is the fact of *not* being the same Frenchman as him, and the fact
that our "Frenchness" is never, nowhere, in no essence, in no figure,
brought to completion. This is not the absence of a figure, but a
plan always being sketched out, a fiction always being invented, a
mêlée of traits. And it is not that identity is always "on the way," projected onto the horizon like a friendly star, like a value or a regulative idea. It never comes to be; it never identifies itself, even as an
infinite projection, *because it is already there*, because it is the *mêlée*.

I already am when my mother and father come together [*se mê-
lent*]; I bring them together [*qui les mêle*]; I am their *mêlée*, and
thus I do not bring myself to be.

What is a people? Certainly there are such things as ethnic traits.
A Sicilian could rarely be mistaken for a Norwegian (even though
the Normans did, in the past, forcibly mix themselves into Sic-

ily . . .). But what about a Sicilian "of the people" and a Sicilian of the upper echelons of society? Could they be confused? It would, in fact, be more likely that, in Chicago, one would confuse a Sicilian "of the people" and a Pole "of the people," or that elsewhere, one would confuse someone from the Palermo upper class and someone from the upper class of Lyon. Under the pressure of wanting to have nothing more to do with *classes*, one ends up denying the most common, everyday evidence. Undoubtedly a class cannot be thought of as an identity, and, indeed, certain varieties of totalitarianism (perhaps all) were made possible by configuring classes according to identity and not according to their conditions. But it is precisely not a question of playing one identity off another. It is a question of practicing singularities, that is, that which gives itself and shows itself only in the plural. The Latin *singuli* means "one by one," and is a word that exists only in the plural. Ipseity exists only as singularly distributed. Insofar as one can speak in the following way, ipseity is "itself" distribution, dissemination, the originary sharing of that which never *is*—*ipse itself*—and is nowhere present as such, "in person." *Ipse* "is" its own dispersion.

It is not nothing—indeed, it is everything—but it remains for us to think this totality of dispersion, of this all-one [*tout-un*] that is all mixed up.

~

The mélange does not exist any more than purity exists. There is no *pure mélange*, nor is there any purity that is *intact*. Not only is there no such thing, this is the very law of *there is not*: if there were something that was pure and intact, there would be nothing. Nothing exists that is "pure," that does not come into *contact* with the other, not because it has to border on something, as if this were a simple accidental condition, but because touch alone exposes the limits at which identities or ipseities can *distinguish themselves* [se démêler] from one another, with one another, between one another, from among one another.

The *mêlée* is not accidental; it is originary. It is not contingent; it is necessary. It *is* not; it happens constantly.

This is the *mêlée* of Ares and the *mêlée* of Aphrodite, the *mêlée* of the one and the other: whether this comes to blows and intertwinings, assaults and cease-fires, rivalry and desire, supplication and defiance, dialogue and contention [*différend*], fear and pity, and laughter too. And, on the flip side, it is the *mêlée* of Hermes, a *mêlée* of messages and paths, bifurcations, substitutions, concurrences of codes, configurations of space, frontiers made to be passed through, so that there can be passages, but ones that are shared—because there is never any identity that is not shared: that is, divided, mixed up, distinguished, entrenched, common, substitutable, insubstitutable, withdrawn, exposed.

Why is it that an "identification photo" is most often poorer, duller, and less "lifelike" than any other photo? And even more, why are ten identity photos of the same person so different from one another? When does someone resemble *himself* [in a photo]? Only when the photo shows something of him, or her, something more than what is identical, more than the "face," the "image," the "traits" or the "portrait," something more than a copy of the diacritical signs of an "identity" ("black hair, blue eyes, snub nose," and so on). It is only when it evokes an unending *mêlée* of peoples, parents, works, pains, pleasures, refusals, forgettings, transgressions, expectations, dreams, stories, and all that trembles within and struggles against the confines of the image. This is not something imaginary; it is nothing but what is real: what is real has to do with the *mêlée*. A *true* identification photo would be an indeterminant *mêlée* of photos and scribbles [*graphies*] that resemble nothing, under which one would inscribe a proper name.

∼

Such an *inscription* [légende] would be meant to be read, deciphered, and recounted, but it would not be a myth: to say it more precisely, it would not confer an identity on the *ipse* or on some *one* of whom it would be the *legendum est*, the "this is to be read." What is to be read is what is written. Myth is not written, but projected and pronounced; it is brandished about or springs forth purely, without habitation, without a history. Not only does myth identify, it identifies itself above all: it is the infinite presupposition of its own identity and authenticity. If, in mythic mode, I say the names "Ares," "Aphrodite," "Hermes" or "France," then I have already said more than all that might be said about them, and nothing legitimate could be said about them that would not also already be authenticated by them in advance. Thus, only the very voice of France could express what is French. Myth is a meaning that is its own subject; myth is where the proper name is the idiom of an idiolect [*en tant qu'idosémie d'un idiolecte*].

But what is written, and what is to be read, is that which has not preceded its own habituation; it is the *mêlée* of the traces of a meaning that gets lost in looking for itself and inventing itself. I read that Sarajevo is a city divided into at least three cities, both successive and simultaneous, and that Bosna-Saray is there mixed with Miljacka and Ilidza.

§ The Surprise of the Event

The title of this essay should also be written or read as: "The Surprise: Of the Event." It concerns not only the "surprise," in the sense of its being an attribute, quality, or property of the event, but the event itself, its being or essence. What makes the event an event is not only that it happens, but that it surprises—and maybe even that it surprises itself (diverting it from its own "happening" ["arrivée"],[1] not allowing it be an event, surprising the being in it, allowing it to be only by way of surprise).

But let us begin at the beginning. We will begin with the following sentence, by which something undoubtedly started to dawn on modern thinking; that is, something began to surprise itself in it, something with which we have not yet finished: "*But philosophy is not meant to be a narration of happenings but a cognition of what is* true *in them, and further, on the basis of this cognition, to* comprehend *that which, in the narrative, appears as a mere happening [or pure event*—Trans]."[2] This sentence is found in the second book of Hegel's *Science of Logic*, in a text entitled "The Notion [Concept] in General," which serves as an introduction to "Subjective Logic; or the Doctrine of the Notion."

This sentence can be read in two ways. According to the first reading, which is certainly the most obvious because it closely conforms to what passes for the canonical interpretation of Hegelian thinking, this sentence signifies that the task of philosophy is to *conceive* that of which the event is only the phenomenon. Let us be more precise. For philosophy, there is first of all the truth that is contained in what happens, and then, in light of this truth, the conception of its very production or effectuation, which appears from the outside as an "event, pure and simple (*bloss*)" exactly because it is not conceived. On this account, the event-ness of the event [*événementalité de l'événement*] (its appearance, its coming to pass, its taking place—*das Geschehen*) is only the external, apparent, and inconsistent side of the effective presentation of truth. The advent of the truth as real, which is contained in the concept, disqualifies the event as a simple, narrative representation.

This first reading, however, cannot hold. With all due rigor, the *logic of the concept*[3] in which one is engaged here should not be understood as a logic of the category or the idea thought of as an "abstract generality" (as in Kant); on the contrary, it is a logic of "the identity of the concept and the thing" (as Hegel's text says a little further on). According to this logic, the concept conceives (understands, puts forth, and founds) all determination, all difference, and all exteriority from the point of view of real effectivity. This is why the concept, understood in this way, is the element in which it is revealed (again, in the same text) that "the Appearance [or phenomenon], is not devoid of essential being, but is a manifestation of essence."[4] In fact, rather than being the opposite of simple, phenomenal truth, the concept is that phenomenon which takes hold of itself as the truth.

It is not obvious, then—staying with the straightforward "canonical" reading—that the expression "event, pure and simple" must be understood only in a unilateral way, as if the predicates could determine the essence of the subject: as if the event as such was only and necessarily "pure and simple" (inessential). On the contrary, maybe it does not remain—and it surely must not—"pure and simple," as that consistency which is proper to the event. In other words, the *conceived* event would remain the *event* conceived, which itself would entail certain consequences.

∽

(Note that this double constraint on the subject of the event comes up elsewhere in Hegel, for whom it undoubtedly constitutes a general law. To give an example, in the introduction to the *Philosophy of History*, Hegel writes, "In the pure light of the divine idea, which is not a simple ideal, there disappears that appearance according to which the world would be an insane event, sheer stupidity [*ein verrücktes, törictes Geschehen*]." Here, too, the question is put forward as to the status of the predicates: Is every event insane [*insensé*]? If the world is a sane [*sensé*] event, then is its meaning independent of its event-ness?)

∼

It is necessary, therefore, to engage in a second reading, paying more attention to the difference that informs this sentence from the *Logic*. It is the difference between, on the one hand, the knowledge of the truth that is found "in" the thing (reality, the subject) that occurs and, on the other hand, and "further" (*ferner*), the conception of that which appears as [a] simple event. In other words, the emphasis is not placed on the thing *which* happens (the content or the nonphenomenal substratum), but on *the fact* that it happens, the event-ness of its event (or else, its event rather than its advent). Undoubtedly, this event-ness, insofar as it is conceived in terms of the truth of the thing, is distinguished from the phenomenon; in fact, it is its opposite, but only in distinguishing itself as the nonphenomenal truth *of the phenomenal itself as such*, that is, distinguished as event, as *Geschehen*.

In this sense, the task of philosophy is broken down into two parts: (1) to know the truth of that which takes place; and (2) to conceive of taking place as such. By means of this difference—a difference that is certainly not immediately apparent and is hardly, if ever, analyzed in itself, but nonetheless remains very clear (*ferner*), Hegel represents the task of philosophy as the task of conceiving the taking place of truth *beyond the true* [outre le vrai]. In other words, it is to conceive of the truth of the taking place of the true—or again, to conceive of the *evenire* of the true beyond its *eventus*, without it failing to be its truth. As a result, it is a truth beyond truth itself.

It is by way of this difference or this surplus of truth—not the truth above the true, but the truth of the taking place of the true—that Hegel opens up modernity, where the opening of modernity is nothing other than the opening of thinking to the event as such, to the truth of the event beyond every advent of meaning. In the opening-up of modernity (or, put another way, in the closure of metaphysics, which is itself nothing other than the event of the opening, the event opening thinking to the surplus that overflows the origin), there is this trace pointed in the direction of the event *as* such.

This is what is at stake: the task of philosophy is not a matter of substituting for the narrative *Geschehen* some substratum or subject that does not happen or occur, but simply is (which, insofar as it is sup-posed [*sup-posé*], has always already been—the "being what it was," the *to ti èn einai* of Aristotle). Beyond the truth of what happens, what is happening, what is in the happening, what has happened, what has always already happened in the happening itself, it is a matter of thinking *that* it happens; it is a matter of the happening or, rather, the happening "it-self," where "it" is not the "self" that "it was," since it has not happened. In other words, it is a matter of thinking sameness itself, as the same as nothing [*mêmeté même, en tant que même que rien*].

This may be why it is, for Hegel, a matter of thinking *Geschichte*, not so much in the sense of "history" as we understand it (and as Hegel himself understands it), but rather [as] the entire Being or act, the entelechy of *Geschehen*. *Geschichte*, then, would not be— that is, not only, or in the first place—the productive succession of the different states of its subject. Rather than an unfolding, rather than a process or procession, the happening or the coming—or, more to the point, "to happen," "to come," "to take place"—would be a nonsubstantive verb and one that is nonsubstantifiable. This is why Hegel refuses to allow philosophy to be identified with the story of an unfolding, that is, identified with all its various episodes [*péripéties*].[5] What he refuses, then, is not the dimension of the "to happen" as such, which he would like to replace with the simple and stable identity of Being and the having-always-already-been. Looking at it more carefully, it is clear that what he does refuse is *Geschehen*—which is the active essence of *Geschichte*, the historiality of history—when it is understood as a simple episode (*blosses Geschehen*). (In fact, one could reread the pages that precede the sentence with which we began from this perspective.) The event is not an episode; it is, if it is at all necessary to say that it is, *that it be* [qu'il y ait]—that is, that there be something, something different than the indeterminacy [*indifférence*] of Being and nothingness, to use the language of the numerical logic of becoming. The event indicates what has to be thought at the very heart of becoming, pointing to it as something more deeply withdrawn and more decisive than the "passage-into" to which it is ordinarily reduced. Insofar as it is understood as "passage-into," becoming primarily indicates that which is passed into, the having-become [*l'être-devenu*] of its result. But in order for the passage to take place, in *step* with the passing [*dans le pas du passer*], there must first be the agitated "unrest" (*haltungslose Unruhe*),[6] which has not yet passed and does not pass as such—but happens.

∼

This is the way in which Hegel wants to think the essence of *Geschehen* as *Geschehen*. Or, at the very least, his thinking tends toward this thought as if toward its own vanishing point. More precisely, Hegel wants to think the essence of what escapes a logic in which essence is understood as substance, subject, or ground, in favor of a logic of the "to happen," the whole essence of which is in the state of "agitation" that consists in not subsisting (*haltungslos*). Moreover, the origin of the word *Geschehen* and its semantic use refer to racing along and leaping, to precipitation and suddenness, far more than to process and what is produced. (In contrast to the French word "événement," this word does not have the sense of a "outstanding or remarkable event," for which there are other words in German, beginning with the closely related term *Geschehnis*, whose slight difference nonetheless brings out the verbal, active, and busy [*passant*] character of *Geschehen*.)

∼

In coming to this recognition, one certainly touches on the extreme limit of what it is possible to make Hegel say. Such is not a matter of exercising interpretive violence, nor is it a matter of making Hegel, contrary to his own maxim, leap over his own time. It is a matter of realizing that he must be made to say this, however surprising that might seem to the "Hegelians" (if there are any left), and a matter of noting that Hegel's own time in philosophy, the time of the modern closure/opening, includes this surprise within itself—a secret [*sourde*] anxiety (*Unruhe*) regarding the event.

Thinking the event in its essence as event surprises Hegelian thinking from the inside. Of course, such a thought closes in on itself just as quickly as it is opened. In short, Hegel lets the *Geschehen* come and go, happen and leave, without seizing it. But he does state, nonetheless, that it happens to him and that it is what is to be thought, although it goes beyond his own discourse.

Or rather, one could just as easily say the following: Hegel seizes the *Geschehen*; he stops it or inspects it in its coming and going; he fixes its concept (it is *Geschichte*). But in doing so, he demonstrates that it is exactly in the seizing that he misses it *as such*. In this way, he opens, *volens nolens*, the question of the "as such" of the *Geschehen*.

The "as such" of the event would be its Being. But then this would have to be the being-happening, or else the being-that-happens, rather than the Being of what happens—that is, of what is happening—or even the Being of the "that it happens." Or to put it another way, it would not be the "there is," but the *that* there is, the *that* without which there would be nothing. The difference between "it is" and "there is" consists precisely in the fact that the *there* marks the proper instance of the taking place of Being, without which Being would not be. That there is = the Being *of* Being, or the transitive Being of the intransitive or substantive Being, the event of Being that is necessary in order for Being to be; it does not in any sense equal the substance, subject, or ground of Being. The event of Being, which is in no way Being, is nonetheless Being "itself"—the same as what *has not been*, as it were, or, more precisely, the same as not having been, the same as nothing. . . .

Therefore, what is opened with the question of the "as such" of the event is something on the order of a negativity of the "as such." How is one to think "as such" where the "as" does not refer to any one "such"? Here, thinking is surprised in the strong sense of the word: it is caught in the absence of thinking [*elle est prise en défaut de pensée*]. This is not to say that it has not identified its object, but rather that there is no identifiable object if "the event" cannot even be said or seen "as such," that is, if one cannot even express "the event" without its losing its event-ness.

∼

Let us dwell upon this characteristic of surprise.

There is, then, something to be thought—the event—the very nature of which—event-ness—can only be a matter of surprise, can only take thinking by surprise. We need to think about how thought can and must be surprised—and how it may be exactly this that makes it think. Or then again, we need to think about how there would be no thought without the event of thinking.

To think the surprise of the event must be something other than questioning the unthinkable, in whatever mode this might occur, and also, of course, something other than winning over surprise in order to detach it from its (sur)prise by assigning it a place under a concept. This undoubtedly comes down to thinking through the leap that is taken at the very core of the Hegelian *Geschehen*, the dialectical spring located at that point where, before being the means of the [dialectic's] driving force, it must be its relaxation or release, and, therefore, its *very* [elle-même] negativity. As such, it is less a matter of the concept of surprise than of a surprise of [*à même*] the concept, essential to the concept.

In going much farther back than Hegel, as far back as the Platonic and Aristotelian *topos* of "wonder," what may need to be understood is the fact that this task is the task of philosophy, and that philosophy is *surprised thought* [la pensée surprise]. We come back to this *topos* again and again, as if to awaken the idea of a first "wonder," which is both a sort of rapture and an admission of ignorance, and which starts such "wonder" on its way toward its own self-appropriation, that is, its self-resorption.

If we pay close attention to the *Metaphysics* (specifically A2), what Aristotle tells us is that "philosophy" is the science which is neither "practical" nor "poetic," and the science which proceeds from wonder—*insofar as* this is exactly what provides access to that science which is its own end. Wonder, then, does not appear as some ignorance to be overcome or as an aporia to be surmounted, which would be a situation wherein one science could not really be distinguished from the others; instead, wonder appears as a disposition toward *sophia* for its own sake. Wonder, then, is properly philo-sophical. One could even appeal to this interpretation in saying that wonder is already, by itself, found within the element of *sophia* or, in a parallel manner, that *sophia* holds within itself the moment of wonder. (In the same passage, Aristotle declares that the *philomuthos*, that lover of myths and their astonishing wonders, is also, in some way, a *philosophos*.) In as much as it is contained within *sophia* and not suppressed, the moment of wonder is that of a surprise kept at the very core of *sophia* and constitutive of it, insofar as it is its own end. On the one hand, knowledge that is not ordered or arranged by anything else is valuable only as its own appearing; on the other hand, and reciprocally, the appearing itself is the only true object of knowledge—if it can, in fact, be an object. *Sophia* must surprise itself, and the surprise must be "known."

Thus, the surprise of the event would not only be a limit-situation for the knowledge of Being, it would also be its essential form and essential end. From the very beginning of philosophy to its end, where its beginning is replayed in new terms, this surprise is all that is at stake, a stake that is literally interminable.

Again, it is necessary to stay precisely within the element of wonder—that is, within what could never properly be made into an "element," but is instead an event. How is one to stay in the event? How is one to hold onto it (if that is even an appropriate expression) without turning it into an "element" or a "moment"? Under what conditions can one keep thinking within the surprise, which is its task to think?

We will examine some of these conditions, at least in a preliminary way.

∽

Let us begin again with this: "the surprise of the event" is a tautology. And it is precisely this tautology that must first be expressed. The event surprises or else it is not an event; so it is all a matter of knowing what "surprise" is.

In a birth or in a death—examples which are not examples, but more than examples; they are the thing itself—there is the event, some[thing] awaited, something that might have been able to be. It can also be formulated like this: what is awaited is never the event; it is the advent, the result; it is what happens. At the end of nine months, one expects the birth, but that it takes place is what is structurally unexpected in this waiting. Or more precisely, the unawaited—and the unawait*able*—is not "the fact that" this takes place, in the sense that this "fact" may itself be circumscribed within the sequence of a process and be a given of the experience. It is not "the fact that"; it is the *that* itself of the "that it happens" or the "that there is." Or even better, it is the "it happens" as distinct from all that precedes it and from everything according to which it is codetermined. It is the pure present of the "it happens"—and the surprise has to do with the present as such, in the presence of the present insofar as it happens.

That it happens is a *quidditas*, which is neither that of "what happens" nor of the "it happens." It is not even that of the succession or simultaneity of the "that" at the heart of all "that's." As Kant says, in order to think of some thing that occurs in a series, it is necessary to conceive of it as the change of a substance (which [itself] remains identical, as in the "First Analogy of Experience"), and it is necessary to refer this change back to causality ("Second Analogy of Experience"). "[The] concept of alteration supposes one and the same subject as existing with two opposite determinations, and thereby as abiding."[7] Outside this concept of change, there is simply no concept of "some thing," for then there would be "coming into being and passing away of substance," which cannot take place "in time," but rather must take place exclusively *as time itself.* Yet, "time cannot be perceived in itself." The pure occurring (*das blosse Enstehen*)—in other words, the *ex nihilo* and also the *in nihilum*—is nothing for which there is a concept; it is time "itself," its paradoxical identity and permanence as "empty time."

The event as such, then, is empty time or the presence of the present as negativity, that is, insofar as it happens and is, as a result, nonpresent—and in such a way that it is not even "not yet present" (which would reinscribe everything in a succession of presents already available "in time"), but is, on the contrary, the sort [of thing] that nothing precedes or succeeds. It is time itself in its appearing, as the appearing that it is.[8]

But empty time or the void of time "as such," a void which is not an emptiness interior to any form, but the condition of the formation of every form, is not a "thing in itself," beyond reach and accessible only to an *intuitus originarius.* "Empty time," or the articulation of the *nihil/quid* as nonsuccessive, as the happening or coming of something in general, is time itself, in that it is not successivity, but that which does not succeed and is not permanent substance. One would have to say it in the following way: it is permanence without substance, the present without presence; rather than the coming [*la venue*], it is the unexpected arrival [*sur-venue*][9] of the thing itself. It is neither (successive) time, nor (distributive) place, nor (extant) thing, but rather the taking place of something—the event. To use a word that is heavy with the weight of an enormous tradition, which it will be necessary to problematize later, it is *creation.*

Empty time, or negativity as time, or the event, makes itself the "in itself" of the "thing in itself." Undoubtedly, this is exactly what Kant was unable to grasp. It is also what Hegel and those of us who come after him, within the insistent tradition of passing along a thinking of the event, are constantly addressing. "Time" or "the event" (both of these terms are still too firmly rooted in a thematic of continuous-discontinuous succession) mark out, or just are, the "position of existence" as such: the *nihil/quid* that cannot even be expressed as "from the *nihil* to the *quid.*" This is the event of Being, neither as an accident nor as a predicate, but as the Being of Being [*l'être de l'être*].

According to these conditions, the event is not "something" beyond the knowable or the sayable—and, as such, restricted to the beyond-speech and beyond-knowledge of a mystical negativity. It is neither a category nor a metacategory distinct from Being.[10] Rather, it is right at [*à même*] Being, the necessary condition for the categorization of Being: for saying it, addressing it, summoning [*interpeller*] it to the level of the surprise of its unexpected arrival. As such—*als Geschehen, als Entschehen, als Verschwinden,* as taking place, appearing, disappearing—the event is not "presentable." (In this sense, it exceeds the resources of any phenomenology, even though the phenomenological theme in general has never been more magnetized by anything else). But it is not, for all that, "unpresentable" like some hidden presence, for it is the unpresentable or, rather, the unpresentifiable of the present that is right at the present itself. The unpresentifiable of the present is the difference that structures the present, as has been known from the time of Aristotle right up until the present day, via Husserl and Heidegger. That this difference of the present is not presentable does not mean that it is not thinkable—but this could mean that thinking, in order to be thought, must itself become something other than a seeing or knowing; it must make itself the surprise of/in its "object." In Deleuzian terms, a becoming-surprise of thinking must correspond to the unexpected arrival of the present (of Being).

～

In this formulation, there is no event "as such." This is because the event as event—that is, *quo modo* or according to its own mode (*evenire quo modo evenit*), the event according to the appropriateness and measure of the event itself—is not what is produced or could be shown (as the spectacular, as the newborn infant, as the dead man). Rather, it is the event *as* it comes about [*é-vient*], *as* it happens. Almost immediately, one can discern that in similar circumstances the modal *as* is confused with the temporal *as* (the one that is used when one says "as it happened, there was a flash of lightning" ["comme il arrivait, il y eut un éclair"]). Here, *quo modo* = *quo tempore*.

The mode of the event, its "as such," is time itself as the time of

the unexpected arrival. And the time of the unexpected arrival is
"empty" time. The void of time, or better still, the void as time, the
void in the mode of time, is "negativity for itself" (the phrase by
which Hegel defines time in the *Encyclopedia* in §257). But this is
not negativity understood as Hegel understood it, as "abstractly related to itself" (which, in short, amounts to the Kantian "void").
In this case, one would remain firmly rooted in a model of the succession of presents, a succession divided up and reconnected by
this abstract negativity. Rather, the relation of negativity to itself—
"birth and death," as Hegel says in the same section—must be understood as the nonabstract, itself understood as not the result [of
some process]. (This is exactly what Hegel lets fall by the wayside,
but also what he is very close to when he names time "the abstract
being"). What is neither abstraction nor result is the unexpected
arrival; in fact, it is negativity "for itself," but for itself only insofar
as it is the position of Being or existence.

This positivity of negativity is not its dialectical fecundity. In order to avoid reopening the whole issue of deconstructing the dialectic, let us just say that this positivity is the exact reverse of this
fecundity, without going so far as to say that it is its dialectical
sterility. It is Being or existence that exists, [which is] neither engendered nor unengendered, but which arrived unexpectedly, ar-
rives unexpectedly—or again, is "created."

Negativity, here, does not deny itself and is not raised up out of
itself. It does something else; its operation, or its in-operation, is
otherwise and obeys another mode. One could say that it becomes
strained: tension and extension, the only means by which something could appear as "passing-through" and "process," the non-
temporal and nonlocal extension of the *taking-place as such*, the
spacing through which time appears, the tension of nothing which
opens time. As Heidegger put it: *Spanne*.

The unexpected arrival: the nothing stretched to the point of
rupture and to the leaping-off point of the arrival, where presence
is presented [*pres-ente*].

There is a rupture and a leap: rupture, not in the sense of a break
with the already presupposed temporal continuum, but rupture as

time itself, that is, as that which admits nothing presupposed, not even, or especially not, a presupposition. To do so would be to admit an antecedent of time [in]to itself. The rupture of nothing, the leap of nothing into nothing, is the extension of negativity; or to be more precise, since the negative is not something that can be stretched like a rubber band, [it is] negativity as tension, a tension that is not itself progressive, but is all in one go, in a single stroke, the tension/extension of Being, "that there is."

If the event of the "that there is" has negation as its corollary "and not nothing," it does not have it as its negative—which is to say, not as just another inverse and symmetrical possibility: that there be "nothing" *in the place of* something. This is because there is no place for the taking place of a "nothing" in the guise of "something." "And not nothing," as it is used above, does not mean that this is not "nothing" which exists. On the contrary, it says that nothing exists except for "something," and that "something" exists with no presupposition other than its own existence, the extension of "nothing" as the tension of its becoming-present, of its event.

(In this, it must be conceded that the thinking of existence would prove "nothing." But the proof of nothing is not necessarily, or exclusively, the anguish of nothingness—which always runs the risk of projecting this "nothingness" as the abysmal presupposition (and postsupposition) of Being. Instead, the experience [*preuve*] of nothing is what we are trying to approach: the thinking-surprise [*pensée-surprise*] of the event.)

～

What, then, is the surprise?

This is exactly what can no longer be asked. The surprise *is not* anything. It is not some newness of Being that would be surprising in comparison to the Being that is already given. When there is the event (whether there is the event only for the totality of beings or for diverse, dispersed, and uncertain beings—which comes down to the same thing), it is the "already" that leaps up, along with the "not yet." It leaps [over] every presented or presentable present, and this leap is the coming, or the pre-sence or *prae-sens* itself without a present.

When "the infant is born," as Hegel says in the famous passage from the *Phenomenology*, the event is not that the infant is born, because this was already well established in the order of process and the modification of substance. Instead, the event is the interruption of the process, that leap which Hegel represents as the "qualitative leap" of the "first breath" (or even, as he says elsewhere, as the "trembling" which crosses through and divides the maternal substance *in utero*). To use Heidegger's language, to be born or to die is not "to be," but to be "thrown into Being."

Thinking the leap can only be accomplished by a leap of thought —by thought as a leap, as the leap that it knows and is aware of being, necessarily. But it knows itself and is aware of itself *as surprise* (surprise in its knowledge and awareness, surprise as knowledge and awareness). The surprise is nothing except the leap right at [*à même*] Being, this leap where the event and thinking are "the same." In a certain way, the thinking of the surprise repeats the Parmenidian sameness of Being and thinking.

It leaps; but who or what is this "it"? Nothing, no one. "It" only is in the leap. That is, it exists—if the ek-sisting of existence is made of the tension and extension between Being and the being, between nothing and something. It leaps into nothing, and this is how it exists. It is to leap into nothing. It is itself the articulation of the difference between nothing and something, and this difference is also a *différend* (*ein Austrag*, dispute, conflict, distribution, sharing—as Heidegger lays out in the second volume of his Nietzsche lectures). There is a disagreement between Being and the being: Being is in disagreement with the present, given, disposed being-ness [*étantité*] of the being, and the being is in disagreement with the substantial, founding essentiality of Being. The disagreement is a disagreement with that which, *by according Being to the being, would have eased the tension of ek-sisting.* Disagreement, then, constitutes the event: the nonpresence of the coming to presence, and its absolute surprise.

But this is not a surprise for a subject. No one is surprised, just as no one leapt. The surprise—the event—does not belong to the order of representation. The surprise is that the leap—or better the "it," the "someone" who occurs in the leap and, in short, occurs as the leap "itself"—surprises itself. It *is* surprised; it is insofar as it is surprised that it is—and it is as surprise, surprising itself in the glaring absence of being-present. It surprises itself precisely insofar as it represents neither "itself" nor its surprise. The leap coincides with the surprise; it is nothing but this surprise, which still does not even "belong" to it.

The tension or extension of the leap, that is, the spacing of time, the discord of Being as its truth: this is the surprise. The *Spanne* is not surprising in that it comes to trouble or destabilize a subject that was there, but in its taking someone there *where he is not*, or insofar as it overtakes him, seizes him, paralyzes him *insofar as he is not there*.

This "not being there" is exactly the most appropriate mode of "being there," since it is a matter of "leaping into Being," or a matter of existing. "Not to be there" is not to be already there, but to be the there itself (which is the principal existential condition of *Dasein*). The "there" is the spacing of the tension, of the ex-tension. It is space-time; it is not space, not time, not a coupling of the two, not a source-point outside the two, but the originary division [*coupe*] and chiasm that opens them up to one another.

The surprise is the leap into the space-time of nothing, which does not come "before" or from "elsewhere"; as such, it is the leap into the space-time of space-time "itself." It is the taking place of place, of the there that is not a place "for" Being, but Being as place, being-the-there. It is not present Being, but the *present of Being insofar as it happens*, and therefore insofar as it is not.

It is in this way that the surprise of the event is negativity—but not negativity as a resource, as an available foundation, as nothingness or an abyss from the depths of which the event would come; for such an "event" would still be a result. The nothing (in order to keep this dried-up word and to make it incisive for every "abyss" and all their various depths), which is "at bottom" ["au fond"] nothing and no more than the nothing of a leap into nothing, is the negativity that is not a resource but the affirmation of ek-sistent tension: its intensity, the intensity or surprising tone of existence.

~

According to these conditions, if a schematism of the surprise were necessary—and it is necessary; it is what concerns us here; it is necessary to give the a priori conditions of grasping the surprise as such, the conditions of a surprise seizure of surprise—it could be said that the surprise is the schematism itself. For if the schematism is the production of a "pure vision," anterior to every figure, and if "pure vision" is itself the ex-position of time as "pure auto-affection,"[11] it is in pure auto-affection that vision sees itself seeing and, *in this way*, sees—(the) nothing. In general, the schematism is principally the visibility of nothing as a condition for the possibility of any visibility of something. In every vision of something, the vision first of all sees itself as pure vision, seeing nothing, seeing nothing there—and yet, it is already "vision," and as such is ahead of itself or outside itself, not a figure and the figure of the nothing—this surprising figure without figure that the event of Being traces in a flash.

Therefore, the schematism—and along with it, all transcendental imagination—would neither be some sort of "image" (as is already well known) nor some sort of arche-image, any more than it would be a sort of sublime abyss of the breaking down of these images. More simply, more unimaginably, it would be the event-schema, the lighting of the trace stretched out right at nothing and the pure affirmation of existence. Finally, it would not even be "birth" or "death," but only what these incisions dissect: the Being of a being, its event.

Will it be said, then, that this event is unique—in the sense in which Heidegger speaks of the "fundamental event of Dasein"?[12] Certainly. In a certain respect, there is nothing apart from an event, and there is nothing "of the event" that is scattered here and there with no connection to essential event-ness. There is an event, a surprise. What exists does not recover; it does not return. It is to exist.

But the unity of the event is not numerical. It does not consist in being gathered at a point of origin (for ontology, there is no Big Bang). Because it is or creates surprise, its nature and structure are such as to be dispersed in the flow [*l'aléa*] of events, and, as a result, also in the flow of that which does not constitute an event and withdraws discreetly into the imperceptible continuum, into the murmur of "life" for which existence is the exception.

If the event were fundamental and unique in the ordinary—or "metaphysical"—sense of these words, it would be given, and this giving would also be the originary dissolution of all event-ness. There would be no surprise. Only because it is not given, but instead happens, is there surprise and an unpredictable [*aléatoire*] multiplicity of what might now be called the arrivals (or the "arrivings") of the unique event. In this sense, there are only events, which means that "there is" is eventlike [*événementiel*] (*Sein, Ereignis*). This means they are not only diverse, discrete, and dispersed, but also rare. Or, in other words: the event is simultaneously unique, innumerable, and rare.

It never stops happening—and surprising. Thinking never stops catching itself in the act [*se surprendre à*] of seeing it coming, its open look turned upon the transparency of nothing. A thought is an event: what it thinks happens to it there, where it is not. An event is a thought: the tension and leap into the nothing of Being. It is in this sense that "Being and thinking are the same" and that their sameness takes place according to the incisive ex-tension of ek-sistence.

It is also in this sense that it might be said that the creation of the world is the thought of God. [We could say this] if from now on—given that the unconditioned is no longer subjected to the condition of the supreme being—it were not also necessary for us to think this without "God" and without a "creator": this is what is meant by the demand to think of the event as we have inherited it from Hegel.

[Since Hegel] at the very least—it might be necessary to pay some renewed attention to the work of Parmenides himself, particularly to how ontological truth is inscribed there in the recitation of an event. After all, the poem immediately opens onto the present with "the horses which carry me," where nothing indicates a stopping point in any formal way. In fact, the speaker's chariot enters the domain of the goddess, but this domain is only presented as the road opened wide by the gaping opening that Diké agreed to open. He, the "young man," the one who "knows" or "sees" his road "pass through all the cities," does not come down from his chariot. He is instructed by the goddess along the way, without stopping, instructed not about Being but about the "it is." Passing through the opening, he sees that there is; that is all that happens to him, and nothing else ever happens—when something happens.

It is precisely this that must be said and thought—there is nothing but this to say and to think; all meaning is there.

What meaning, then? The meaning that makes it the case that "there is"; that which destines or provokes Being into happening; that which sends Being on its way into happening—into happening/arriving/leaving. What is this? This cannot be represented as an axiom, or as a fact. It will be said that it is an "it must."

Written beneath the title of the last movement of Beethoven's Quartet, op. 135—"the decision made with difficulty"—he added this well-known note: "*Muss es sein? Es muss sein.*" (This could be interpreted in the following way: "Must it (be)? It must (be)" ["Le faut-il (être)? Il le faut (être)"]). If Being simply were, nothing would ever happen, and there would not be any thinking. In addition, the "it must" is not the expression of a simple, immanent necessity (of a nature or destiny). Necessity itself can only be the decided response of thinking to the suspense of Being wherein it is surprised: *Muss es sein?*

§ Human Excess

Measure is the name for the propriety [*convenance*] of one Being to another, or to itself. On the one hand, as propriety to another, measure is that "dimension" for which there is no prescribed propriety except for that of convention. Systems of measurement [*mesure*] are all grounded, at least in part, on considerations of use (which are more or less mixed up with various kinds of symbolism).

On the other hand, apart from every intention toward some sort of use, it is always possible to measure the average life of a man in millionths of a second, or in definite fractions of the time it takes for the light of a distant star to reach us. This is how the curiosities that fill almanacs are obtained (the height of the column formed by all the books in the Bibliothèque Nationale . . .), facts devoid of meaning but not of truth, albeit infinitely impoverished truth. Within this order of truth, excess is impossible. Quite to the contrary, it is the perfect domain of large numbers, shifts in scale, incommensurables, all the surpluses with regard to averages, and so forth. Seven million six hundred thousand pounds sterling for Canova's *The Graces* is a commercial truth that is neither measured nor excessive. Ten billion people on Earth is a prospective demographic truth, which is neither measured nor excessive as such.

In turn, these figures themselves measure something: the engagement with certain evaluations within a market, the engagement with a certain number of risks and tasks in a world (in a world that becomes worldly by this very engagement). In other words, each time these figures measure a responsibility.

Taking account of the "excess" of large numbers sometimes comes down to simply establishing a propriety that has no sense of "excess" with relation to itself (as is the case with curiosities from almanacs, record books, or the purely spectacular exhibition of the universe's dimensions—all of it science and truth for fools). But sometimes, it is also a matter of bringing a certain responsibility to light. Each of these gestures is the reverse of the other, so that the proliferation of large numbers in our culture, our interests and our needs (the size of a computer memory, the price of a nuclear submarine, and so on) also defines the exponential growth of such responsibility.

(Sergio Moravia had this feeling, albeit in a form that was still imprecise and too Manichean, when he wrote: "Evil today is called 'Number'. . . . Nuclear weapons, weapons of mass homicide, were born of Number. Without Number, their invention would have been meaningless. Thus, the Number of the species is opposed to the Number of the end of the species."[1])

It is not without reason that the figures for genocide and other forms of extermination have become, if not names properly speaking, at least the *semantemes* of modernity. "Six million" is indissociable from the Shoah. "Six million" (as well as figures for other exterminations and massacres), as it is used, does not mean the same as being "very big" or "too high," excessive or out of proportion. Would it be "within measure" to kill ten Jews, or a hundred Armenians, or twenty-five Tutsis? Is it "within measure" to let two people die of hunger rather than a million? These figures do not designate a surpassing or going beyond [*dépassement*] (of what norm? of what average?). They indicate an order, a register appropriate to engagement and responsibility, of which they are themselves a part.

(Of course, one must trace back to Marx the role large numbers play in what might be called moral exposition. In order for the function these numbers serve to jump out in front of our eyes it is enough to glance through any number of chapters from *Capital,* for example, the chapter on the "General Law of Accumulation."

The figures are there not only as elements of the discourse; they precede it. In a certain way, they indicate its meaning in advance of all its articulated significations. "Capital" itself may also be absolutely general exposition and exponentiality.)

Just as in the vain exercise of curiosity (or its exact opposite), here too, "excess" is its own propriety and forms the measure of an "unheard-of" ["inouïe"] measure. It measures itself; that is, it is engaged as totality. In today's world, excess [*la démesure*] is not an excess [*un excès*], in the sense that it is indeterminant with relation to normative structures; it does not form a monstrous excrescence and, as such, is not doomed to perish. It constitutes a tendentious, continued approximation of totality. It indicates not so much the degree or quantum of its magnitude [*grandeur*] (six or ten or forty million, or even 13 or 20 meters square of arable land per person by the year 2050), but magnitude itself as an absolute which touches upon another propriety of Being (or the human, or meaning—however we want to say it). This can be illustrated in the following way: the Big Bang is not about "very large" quantities (of time, energy, the dimensions of the Universe, and so on), it is about a magnitude (the Universe) that is entirely its own measure, and the measure of no other.

This magnitude, which is its own "excessive" measure or measured excess, also provides the scale of a total responsibility: when it is thoroughly analyzed, the whole matter of the Big Bang concerns the fact that the true "measure" of the universe is found in the "excessive" responsibility that we have for it, or which we take on from that very moment we measure in this way. Man as the measure of all things has taken on a new, excessive meaning: far removed from every relation to the human as some mediocre standard, and also far removed from its remnants, this meaning relates humans themselves to an immensity of responsibility.

In an age where humanity is understood as the population of a very large number of people, the *humanitas* of humanity itself appears as an excess that gives the measure or sets the standard against which we must measure ourselves. As such, a murder is excessive in relation to the ordinary mores of a social group. But an extermination (the name of which indicates all too well what it is saying: to go to term, exhaust the account [*épuiser le compte*], to measure a people only against its existence within totality), this itself measures a social relation, or its absence, as it were. The opposite of an extermination cannot be found [by looking for some] "just measure": it must reclaim the same totality. This is also the meaning of demographic mastery: humanity as totality clearly comes down to being humanity's responsibility. This responsibility is given without measure, because the question is not how many people the Earth or the universe can support, but rather which people it can support, which existences. Number, here, immediately converts its magnitude into moral magnitude: the size of humanity becomes indissociable from its dignity.

⁓

But this dignity, this *humanitas*, is not itself given as a measure (to believe that it is constitutes the notorious weakness of all discourses of "measured" and measuring humanism). In a certain way, all calls to "measure" are in vain, since there is no excess that can be determined with relation to a given measure, norm, scale, or mean. Thus, the use and/or rule that gives the measure must itself be invented.

In our culture, a long period of rule was needed in order to recall how much the ancient world was a world of measure, and how it was that under this heading, perhaps more than any other, it had to be a model for us (model and measure, model of measure, and measure of the model: this all makes up a large part of our history and metaphysical constitution). It was a world of well-defined limit, a world of the horizon, of *phronesis, mesotes,* and *metron. Hubris* was the measurable excess par excellence, and one knew, or could know in principle, if Ajax, Antigone, or Creon, Caesar or Brutus surpassed the measure and one could know which measure was exceeded. Thus, measure is the propriety of Being to itself. It is its mode (its temperament, its rhythm, its own [*propre*] coherence), not its dimension.

It is not important whether this interpretation of the ancient world is accurate or not. What is important is that we have set up this model—and that it gets exhausted. It is exhausted because it does not take into account (as the proper mode, as the propriety of Being to itself) that the measure of the modern world is itself the "excessive" mode of infinity.

Its origin [*provenance*] is undoubtedly Christian; or rather, Christianity was only ever the installation of this infinite mode of Being. Properly speaking, Christianity had long concealed the truth of this infinite mode under the apparent preservation of a measurable measure, the measure of the created Being [*l'être créé*]. As a creature, Being had to observe the propriety of its dependence. But insofar as the whole of creation essentially carries the mark or vestige of its creator as its proper mode (man in the image of God was nothing more than the pinnacle of this structure or process), it itself has as its propriety the immensity, the nonmeasure, of the creator. To put it more precisely, this is the nonmeasure of the act of creation (where the subject creator is nothing other than its act), which has as its property the lack of measure and the fact that it operates without measure, as distinct from all cosmogony. In fact, creation means the nonorigin [*non-provenance*] of existence as such, with no other measure or mode, and it means Being's absolute and exclusive propriety to itself.

As for "God," he is only the interpretation of this excess in terms of a process and as the agent of production. But this is also why, even within the framework of this interpretation, creation has brought about so many complex elaborations on the structure and extent of his act: on the "ex nihilo," on God's expansion out of himself or retreat into himself, on the various themes of love, glory, giving, or abandonment. All these considerations gravitate toward the following: "creation" is the absolute measure, the Being which is, unto itself, the pure and simple propriety of its existence.

The result is that the formula for God, as the measure of all things, does not have the same meaning for Plato as it does for Hegel. For Plato, God is the measure of a relation between each existing thing [*existant*] and its own mode of being; as such, God is the absolute measure of the modalization of beings. For Hegel,

God is the excessive measure [*(dé)mesure*] according to which Being
is modalized as Being, essentially and in every existing thing (which
also implies that his own mode has just as much to do with nothingness and becoming). Up to a certain point, Hegel represents this measure—the being-
modal [*l'être-mode*] of Being itself—as an absolute measure, as an
absolutely finished or accomplished infinity. This can be transcribed into another register in the following
way: for Hegel, as well as for Plato, there is an absolute justice to
absolute measure. In modalizing itself, Being confers on itself the
right modes [*justes modes*] of its modalities (and precisely because
it modalizes itself, or because its structure is subjectivity). In principle, then, this justice in itself defines the good. What follows
from this is that there is, of itself, a just social order and a just sovereignty. For us, in turn, the modalization of Being is that of the
without-measure [*sans-mesure*] as such. What we still interpret in
the ancient or Christian ways as "excessively large," whether it be
speed, population, massacres, poverty, the universe, or nuclear
power, for example, is only the modalized translation of the following: "creation" is now understood as the act of Being which is
without measure its own measure [*comme l'acte de l'être qui est sans
mesure sa propre mesure*].

Perhaps we can also understand the universal constants of modern physics in this way, for example, the speed of light or *quantum*
of energy. These do not measure themselves against other things,
but, on the contrary, are the origin of all possible measure. These
days, *fait lux* means that there is a "speed" against which all speed is
measured and which is not measured against anything superior
(that is, it is fixed merely by convention). It is no longer the word
of God [a creator] who would have measured this speed in advance. It is no longer a word at all. But the universe that has this
constancy is "creation." Being [*étant*] without a creator is not creation; creation is simply Being. Creation is that there is Being in
this way, and not otherwise. Being, then, is finite, in the sense that
there is no "infinite speed," but its finitude has no measure; it is its
own total measure of Being. In this sense, it is infinite, but an in-

finitude that consists in being its own excessive measure. The result is not Being as a substance, but Being as responsibility.

To be responsible is not, primarily, being indebted to or accountable before some normative authority. It is to be engaged by its Being to the very end of this Being, in such a way that this engagement or *conatus* is the very essence of Being. ("Engagement" is, after all, a good translation of "conatus.")

The epoch that appears to us as the epoch of very large numbers, the one we can describe as that of "exponential Being," is in fact the epoch of Being which is exposed to and as its own immensity in the strictest sense: nothing measures it, and it is precisely that which measures the existence which engages it, and which it engages in the mode of a responsibility that is itself immense. "Humanity" and "globalness" ["mondialité"] now mean this engagement without measure [or this measureless engagement].

Either the time to come will know to take the measure [of things], or there will be the loss of all measure, and existence along with it. In both a disturbing and exhilarating way, this is what is immensely grand in what is happening to us today, to the extent [*à mesure*] that we are exposed to it.

Cosmos Baselius

Nomos basileus. . . .

—Pindar

The unity of a world is not one: it is made of a diversity, and even disparity and opposition.[1] It is in fact, which is to say that it does not add or subtract anything. The unity of a world is nothing other than its diversity, and this, in turn, is a diversity of worlds. A world is a multiplicity of worlds; the world is a multiplicity of worlds, and its unity is the mutual sharing and exposition of all its worlds—within this world.

The sharing of the world is the law of the world. The world has nothing other; it is not subject to any authority; it does not have a sovereign. *Cosmos, nomos.* Its supreme law is within it as the multiple and mobile trace of the sharing that it is. *Nomos* is the distribution, apportionment, and allocation of its parts: a piece of territory, a portion of food, the delimitation of rights and needs in each, and at every time, as is fitting [*il convient*].

But how does it fit? The measure of the suitability [*la convenance*][2]—the law of the law, or absolute justice—is only in the sharing itself and in the exceptional singularity of each—of each instance [*cas*], each according to this sharing. Yet, this sharing is not given, and "each" is not given (that which is the unity of each part, the occurrence of its instance, the configuration of each world). This is not an accomplished distribution. The world is not given. It is itself the giving [*le don*]. The world is its own creation (this is what "creation" means). Its sharing is put into play at each instant: the universe in expansion, the un-limitation of individuals, the infinite need of justice.

~

"Justice" designates what needs to be *rendered* (as one says in English, "to render justice"). What needs to be restored, repaired, given in return to each existing singular, what needs to be attributed to it again, is the giving which it is itself. And this also entails that one not know exactly (that one not know "au juste," as is said in French) what or who is an "existing singular," neither where it begins nor where it ends. Because of the incessant giving and sharing of the world, one does not know where the sharing of a stone starts or finishes, or where the sharing of a person starts or finishes. The delineation is always more ample and, at the same time, more restricted than one believes it to be (or rather, if one is attentive, one knows all too well how much the contours are trembling, mobile, and fleeting). Each existence [*existant*] appears in more ensembles, masses, tissues, or complexes than one perceives at first, and each one is also infinitely more detached from such, and detached from itself. Each opens onto and closes off more worlds, those within itself just as those much as outside of, bringing the outside inside, and the other way around.

Suitability, therefore, is defined by the proper measure in each existence *and* in the infinite community (or communication, contagion, contact), or in the indefinite opening, circulation, and transformation of all existences [*les existences*] among themselves. This is not a double suitability. It is the same one, for community is not added to existence. Community is not some proper consistency and subsistence of existance as it stands apart from it: existence has such only as the sharing of community. This (which no longer has anything to do with subsistence by itself, that is, with contact, encounter, porousness, osmosis, and rubbing up against, attraction and repulsion, and so forth) is cosubstantial with existing: in each one and in every one, in each one as in every one, in each one insofar as in every one. Translating it into a certain language, it is the "mystical body" of the world; in another language, it is the "reciprocal action" of parts of the world. But in every case, it is the coexistence by which it defines itself as existence itself and a world in general—both, at once.

~

Coexistence holds itself just as far from juxtaposition as it does from integration. Coexistence does not happen to existence; it is not added to it, and one can not subtract it out: it is existence. Existence is not done alone, if one can put it this way. It is *Being* that is alone, at least in all the ordinary senses which are given to Being. But existence is nothing other than Being exposed: beginning from its simple identity in itself and from its pure position, exposed in appearing, in creation, and, as such, exposed to the outside, exteriority, multiplicity, alterity, and change. (And in one sense, to be sure, this is not anything other than Being exposed to Being itself, in its own "being," and, as a consequence, Being exposed as Being: exposition as the essence of Being.)

~

Justice, therefore, is returning to each existence what returns to it according to its unique, singular creation in its coexistence with all other creations. The two standards [*les deux mesures*] are not separate: the singular propriety is equal to the singular trace, which joins it to other proprieties. That which distinguishes is also that which puts "with" and "together."

Justice needs to be rendered to the trace of the proper, in the carving up of it that is appropriate each time—a carving up which does not cut up or deduct from a foundation, but a common carving up that, all at once [*d'un seul coup*], constitutes distance and contact, such that the coexistence which indefinitely intertwines with it is the only "foundation" upon which the "form" of existence is [*s'enlève*]. Therefore, there is no foundation: there is only the "with"—proximity and its distancing—the strange familiarity of all the worlds in the world.

~

For each one, its most appropriate horizon is also its encounter with the other horizon: that of the coexistent, of all the coexistences, of the whole of coexisting. But "encounter" is still to say too little, especially if one does not understand that all the horizons are sides of the same carving up, of the same winding and lightning-fast trace of the world (its "unity"). This trace is not proper to any existant, and still less to an other sort of substance that hangs over the world: it is the common impropriety, the non-membership [*la non-appartenance*], the nondependence, the absolute errancy of the creation of the world.

Justice, then, needs to be rendered at once to the singular absoluteness of the proper and to the absolute impropriety of the community of existences. It needs to be rendered equally [*exactement*] to both, to the one and the other: such is the play (or the meaning) of the world.

As a consequence, infinite justice needs to be rendered at once to the propriety of each one and to the common impropriety of all: to birth and to death, which hold between them the infinity of meaning. Or rather: to birth and to death, which are, one with the other and one in the other (or one through the other), the infinite overflowing of meaning and, therefore, of justice. Birth and death about which there is nothing fitting to say—since this is the strict justice of truth, but where all true speech distractedly aims at the just measure.

This infinite justice is in no way visible. On the contrary, intolerable injustice arises everywhere. There are earthquakes, infectious viruses, and people are criminals, liars, and torturers.

Justice cannot be disengaged from the gangue[3] or haze of injustice. Neither can it be projected as a supreme conversion of injustice. It constitutes part of infinite justice that it would fail to deliver a decisive blow to injustice. But there are no reasons that can be given for how and why this constitutes part of it. It is not subject to those interrogations that concern reason or the demand for meaning. This constitutes part of the infinity of justice, and of the interrupted creation of the world: in such a way that the infinity is never anywhere called upon to accomplish itself, not even as an infinite return of itself in itself. Birth and death, sharing and coexistence, belong to the infinite. Itself, if one can say it like this, ap-

pears and disappears; it divides itself and coexists: it is the movement, the agitation and general diversity of the worlds that make
up the world (and unmake it as well).

This is also why justice is always—and maybe principally—the
need for justice, that is, the objection to and protest against injustice, the call that cries for justice, the breath that exhausts itself in
calling for it. The law of justice is this unappeasable tension with regard to justice itself. In a parallel manner, the law of the world is an
infinite tension with regard to the world itself. These two laws are
not only homologous, they are also the same and singular law of absolute sharing (one could say: the law of the Absolute as sharing).

Justice does not come from the outside (what outside?) to hover
above the world, in order to repair it or bring it to completion. It is
given with the world, given in the world as the very law of its
givenness. Strictly speaking, there is no sovereignty, or church, or
set of laws that is not also the world itself, the severed [or carved-
up] trace that is both inextricable from its horizon and unaccom-
plishable. One might be tempted to say that there is a justice for
the world, and there is a world for justice. But these finalities, or
these reciprocal intentions, say rather poorly what such justice is.
In itself, the world is the supreme law of its justice: not the given
world and the "such that it is," but the world that springs forth as
a properly incongruous incongruity.

Reference Matter

Notes

[Epigraph]

EPIGRAPH SOURCE: Friedrich Nietzsche, *Thus Spake Zarathustra*, trans. R. J. Hollingdale (New York: Penguin Books, 1969), 102.

1. In opting for "the human" as a translation of *l'homme*, we elect a more gender-neutral translation. At the same time, however, we lend the text a few connotations that Nancy himself clearly wants to avoid. In reading "the human," then, one must read it in such a way as to not hear the same sort of "humanist" tone that is out of the question in all the texts that follow.—Trans.

2. Friedrich Nietzsche, *The Gay Science*, trans. Walter Kaufmann (New York: Vintage Books, 1974), 180.

3. *La terre des hommes* literally means "the earth of men." The French expression is a common one, referring to the earth in its specific character as the milieu inhabited by humans.—Trans.

Preface

1. Throughout the work, we translate *l'être*—which coincides with the German *Sein*—as "Being," in keeping with an established, if not entirely satisfactory, tradition. We do this only when *l'être* stands alone, however, and only so as to make Being easily distinguishable from being [*l'étant*]. The difficulty is that the capital letter has the distracting and often misleading effect of making "Being" appear as a proper name, suggesting that Being is somehow quite independent of beings. This becomes par-

ticularly uncomfortable when the author uses compound expressions such as *être-avec* or *être-ensemble*, which clearly refer to the concrete conditions in which beings always do find themselves. Therefore, we have chosen to translate those compounds as "being-with," "being-together," and so forth.—Trans.

2. If, as the author points out in the following paragraph, language does not easily accommodate itself to the logic of "with," then the English language is even less giving than French in this regard. In order to capture all its plurality, one would have to translate *être-les-uns-avec-les-autres* literally as "being-the-ones-with-the-others," but we have opted for the slightly less plural, but far less painful, "being-with-one-another."—Trans.

Of Being Singular Plural

1. It is easy to see the reference here to §32 of Martin Heidegger's *Being and Time*, trans. John Macquarrie and Edward Robinson (New York: Harper, 1962). In a general way, and except when it is quite necessary, it is less to develop a commentary on Heidegger than to move on from him, and from some others—from *us*. In this us and in the relation to Heidegger, one must remember the singular role played by Hannah Arendt and her reflection on "human plurality."

2. Since the emphasis in this essay is on "with," we have almost invariably translated *partager* as "to share," but it is important to remember that it also means "to divide" or "share out." It is also worth bearing in mind that the adjective *partagé* is used to describe, among other things, a requited love, a shared meal, and a divided country.—Trans.

3. *À même* refers to a relation that becomes crucial at several points in this book, but the phrase resists easy description in English. An undershirt is worn *à même* the skin; someone sleeping outdoors might sleep *à même* the ground. Nancy himself has written about a heart his body received in a transplant operation, but later rejected, as being *à même* his body. The relation is one of being right next to, right at, or even in, without being wholly a part of. See also Brian Holmes's translator's note in Jean-Luc Nancy's *The Birth to Presence* (Stanford, Calif.: Stanford University Press, 1993), 396, n 12.—Trans.

4. "Between the 'us all' of abstract universalism and the 'me, I' of miserable individualism, there is the 'we others' of Nietzsche, a thinking of the singular case that thwarts the opposition of the particular and the uni-

versal" (François Warin, *Nietzsche et Bataille: La parodie à l'infini* [Paris: Presses Universitaires de France, 1994], 256).

5. *Se passer* is most commonly used to mean "to happen," but translating it as we do here has the advantage of emphasizing what happens as relation, while retaining the link with "passing" and "passage" in the previous section.—Trans.

6. We have forsaken the colloquial translation of *propre*—"own"— for the more stilted "proper" in order to maintain the association with "properly," "appropriation," and so on, which becomes significant in the course of the work.—Trans.

7. "Les gens sont bizarres." The word *bizarre* is translated as "strange" throughout the text in order to preserve the idiom. This presents a particular difficulty only in the final sentence of the first paragraph of p. 10 where Nancy draws attention to the etymology of the French (and also the English) word *bizarre.*—Trans.

8. Heidegger's *das Man* is generally translated into French as *le 'on'* but has generally appeared in English as the "they." We have avoided that habit here because a plural pronoun is unwarranted and would only serve to confuse what is, after all, an analysis of singularity and plurality. Translating it as the "one" has the added advantage of preserving echoes of both the author's French and Heidegger's German.—Trans.

9. Although the exercise might be instructive, I will not stop here to examine what "people" and "one" designate in various languages, or the history of the word "people" ["les gens"] (*gentes,* "Gentiles," nations, and so on).

10. This *argot* expression means "his head in the clouds" or "not down-to-earth," or even "out of his mind," but we have used the literal translation as the only way to preserve the author's play on "beside" [*à côté*].—Trans.

11. Although reasonably accurate, "appears" is a somewhat pale translation of *surgit,* so some additional connotations should be born in mind: appears suddenly, abruptly, even violently, emerges, wells up, surges forth. The emphasis, however, here and elsewhere, is on the moment of appearing.—Trans.

12. *Bizarre* is the French word we have translated as "strange" throughout this passage.—Trans.

13. Having, gaining, and being access is what is at issue here, but it should be remembered that *accéder* also means "to accede to" or "to accommodate."—Trans.

14. Let me be quite clear that the allusion to Lacan is deliberate.

15. Immanuel Kant, *Critique of Pure Reason*, trans. Norman Kemp Smith (New York: St. Martin's Press, 1965), 504. Also presupposed here is Martin Heidegger's *Kants These Über das Sein* (Frankfurt am Main: Vittorio Klostermann, 1963).

16. The complex ambiguity Nancy emphasizes here is not easily captured in English. It operates along two axes, one having to do with the expression *à la verité*, the other with the verb *accéder*. The phrase could be rendered as "We have access to the truth," or as "Truly, we have access," but either "We accede to the truth" or "Truly, we accede" would also be warranted. In Bataille's text, the latter axis is dissolved (indeed, does not arise) but, as the note below makes clear, Nancy will not allow the connotations of accession or accommodation to disappear.—Trans.

17. Georges Bataille, *Histoire des rats. Oeuvres complètes, III* (Paris: Gallimard, 1971), 114. As a matter of fact [*à la verité*], my memory fails me and Bataille writes "we attain" ["nous atteignons"]: to attain, to gain access [to accede]: as the splitting of the "almost there" ["l'a-peu-pres"] character of reaching the origin. But I must cite the whole passage from Bataille: "We do not have the means of attaining at our disposal: we attain to truth; we suddenly attain to the necessary point and we spend the rest of our days looking for a lost moment: but we miss it only at times, precisely because looking for it diverts us from it, to unite us is undoubtedly a means of . . . forever missing the moment of return. Suddenly, in my night, in my solitude, anxiety gives way to conviction: it is sly, no longer even disturbing (by dint of its being disturbing, it no longer disturbs), *suddenly the heart of B. is in my heart.*"

18. In Section 2, we translated *toucher à* as "to touch" since the context specified surfaces that touch one another. Here, the primary sense is of reaching or attaining an end, but it is also important to bear in mind the tactile sense, as well as the more common sense of "being in touch with."—Trans.

19. When the author presented this section (along with Sections 5 and 6) as part of "Openings: The Space of Thinking," a conference at Vanderbilt University in January 1996, he added the following quotation from Kant as an epigraph: " . . . if we were entitled to regard material beings as things in themselves . . . the unity that is the basis on which natural formations are possible would be only the unity of space, and yet space is not a basis [responsible] for reality of products but is only their formal condition; space merely resembles the basis we are seeking inas-

much as no part in space can be determined except in relation to the whole (so that [in its case too] the possibility of the parts is based on the presentation of the whole)" (Immanuel Kant, *Critique of Judgment*, trans. Werner S. Pluhar [Indianapolis, Ind.: Hackett Publishing Company, 1987], 293).

20. See Jean-Luc Nancy's *La deconstruction du christianisme*, forthcoming.

21. The recent book by Serge Marcel, *Le tombeau du dieu artisan* (Paris: Les Éditions de Minuit, 1995) is an amazing rereading of the *Timaeus*, which may offer something quite close to the notion of the Platonic demiurge of "creation" I am trying to bring out here.

22. *Éclat* is a difficult word to translate, exactly because it has many different meanings that do not come together easily in one English word. In all the essays that constitute this book, we have translated it as "brilliance," which only captures part of its sense. Other elements of the word suggest that "brilliance" could be, and maybe even should be, predicated with any of the following adjectives: shining, flashing, glaring, explosive, shattering, and so forth. These adjectives, in turn, could be made into nouns, any of which would also suffice as an English translation. The point is that the *éclat* is both sudden and radiant.—Trans.

23. Benoit Goetz uses this theme of spacing in his "La dislocation: Architecture et expérience" (thesis, Université de Strasbourg, 1996); he discusses it in relation to a discourse about generalized "architecture" and its becoming "existential."

24. See §36, §37, and §68c of Heidegger's *Being and Time*. In lowering the status of curiosity by measuring it against thinking, which is a fairly traditional gesture, Heidegger completely misunderstands and cheapens an element of the modern world: science and technology. In this way, he challenges what he otherwise pretends to affirm as belonging to the "sending" of Being. In relation to the role of curiosity within modernity, see Hans Blumenburg's classic book *Der Prozess der theoretishen Neugierde* (Frankfurt au Main: Suhrkamp, 1966).

25. In certain regards, what follows pursues the dialogue proposed by Jacques Rancière in his book *Disagreement: Politics and Philosophy*, trans. Julie Rose (Minneapolis: University of Minnesota Press, 1999).

26. André Tosel, *Démocratie et libéralismes* (Paris: Kimé, 1995), 203. See also the chapter entitled "L'égalité, difficile et nécessarire."

27. Étienne Balibar, "La proposition de l'égaliberté" (paper delivered at Les conférences du Perroquet, no. 22, Paris, November 1989).

28. I agree, then, with Jacques Derrida's critique of fraternity in his *Politics of Friendship*, trans. George Collins (London: Verso, 1997). But I must point out that I have also, on occasion, raised the question of Christian fraternity. Moreover, I have reversed my position again and again on the possibility of looking into whether fraternity is necessarily generic or congenital. . . .

29. See "L'insacrifiable," in Jean-Luc Nancy, *Une pensée finie* (Paris: Galilée, 1990).

30. François Raffoul's *Heidegger and the Problem of Subjectivity* (Highlands, N.J.: Humanities Press, 1997) is one of the first works that engages in opening up a path for a reevaluation of *Mitsein*, and it does so in a remarkable way.

31. Heidegger, *Being and Time*, 161.

32. Jean-François Marquet's *Singularité et événement* (Grenoble: Jérome Millon, 1995) gives a full account of the tradition of thinking about the one, in the sense of each one and the singular, and what differences there are among our various perspectives. But even before going there, one should look at those texts where this preoccupation comes to us in the first place: the texts of Gilles Deleuze along with those of Jacques Derrida (and this *with* will demand its own commentary some day). Basically, this preoccupation travels in the same direction as that undertaken by Giorgio Agamben, on one side, and Alain Badiou, on the other (even if Badiou wants to put the question in the form of an opposition by playing multiplicity against the One). All of this is to make the point that we are only thinking about the ones *with* the other [*les uns* avec *les autres*] (by, against, in spite of, close to, far from, in touch with, in avoiding it, in digging through it).

33. See Part 1, §3 of Immanuel Kant's *Der einzig mögliche Beweisgrund: The One Basis for a Demonstration of the Existence of God*, trans. Gordon Treash (New York: Abaris Books, 1979).

34. G. W. F. Hegel, *Hegel's Logic*, trans. William Wallace (Oxford: Oxford University Press, 1975), 31.

35. Edmund Husserl, *Cartesian Meditations: An Introduction to Phenomenology*, trans. Dorion Cairns (The Hague: Martinus Nijhoff, 1977), 140.

36. Descartes himself attests to this, that we all participate in the process and discourse of the *ego sum*: " . . . by that internal awareness which always precedes reflective knowledge. This inner awareness of one's thoughts and existence is so innate in all men that, although we may pre-

tend that we do not have it . . . we cannot in fact fail to have it" ("Author's Replies to the Sixth Set of Objections," *The Philosophical Writings of Descartes, Volume II*, trans. John Cottingham, Robert Stoothoof, and Dugald Murdoch [Cambridge: Cambridge University Press, 1984], 285).

37. In a sense, Levinas testifies to this problematic in an exemplary manner. But what he understands as "otherwise than Being" is a matter of understanding "the ownmost of Being," exactly because it is a matter of thinking being-with rather than the opposition between the other and Being.

38. Martin Heidegger, *Beiträge zur Philosophie* (Frankfurt am Main: Vittorio Klostermann, 1989), 319.

39. Jean-Jacques Rousseau, *The Social Contract*, trans. Maurice Cranston (New York: Penguin Books, 1968), 65.

40. Friedrich Nietzsche, *Thus Spake Zarathustra*, trans. R. J. Hollingdale (New York: Penguin Books, 1969), 229.

41. This is, of course, an expression that is dear to Bataille. One could even say that this constituted his expression, absolutely.

42. See Antonio Negri's "La crise de l'espace politique," and the rest of the articles gathered in number 27, "En attendant l'empire," of *Futur Antérieur* (Paris: l'Harmattan, January 1995).

43. See the work gathered together not long ago in *Retreating the Political*, ed. Simon Sparks (London: Routledge, 1997), and in *Rejouer le politique* (Paris: Galilée, 1983).

44. For a deconstructive reading of the "as such" of Being in fundamental ontology, see the work of Yves Dupeux (thesis, Université de Strasbourg, 1994).

45. The translation of the following three sections, "Coexistence," "Conditions of Critique," and "Co-appearing," benefited from our review of the translation of these offered by Iain MacDonald in the *University of Essex Theoretical Studies Working Papers* (March 1996).

46. See Marc Augé's *A Sense for the Other: The Timeliness and Relevance of Anthropology*, trans. Amy Jacobs (Stanford, Calif.: Stanford University Press, 1998).

47. Marc Crépon's recent work, "La problème de la diversité humaine. Enquête sur la caractérisation des peuples et de la constitution des géographies de l'ésprit de Leibniz à Hegel" (thesis, Université de Paris-X-Nanterre, 1995) is the first work of importance in the field.

48. We have translated *droit* as "right" in this passage, for the sake of consistency and in order to preserve something of Nancy's play on the

word. To understand the passage, however, the reader must remember that *droit* carries many connotations that, in English, attach to the word "law."—Trans.

49. I am just going to consider it a symptom in itself, which is a still more remarkable symptom given the unexpected return to favor it has had since the death of Guy Debord in 1995. One would have to cite the articles that appeared at the time to show how the reference to Debord could appear to be necessary and important, could appear as the last critical resource of a world without critique. On the question of fetishism and critique, see Jacques Derrida, *Specters of Marx: The State of Debt, the Work of Mourning, and the New International,* trans. Peggy Kamuf (New York: Routledge, 1994).

50. "Le football rend insignifiante toute autre forme d'art." This was an advertisement for Nike in the Paris Metro in August 1995. I should point out, whether intentionally or not, the word "insignificant" was in fact written in the masculine [where as "art form" would require the feminine; in the above text, Nancy corrects the mistake, making the footnote necessary—Trans.].

51. Of course, the Greek *sumbolon* was a piece of pottery broken in two pieces when friends, or a host and his guest, parted. Its joining would later be a sign of recognition.

52. A trinitarian God represents a Being-together as its very divinity: and it is clear, therefore, that he is no longer "God," but Being-with of the onto-theological species. Here, another motif of the "deconstruction of Christianity," which I invoked in relation to the Creation, is touched upon. It is also possible to discern here the intimate connection of all the great motifs of Christian dogma, none of which deconstruction can leave intact.

53. Husserl, *Cartesian Meditations,* 139. It is undoubtedly here, more than anywhere else, that Husserl shows how phenomenology itself reaches its limit, and exceeds it: it is no longer the egoistic kernel, but the world "as a constituted sense" that shows itself to be constitutive (137). The constitution is itself constituted: in these terms, this is undoubtedly the ultimate structure of "language" and of the "with," of language *as* "with." The immediate context of the passage shows how Husserl means to give his most direct reply to Heidegger and to a thinking of *Mitsein* still insufficiently founded in the "essential necessity" of the "given Objective world" and its "sociality of various levels" (137). A highly remarkable chiasma is produced, here, between two thoughts that provoke and cross through one another according to what can only be called *two styles*

of the essentiality of the with. Broadly speaking, they might be described as the style of cobelonging (in *Being as truth*, Heidegger) and the style of correlation (in *ego as meaning*, Husserl). But these somewhat schematic characteristics could just as easily be reversed. This is not what is most important. What is important is in the *common* testimony of the era (with Freud, with Bataille, with . . .), according to which ontology must, from that point on, be the ontology of the "with," or of nothing.

54. As Francis Fisher, a longtime companion in the recognition of this demand, said, "The 'with' is a strict determination of the inessence of existence. Being-at is immediately 'with' because *Dasein* has no essence" ("Heidegger et la question de l'homme" [thesis, Université de Strasbourg, 1995]).

55. One should keep in mind that "coappear" translates *com-parution*, the exact English equivalent of which is "compearing." This itself is a legal term that is used to designate appearing before a judge together with another person.—Trans.

56. See the forthcoming volume *L'éthique originaire* (which starts with Heidegger).

57. For instance, see the title of Paul Ricoeur's *Oneself as Another*, trans. Kathleen Blamey (Chicago: University of Chicago Press, 1992).

58. A major part of the work of Philippe Lacoue-Labarthe is devoted to the deconstructive analysis of this originary *mimesis*.

59. This is true only up to a certain point. After all, Rousseau did have a keen sense of the necessity of the spectacle he so condemned, and he wished to think a sort of self-surpassing of spectacular-representational exteriority, both in terms of "civil religion" and in terms of literature. In this way, "literature" (along with "music," or "art" in general), and "civil religion" (that is, the presentable figure of secular sociality) are the terms that serve as precursors to our problem concerning meaning-with. "*To show* a man to those like himself . . . ,'" on the one hand, and to celebrate, on the other—since we could not live the event itself—is the institutive pact of humanity itself. The model is everywhere and nowhere, singular plural. This is also why, from the very beginning, the problem is set up as a convergence of *and* a division between "art" and "civil religion". . . .

60. This is not to say that any spectacle whatever would be "good on the whole." On the contrary, a society for which the spectacular form is no longer codified poses, and must pose for itself, the most difficult problems concerning the spectacle: not only must it confront its subject with a multitude of ethical, practical, economic, aesthetic, and political decisions, but it must also, first of all, recapture and found anew the thinking

of the "spectacle" as such. More often than not, the general critique of the "spectacular"—of mediatization, television, and so on—provides an alibi and stage for a very poor ideology. Whether it is belligerent, whining, or disdainful, it is most interested in propagating the notion that it possesses the key to what is an illusion and what is not. For example, it pretends to know that "people" are "fools" because of "television," which is to say, because of "tele-cracy." But this ideology knows nothing about the genuine use "people" make of TV—a use that is, perhaps, much more distanced than the critics would like to admit—or anything about the real state, sometimes genuinely "foolish," of the popular cultures of earlier times. The critique of the spectacular has been performing its routine for some time—but now it is beginning to get old.

61. If *physis* = what presents itself and what accomplishes itself by itself, then the "with" is of a different order. Even "in nature," species proliferate and live alongside one another. *Technē* would always have to do with what neither proceeds from nor to itself, with disparity, contiguity, and, thus, with an unachieved and unachievable essence of the "with."

62. All this refers, obviously, to the work of Derrida and Lacoue-Labarthe on *mimesis*, and to the work of Etienne Balibar in *The Philosophy of Marx*, trans. Chris Turner (London and New York: Verso, 1995), which insists on the intrinsic connections between "the necessity of appearance" and the "social relationship," and on the demand that an "ontology of the relation" be elaborated according to these conditions.

63. The [French] Revolution and the German Romantics did present another, republican Rome as the political theater that was immediate and without theater, which is to say, the theater of the toga and the Senate.

64. Although the French word *exposition* is more often translated as "exhibition," we have translated it here, and in the other chapters, as "exposition." We have done so in order to maintain, as much as possible, the play between it and other words that share its root, including "pose," "posed," "position," and so on.—Trans.

65. Husserl, *Cartesian Meditations*, 156.

66. Daniel Giovannangeli, *La passion de l'origine: recherches sur l'esthétique de la phenomenologie* (Paris: Galilée, 1995), 133.

67. Leviticus 19:18, which is taken up again in Matthew 22:39 and James 2:8, "apapéseis ton plésion sou ôs seautov," "diliges procimum tuum sicut teipsum": love others as you love yourself—the "golden rule," or commandment, which summarizes, together with the commandment to love God, "all the laws and prophecies."

68. I will not stop to consider here the intricacies of ideas that include "love" at the core: *ros, agap, caritas*. Nor will I consider the Judeo-Christian intricacy of the relation between love and law. It is obvious what an enormous field of investigation this represents. One invites punishment in trying to think about it in conceptual terms, especially where there is little to say when the whole of our tradition—all our thinking about "us"—will have to revolve around it. The task is this: the deconstruction of theological and/or sentimental Christianity, of the "love one another."

69. This also underlies the logic of the "politics of friendship" of the form Derrida proposes to deconstruct.

70. Heidegger, *Being and Time*, 156–63.

71. Ibid., 164–65.

72. Ibid., 160. *Umwillen* may be translated as "with regard to," "for," "in view of," "according to," "in favor of," "for the love of" (*um Gottes Willen!*).

73. In almost every case, the variations of "to disclose" found in this paragraph are translations of some variation of *ouvrir*, which means "to open." We have stayed with "disclose" because it is more consistent with the extant translations of Heidegger's work, and because Nancy is clearly interested in marking a certain relation to the Heideggerian text.—Trans.

74. In most of the other essays, we have translated *surgir* as "to appear," doing so in order to maintain a certain consistency with the context. In this particular essay, we switch back and forth between "to appear" and "to spring forth"; we chose the later in those cases where its relation to growth and surprise is important.—Trans.

75. Jean-Luc Nancy, *Corpus* (Paris: Anne-Marie Métailié, 1992), 32.

76. "*Language*, whether *spoken or silent*, is the first and most extensive humanization of the being. Or so it appears. But *this* is precisely the most originary dehumanization of man as *being living present-there* and 'subject,' and also the whole of what has occurred to this point" ["Sprache, *ob* gesprochen oder geschwiegen, *die erste und weiteste Vermenschung des Seienden. So scheint es. Aber* sie *gerade die ursprüng lichste Entmenschung des Menschen als* Vorhandenes Lebenwesen *und 'Subjekt' und alles Bisherigen*"] (Martin Heidegger, *Beiträge zur Philosophie* [Frankfurt am Main: Vittorio Klostermann, 1989], 510).

77. Giorgio Agamben, *The Coming Community*, trans. Michael Hardt (Minneapolis: University of Minnesota Press, 1993), 98–100.

78. Maurice Blanchot, "Literature and the Right to Death," in *The Work of Fire*, trans. Charlotte Mandel (Stanford, Calif.: Stanford Univer-

sity Press, 1995). But this is the whole of Blanchot's work, which never stops talking about this talk of death, that is, the "unique birth" of the language of work, where work unworks itself. See his "Communication and the Work," *The Space of Literature*, trans. Ann Smock (Lincoln: University of Nebraska Press, 1982).

79. Heidegger, *Being and Time*, 308.

80. It would be easy, but tedious, to furnish the overabundant evidence for this.

81. I have in mind, here, the indications from Heidegger's *Beiträge zur Philosophie* from page 319 to the end, in order to, then, take up again the ensemble of known indications from *Being and Time*, with the aim of suggesting a recomposition in which *Mitsein* would be *actually* coessential and originary. It is necessary to rewrite *Being and Time*: this is not a ridiculous pretension, and it is not "mine"; it is the necessity of all the major works, insofar as they are *ours*. One can guess without much trouble that this necessity also belongs to the stakes of a political rewriting.

82. In using the word *l'écartement*, Nancy is laying out explicitly the connection to his earlier use of the word *écart*. So, although we have consistently translated *l'écartement* as "the dispersal," so as to maintain a certain fluidity with his use of "dispersion," one should keep in mind that what is contained therein is the reference to something like "a dispersal of explosive brilliance."—Trans.

83. *Bei sich*: one would have to respond, ever since Hegel at least, to the constant crossing over, the mutual intrication and distancing, in the fundamental structure of the "self," of the "in itself," of the "near to itself," and of the "right at itself." The "for itself," since it occurs and if it occurs, is only the result.

War, Right, Sovereignty-Technē

1. Published in *Les Temps Modernes* no. 539 (Paris, June 1991). Given the fact that this text is firmly bound up with the events of the day, I have not allowed myself to modify it, apart from some tiny editorial details. It holds as well for what ensued.

Since published as "War, Law, Sovereignty—Technē," *Rethinking Technologies*, ed. Verena Andermatt Conley (Minneapolis: University of Minnesota Press, 1993). Our translation benefited greatly from a review of the translation offered by Jeffrey S. Librett in the above text.—Trans.

2. It almost certainly goes without saying that translating the French word *le droit* is a difficult task, exactly because it means both "right" and

"law." Within this text, it is almost invariably the case that when either the word "law" or the word "right" appears it is as the translation of *droit.* We have done our best to remain attuned to the course of the text and to choose the appropriate translation in each instance.—Trans.

Eulogy for the Mêlée

1. This essay appeared in German in *LettreInternationale* no. 21 (Berlin, 1993), and in Serbian in *Mostovi* (Belgrade, March 1993); the French text appeared in *Transeuropéennes* no. 1 (Geneva: Centre européen de la culture, 1993) and was reprinted in *M/mensuel, Marxisme, mouvement* no. 71 (Paris, July 1994). The request for the piece originally came from Ghislaine Glasson-Deschaumes, director of *Transeuropéennes.*

2. The French word *mêlée* has entered the English language in an impoverished form. Throughout this piece, it should not be read as meaning only a confused fight, a fray, scrap, skirmish, or scuffle, that is, as a word in English. Rather, it remains an untranslated French word meaning a fight, but also a mingling of a more sexual nature. In addition, as its connection to the verbs *mêler* and *se mêler* ("to mix") make clear, the ideas of mixture, mixing, motley, and variegation are also implied.—Trans.

3. Again, we leave the word *mélange* untranslated, but one should read here its connection to the above-cited *mêlée,* as well as its saying something like "mixture" or "muddle." It is this latter definition that seems to inform the transition Nancy wants to make from *mélange* to *mêlée.*—Trans.

4. Fernand Braudel, *The Mediterranean and the Mediterranean World in the Age of Philip II,* trans. Siân Reynolds (Berkeley and Los Angeles: University of California Press, 1995). Nancy's essay, as it appears in the original French edition, does not give the page number of this quotation from Braudel. Seeing as the whole of Braudel's book is more than 1,500 pages, the translation offered of the quotation is ours, and not from the above English edition.—Trans.

The Surprise of the Event

1. In almost every case, what we translate here as "happen," "happening," and "happened," is some version of the French word *arriver.* One should also keep in mind the various other translations that might be offered of the same word, translations which suggest other important connotations: "to occur," "to arrive," "to come," "to be on the way," and so forth.

2. G. W. F. Hegel, *Hegel's Science of Logic*, trans. A. V. Miller (Atlantic Highlands, N.J.: Humanities Press International, 1989), 588. The translation offered by Miller, the one we have used in this essay, has a different emphasis than the one given in the French translation of the same sentence. The French translation says something more like the following: "Philosophy must not be a story of what happens, but a knowledge of what, in such happening, is true, and beginning from the true it must also conceive of what in the narrative appears as a pure event." The significant difference comes in the last phrase, which in Miller's translation says "mere happening" and in the French translation says "pure event." ["Aber die Philosophie soll keine Erzählung dessen sein, was gesehiet, sondern eine Erkenntis dessen, was *wahr* darin ist, und aus dem Wahren soll sie ferner das begreifen, was in der Erzählung als ein bloßes Geschehen erscheint."] (G. W. F. Hegel, *WissenschaftderLogic* [Frankfurt am Main: Suhrkamp Verlag, 1969], 260).—Trans.

3. In the French edition, "Logique du concept" is the title of the second volume of Hegel's *Science of Logic*, which is translated by "Subjective Logic; or the Doctrine of the Notion" in the above English edition.—Trans.

4. Ibid., 591.

5. The most common translation of the word *la péripétie* would be "the event," but we have chosen the word "episode" to reserve the specificity of the term "event" for translating *l'événement.* But one should also keep in mind Aristotle's use of *peripeteia.*—Trans.

6. Hegel, *Hegel's Science of Logic*, 91.

7. Immanuel Kant, *Critique of Pure Reason*, trans. Norman Kemp Smith (New York: St. Martin's Press, 1965), 218.

8. Therefore, it is a matter of "originary temporality," the major concept of *Being and Time.* Is such a concept itself again subordinated to the concept of the time of presence (already present and homogenous with itself), or does it exclude itself from it? This is the most important thing at stake in a debate entirely internal to Heidegger, and then opened between Derrida and Heidegger, and indeed between Derrida and himself. For example, compare *"Ousia and Grammē*: A Note on a Note from *Being and Time," Margins of Philosophy*, trans. Alan Bass (Chicago: University of Chicago Press, 1982), and portions of *Given Time: I. Counterfeit Money*, trans. Peggy Kamuf (Chicago: University of Chicago Press, 1992). Perhaps it is necessary to think that it is presence which precedes itself—that presents itself—heterogeneous to itself, and that the event (of Being) is here.

9. *Survenir*, which we translated earlier as "to occur," also has the connotation of occurring unexpectedly, and the noun *le survenue* means "a sudden or unexpected arrival."—Trans.

10. Even and especially if it "reveals the that-which-is-not-being-asbeing." Alain Badiou, *L'être et l'événement* (Paris: Éditions du Seuil, 1988), 211. It is "not-Being-as-being," then, that is the condition of Being, or to be more precise, the existent condition of Being (or the "existential" of Being itself). No doubt all parties to the *disputatio* would agree on this as an (essential) minimum—at least insofar as this is only the beginning of expressing such a minimum.

11. See §22 and §35 of Martin Heidegger's *Kant and the Problem of Metaphysics*, trans. Richard Taft (Bloomington: Indiana University Press, 1990).

12. Martin Heidegger, *The Fundamental Concepts of Metaphysics*, trans. William McNeill and Nicholas Walker (Bloomington: Indiana University Press, 1995), 501 ff.

Human Excess

1. Sergio Moravia, *Journal européen*, trans. Denis Fernandez-Récatala and Gianni Burattoni (Paris: Écriture, 1984), 48. The translation into English is ours.—Trans.

Cosmos Baselius

1. This text was first published in *Basileus*, an Internet philosophy journal, ed. Paul Minkkinen (http://www.helsinki.fi/basileus, March 1998).

2. In the previous essay, "Human Excess," we translated the word *covenance* as "propriety" in order to maintain a certain proximity with the French words *propre* and *provenance*. In the above text, we have rendered it as "suitability" in order that it follow more closely from the verb *convenir*, which means "to be suitable," or "to be fitting." However, in a few cases, we have once again translated *covenance* as "propriety," but these instances are marked in the text.—Trans.

3. The word "gangue" exists both in French and English, but it is not often used except in certain specialized discourses. It is the worthless rock or vein matter from which valuable metals or minerals are extracted.—Trans.

M E R I D I A N

Crossing Aesthetics

Louis Marin, *Sublime Poussin*

Philippe Lacoue-Labarthe, *Poetry as Experience*

Jacques Derrida, *Resistances of Psychoanalysis*

Ernst Bloch, *Literary Essays*

Marc Froment-Meurice, *That Is to Say: Heidegger's Poetics*

Francis Ponge, *Soap*

Phillipe Lacoue-Labarthe, *Typography: Mimesis, Philosophy, Politics*

Giorgio Agamben, *Homo Sacer: Sovereign Power and Bare Life*

Emmanuel Levinas, *Of God Who Comes to Mind*

Bernard Stiegler, *Technics and Time, 1: The Fault of Epimetheus*

Werner Hamacher, *pleroma—Reading in Hegel*

Serge Leclaire, *Psychoanalyzing*

Serge Leclaire, *A Child Is Being Killed*

Sigmund Freud, *Writings on Art and Literature*

Cornelius Castoriadis, *World in Fragments: Writings on Politics, Society, Psychoanalysis, and the Imagination*

Thomas Keenan, *Fables of Responsibility: Aberrations and Predicaments in Ethics and Politics*

Emmanuel Levinas, *Proper Names*

Alexander García Düttmann, *At Odds with AIDS: Thinking and Talking About a Virus*

Maurice Blanchot, *Friendship*

Jean-Luc Nancy, *The Muses*

Massimo Cacciari, *Posthumous People: Vienna at the Turning Point*

David E. Wellbery, *The Specular Moment: Goethe's Early Lyric and the Beginnings of Romanticism*

Edmond Jabès, *The Little Book of Unsuspected Subversion*

Hans-Jost Frey, *Studies in Poetic Discourse: Mallarmé, Baudelaire, Rimbaud, Hölderlin*

Pierre Bourdieu, *The Rules of Art: Genesis and Structure of the Literary Field*

Nicolas Abraham, *Rhythms: On the Work, Translation, and Psychoanalysis*

Jacques Derrida, *On the Name*

David Wills, *Prosthesis*

Maurice Blanchot, *The Work of Fire*

Jacques Derrida, *Points ... : Interviews, 1974–1994*

J. Hillis Miller, *Topographies*

Philippe Lacoue-Labarthe, *Musica Ficta (Figures of Wagner)*

Jacques Derrida, *Aporias*

Emmanuel Levinas, *Outside the Subject*

Jean-François Lyotard, *Lessons on the Analytic Sublime*

Peter Fenves, *"Chatter": Language and History in Kierkegaard*

Jean-Luc Nancy, *The Experience of Freedom*

Jean-Joseph Goux, *Oedipus, Philosopher*

Haun Saussy, *The Problem of a Chinese Aesthetic*

Jean-Luc Nancy, *The Birth to Presence*